ESSENTIAL
CISM

Exam Guide

Updated for the
15th Edition Review Manual

Phil Martin

ISBN 978-1-98068-442-8

Essential CISM

Contents

Contents

v

Contents

Contents

Figures

Tables

About the Exam

The CISM, or Certified Information Security Manager Certification, is one of the most recognized credentials for information security managers and has been awarded to more than 27,000 professionals to-date.

Beyond passing the exam, a CISM Certification requires a minimum of five years of experience in information security, and a minimum of two years of experience as an information security manager. If you have a CISA or CISSP certification, or a post-graduate degree in information security or other related field, then you are eligible to substitute two years of work experience. Finally, you will be required to and agree and comply with the ISACA's Code of Professional Ethics and the CISM Continuing Education Policy.

The exam cost between $625 and $750. If you pay to register as a member with ISACA, you can receive a discount. ISACA offers a free self-assessment exam with 50 questions to test your readiness for the actual exam. You can register for the CISM exam on the ISACA website. The day of the test you must bring a photo ID and the admissions ticket provided after you register.

The CISM exam is given twice per year in June and December. The test will take four hours and includes 200 total questions, giving you just over one minute per question. You are awarded 4 points per each correctly answered question, and a minimum score of 450, or roughly 113 correct questions, is required to pass the test.

Once you pass the test and have the score in-hand, you can submit your CISM application to get your certification. This requires proof of five years of experience of work, with signed verification from your employers.

There is only a 50-60% first time pass rate, so study the material repeatedly and take multiple assessment tests prior to taking the plunge.

How to Use This Book

If you have tried to read the official CISM Review Manual, then you know what a coma feels like. This book has boiled down the contents into a concise and easily-readable format, purposefully avoiding those $100 sentences that take 2 minutes to decipher.

Some simple rules on text formatting...

Underlined and italicized text:

This is a term you should memorize.

Bold text:

This is a concept you should remember.

Normal text:

This is to help you understand the two above. Read this part at least once, and revisit as often as you need.

This book is divided into two sections. **Section 1** covers basic CISM concepts that are covered in more than one domain. **Section 2** covers each of the four CISM domains.

So, let's start with the basics!

An audio version of this print book is available on audible.com!

14

Section 1: The Basics

Before we go into each CISM domain, there are a number of topics we need to cover first. All the subjects in this section are repeatedly referred to in more than one domain. Instead of trying to keep adding sidebars to explain what is going on, you're going to be put through a 'boot camp' in which each topic will be discussed. Later on, when you run across a topic, you'll immediately know what is going on.

Chapter 1: Security Concepts

There are a few security-related concepts that keep coming up across the four domains. We're going to cover them here, so you are prepared when each pops up.

Principle of Least Privilege

The _principle of least privilege_ is an approach that segments all resources so that we can increase access as-needed. This allows us to give people access only to the bare minimum resources they need to do their job. The downside of this approach is that it requires a well-thought-out plan from the very beginning and requires increased attention to ensure resources are properly segmented.

Need-to-Know

Need-to-know is a security approach that requires a person to not only have the proper authority to access resources, but also a valid need to do so. For example, it is not enough to be given authority to read customer files – your role in the company must also require it. This provides an extra layer of security to keep information out of the wrong hands.

Segregation of Duties

Segregation of duties, or _SOD_, is a security mechanism that prevents a single role from having too much power. For example, in a bank, the same person who prints a check should not have the ability to change the name on that check – it should require a different person to execute both actions. This greatly reduces the chance of fraud.

Criticality

Criticality is the impact that the loss of an asset will have, or how important the asset is to the business. For example, if the loss of a specific IT system would prevent orders from being processed until the system is returned to a usable state, it is most definitely critical to the business. On the other hand, payroll processing is not _as_ critical – while the permanent loss of the ability to pay employees would certainly cause a mass exodus of people at some point, we can probably absorb a lengthier downtime.

Sensitivity

Sensitivity is the impact that unauthorized disclosure of the asset will have, meaning that people that should not see information are able to get to it. Consider a scenario in which we want to keep the recipe to our secret sauce from getting out. The leakage of this information would not impact our day-to-day operations, so it is not considered to be critical. But, we would be losing one of our core advantages over competitors, and so the recipe is said to have a high sensitivity.

Assurance

Assurance, related to security information, means that we can manage security risks by keeping vulnerabilities and threats to a level that we can live with. For example, if we deploy a firewall and encryption techniques to help protect access to a database, then we are assuring the database is being kept secure.

TCO

The *total cost of ownership*, or *TCO*, represents the true cost to own an asset, as opposed to just the cost to initially acquire it. TCO at a minimum covers the original cost, any upgrades, ongoing maintenance, support, and training.

Chapter 2: Governance, Goals, Strategies, Policies, Standards and Procedures

You might think that some of these words describe the same thing, but in the world of security each term has its own place and relationship to the others. **Figure 1** provides a diagram to help you understand it.

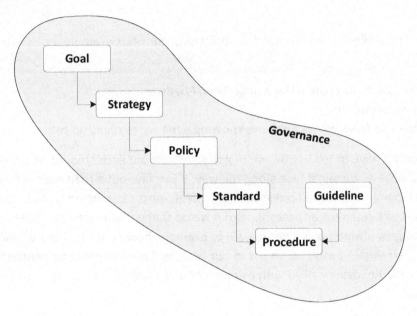

Figure 1: Goals, Strategies, Policies, Standards, Procedures and Guidelines

Governance

In a nutshell, _governance_ is the act of creating a plan on how a company will achieve a goal and then making sure everyone executes that plan. Governance is the responsibility of the board and company executives. These folks at the top might delegate a lot of the footwork, but they are ultimately responsible to ensure the plan is properly implemented. A core tenant of governance is that the people tasked with it must have the authority to enforce it. After all, what good does it do to have the responsibility of something if you don't have the authority to make it happen?

Goal

A *goal* is the result we want to achieve. Let's say we want to colonize Mars - the goal might be to establish a Martin outpost with 100 settlers. A few years ago, this would be an outlandish idea, but in the era of Elon Musk, anything is possible!

Now, how do we reach our goal? We need a strategy!

Strategy

A *strategy* is a plan of action to achieve our goal. Using our Mars example, our strategy might be:

1) Build a spaceship shaped like a huge Tesla Roadster
2) Fill it with colonists
3) Launch it to Mars without anyone knowing what we're really up to

A strategy doesn't have to tell us how we're going to carry out each step, or how long it will take, or the problems we might face along the way. It just lays out a road map of how we are going to reach our goal. If we're honest with ourselves, most of us would want to dive right in at this point and start designing a spaceship. But if we do that without some kind of guiding principles, things will wind up as a hot mess. For example, how do we buy the Vibranium needed to build the spaceship? How do we ship it to our facilities? How do we keep people from finding out that our Tesla Roadster is filled with colonists? The answer is that we need to create policies to provide guidance.

Policy

A *policy* is a high-level statement of what senior management expects and will dictate the direction in which we are heading. In mature organizations, policies are well-developed and remain unchanged for a long time.

A good example for securing information about our spaceship-building activities is the following policy covering access control: "*Spaceship design information shall be controlled in a manner that prevents unauthorized access.*" The policy doesn't say how, or what technology to use, it just describes what needs to happen.

You can think of a policy as part of an organization's 'constitution' – written words that define how an organization operates. If a policy cannot be traced back to strategy elements, something went wrong – either the strategy is incomplete, or the policy is just flat out wrong. The policy we just described can be linked directly to our third strategy element, "Launch it to Mars without anyone knowing what we're really up to". By keeping that information from unauthorized eyes, the policy carries out the strategy.

Most organizations today have an incoherent mish-mash of information security policies born out of reaction to incidents as they occur. There is seldom any mapping back to an actual strategy. This is unfortunate, as policies are one of the primary elements of governance. Not only does this reflect a lack of strategy, it also is indicative of a lack of governance in general.

At times, we may encounter the need to create a sub-policy to address a need separate from the bulk of the organization. For example, one business unit is engaging with an outside party that has some very unique and specific requirements. Rather than adopt those unique policies across the enterprise, a sub-policy is created for this one unit.

A good policy will exhibit several attributes, which are:

- It clearly **describes a strategy** that captures the intent of management
- It states only a **single general mandate**
- It is **clear and easily understood** by all affected parties
- It is no more than a **few sentences long**, except in rare cases
- It is part of a complete set that is **no more than two dozen** in number

In some organizations, effective practices have evolved that are not contained in a written policy. In these cases, the practices themselves should serve as a basis for policy and standards.

Now, if a policy simply reflects where we're heading without being specific, how do we turn that into something useful? Something that we can point to and say 'Yes, we have carried out that policy.' For that, we need a standard!

Standard

If policies are the constitution of governance, then standards are the laws. Strategy results in policies that communicate intent and direction, and standards tell us how to carry out that policy.

As an example, take our policy about securing information dealing with the Tesla Roadster spaceship. If you recall, the policy stated:

"Spaceship information shall be controlled in a manner that prevents unauthorized access."

We could write a standard providing some implementation details that might say:

"Passwords for low and medium security information shall be composed of no fewer than eight characters consisting of a mixture of upper and lower-case letters and at least one number and one punctuation mark."

A standard must provide enough parameters to allow us to confidently state if a procedure or practice meets the requirements. However, we must be careful that standards provide the necessary limits while not limiting our technology options too much. Having said that, standards might change as technologies and requirements change to reflect new capabilities, and there are usually multiple standards for each policy. For example, in the example above we will also need a standard for high security information (such as the existence of Mars colonists on the spaceship), as only low and medium security domains were addressed.

When we encounter a standard for which there is not a readily available technology, or there is some other reason for which we cannot create a process to meet the standard, we must create an exception process. For example, let's assume we want to use a 6-digit pin number to secure some low-security rooms. That does not follow the standard, and we would therefore need to follow some exception process to have it approved.

Another way of looking at policies vs. standards is a strategic vs. tactical viewpoint. Policies are strategic – a high-level view of *where* we want to get to. Standards are tactical – they represent specific tools we use to *get* to where want to go. But a standard by itself doesn't get any work done – it only describes at a medium level how it should work. To actually accomplish real work, we need a procedure!

Procedure

A *procedure* is an unambiguous list of steps required to accomplish a task. It must define the following:

- Required **conditions** before execution
- **Information** displayed
- The expected **outcome**
- What to do when the **unexpected** happens

Whereas standards are left a little vague on execution, procedures must be very clear and exact. The terms used are important and should conform to the following list:

- If a task is **mandatory** use the terms 'must' and 'shall'
- If a task is **preferred** but not mandatory, use the term 'should'
- If a task is purely **discretionary**, use the terms 'may or 'can'

Discretionary tasks should appear in procedures only where necessary, as they tend to dilute the message. Continuing our password example, a procedure would be written to set up a password account, or for resetting passwords, and both cases would provide detailed steps.

Since a procedure is extremely sequential – most often a series of steps to carry out – we need to keep it as simple as we can. But there are always times when we try and execute a step and run into trouble that the procedure does not cover. What do we do then? We turn to a guideline!

Guideline

A *guideline* contains information that is helpful when executing procedures. While standards are usually expressed in very explicit rules and are carried out by procedures, guidelines are a little more flexible to accommodate unforeseen circumstances.

For example, say we have a procedure containing step-by-step instructions on how to pack 100 colonists into a spaceship. Half-way through the loading process someone who is already in the roadster pops their head out and says, "Hey, I forgot my ear phones!" Chances are, the loading procedure will not say anything about what to do in this situation. But, at the bottom of the procedure is a list of *guidelines* that you can reference, including a promising one titled 'Handling Memory-Challenged Colonists". Problem solved!

Bringing It All Together

In summary, we:

1) Identify a worthy **goal**
2) Shape a multi-step **strategy** to reach the *goal*
3) Craft **policies** to carry out each *strategy*
4) Define **standards** to outline how we carry out *policies*
5) Write **procedures** containing step-by-step instructions on how to implement *standards*
6) Fashion **guidelines** to help when a procedure runs into a problem

We can also say the following:

- Goals, Strategies and Policies tell us where we want to go
- Standards provide the tools
- Procedures give us the step-by-step instructions
- Guidelines provide recommendations

Chapter 3: Strategy

Overview

In its simplest form, the term _strategy_ can be defined as…

> …_a plan to achieve a goal._

But if we dig a little deeper, we find that any successful plan must have two components – a well-defined goal and an understanding of the current conditions. Digging even deeper, we discover that a successful strategy involves answering the following four questions:

1) Where are we now?
2) Where do we want to be?
3) What is the gap between the two?
4) What do we need to do to close the gap?

Strategies can fail for a number of reasons – let's walk through them one at a time.

First of all, _overconfidence_ is a leading cause of failure. Research has shown that people have way too much confidence in their ability to create accurate estimates. Most people dislike coming up with estimates that have a wide range and prefer to be precisely wrong rather than vaguely right. Additionally, people tend to be more confident in their abilities than their success history warrants.

Closely related, people tend to be overly _optimistic_ in their forecasts. When you combine overconfidence with optimism, you wind up with estimates that are unrealistically precise and overly optimistic.

If you show a number to a person, he or she will tend to anchor all subsequent estimates to that number, even if the second subject being estimated has nothing in common with the first. This is called _anchoring_ and means that subsequent attempts at estimating will be swayed back to the original number. As an example, if I were to ask you how many brothers and sisters you have, and then ask you how many slices of pizza you can eat before you are full, you will tend to unconsciously _anchor_ your pizza answer to the numbers of siblings you have.

The _status quo bias_ is a phenomenon in which a person will favor a known approach even when it has been demonstrated to be vastly ineffective. People will also show more concern over a possible loss than excitement over a possible gain.

The *endowment effect* makes people hold something they already own at a higher value than if they did not already own it. In other words, if I have a vase that I will not sell for anything less than $20, I probably would not pay someone else $20 for that same vase if I did not already own it.

The *mental accounting effect* is seen when we treat money differently based on where it comes from or how it is spent and is common in boardrooms. For example, senior management may clamp down on costs for a core business but spend freely on a startup. Or, they might create new spending categories with nebulous names such as 'revenue investment'.

The *herding instinct* describes the tendency for people to 'do what everyone else is doing'. It takes a special leader to step out and take a chance when no one else is doing it.

False consensus describes the tendency to overestimate the extent to which other people share our own views or beliefs. When dealing with strategies, this pitfall can cause someone to ignore important threats or to prolong a doomed strategy.

Confirmation bias happens when we seek opinions and facts that support a conclusion we have already reached.

Selective recall occurs when we *remember* only facts and experiences that support our current assumptions.

Biased assimilation is encountered when we *accept* only facts that support our current position or perspective.

Biased evaluation is very similar, but in this case, we go one step further and attack anyone presenting those 'alternative' facts, even to the point of personal attacks.

Groupthink is encountered when we experience pressure for agreement in team-based cultures.

Elements of a Strategy

Once the starting and ending point of a strategy have been defined, what else should we look at? The biggest components are going to be resources and constraints that need to be examined while creating the road map. A typical road map includes elements such as people, processes, technologies and other resources. The interactions between these elements can be quite complex, and so it is probably a smart move to employ a security framework from the beginning.

Getting to the desired state is usually a long-term goal that requires multiple projects and initiatives. It is beneficial to break these down into smaller bite-sized projects that can be executed in a reasonable time-period. While we need a long-term road map, everyone must understand that security sits still for no man, and it is highly likely that some initiatives further down the road may become obsolete by the time we get there, or at least require some serious updating. One advantage of breaking long-term projects into multiple short-term initiatives is that we get built-in checkpoints to revalidate previous assumptions and to make midcourse corrections. They can also provide valuable metrics to validate the overall strategy.

Resources

Resources are defined as mechanisms, processes and systems that are available for use. When considering resources, the strategy must enumerate all available possibilities, but use existing resources if possible. Here is a list of the most commonly used resources:

Policies	Training
Standards	Awareness and education
Procedures	Audits
Guidelines	Compliance enforcement
Architectures	Threat assessment
Controls (technical, physical, procedural)	Vulnerability assessment
Countermeasures	BIA
Layered Defenses	Risk analysis
Technologies	Resource dependency analysis
Personnel security	Third-party service providers
Organizational structure	Other organizational support
Roles and responsibilities	Facilities
Skills	Environmental security

Constraints

Constraints are factors that work against efficiency, and typically include the following ten:

- **Legal**, such as laws and regulatory requirements
- **Physical**, such as capacity, space and environmental considerations
- **Ethics**, where we must consider if a given action is appropriate, reasonable, or customary
- **Culture**, which includes both inside and outside of the organization

- **Costs**, such as time and money
- **Personnel**, where people may be resistant to change or resent new constraints
- **Organizational structure**, where we must consider how decisions are made and by whom, and battle turf protection
- **Resources**, such as capital, technology and people
- **Time**, where we consider windows of opportunity and mandated compliance deadlines
- **Risk appetite**, such as threats, vulnerabilities and impacts that may prevent certain actions

Some constraints, such as ethics and culture, may have already been overcome when developing the desired state. Others may arise as a direct result of developing the road map.

Chapter 4: Risk Appetite, Tolerance and Capacity

Now that we understand all of the high-level greatness of where we want to go, and how we're getting there, it's time to dig into some real-world concepts. Each chapter will be building on the previous content, so be sure you understand the material before moving on.

We're going to really dive deep with the idea of risk in a while, but for now just accept *risk* as the likelihood something bad is going to happen. If there is a 75% chance that a building is going to catch fire, risk is *high*. On the other hand, if we only think there is a 10% chance of a building catching fire, that same risk is *low*.

Some definitions we need to learn are the following:

- *Risk appetite*, which is the amount of risk a business is willing to incur.
- *Risk tolerance*, which is the amount of deviation from the risk appetite a business considers acceptable.
- *Risk capacity*, which is the amount of risk a business can absorb without ceasing to exist.

In general, the following statement must be true:

risk appetite + risk tolerance <= risk capacity

Let's use an example to make this clearer. Let's say the Boring company wants to sell flame throwers. However, there is a risk of customers catching fire while using the tool. The business does a quick calculation and decides it has sufficient money for 7% of customers to file lawsuits before it goes out of business. Therefore, it wants to keep the number of spontaneously combusting customers at 5%. So, we have the following:

- Risk appetite = 5%
- Risk capacity = 7%
- Risk tolerance = (7% - 5%) = 2%

Now, risk tolerance is not correct – yet. It is actually expressed as a *deviation* from the risk appetite, so the value is actually (2%/5%) = .4, or a 40% deviation from risk appetite. Risk tolerance is a 40% deviation.

If risk appetite plus risk tolerance is ever more than risk capacity, then something went wrong. The level of risk must always be equal to or lower than the risk capacity.

A final term to note: _risk acceptance_ occurs when an organization decides that no action is required for a specific risk – it is willing to suffer the consequences instead of expending resources to mitigate it.

Defining these risk values – appetite, capacity and tolerance - is crucial if we hope to arrive at reasonable goals. It is also necessary if we expect to have solid criteria by which risk acceptability will be measured.

Before continuing, we need to introduce another term called a _control_. Basically, a control is something put into effect to reduce risk. For example, let's say the threat of fire is too great, meaning that the risk of fire exceeds our risk tolerance. In this case, we can install some sprinkler systems to reduce the likelihood of fire, bringing the risk of fire down below our risk tolerance level. That sprinkler system is a _control_. While it reduces risk, it also costs money to implement.

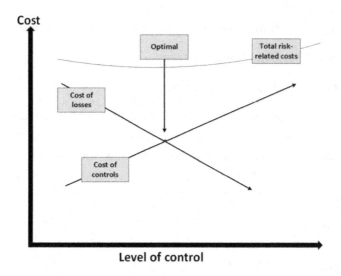

Figure 2: Optimizing Risk Costs

Figure 2 illustrates the relationships between risk, control and the cost of a control. The only way to decrease costs due to a negative incident is to _increase_ the level of controls, which increases upfront control costs. If we _decrease_ the level of controls, we can save money now but the cost after an incursion will go up. The sweet spot is where those two lines cross, representing a happy compromise where our total costs – upfront control costs plus costs after an incident - will be the lowest. But, without a clear idea of what 'acceptable risk' is, it will be exceedingly difficult to know if a given sweet spot is acceptable, or where it even lives.

Let's go back to our sprinkler example to drive this point home. If the cost of fire damage is expected to be $100K and we do not put a control in-place, then our costs after an incident will be $100K. We save a lot of money by not buying a sprinkler system up-front, but we pay for it in the end when a fire breaks out. On the other hand, if we pay $100K for a sprinkler system we may have prevented a fire, but we really didn't do any good – we're still out $100K. The sweet spot is probably going to be when we pay $50K for a cheaper sprinkler system. Maybe it doesn't completely prevent a fire, but it will definitely reduce the amount of damage. And, on the off chance we never have a fire, we just saved ourselves $50K!

Risk is a very complex subject and is extremely difficult to nail down with any real level of precision. We must keep several truths in mind:

1) If there is risk associated with taking some kind of action, there is also risk associated with *not* taking that action.
2) Mitigating one risk will almost *always* increase another risk, or perhaps even create another risk.
3) Risk *always* carries a cost, whether it is controlled or not.

An important factor to consider is something called *business interruption insurance*, which is an insurance policy the organization purchases to cover itself in the event that we exceed our *RTO*. We go into more detail later, but RTO is our *recovery time objective*, or the maximum amount of time we have to get our business back up and running after an incident before our business goes belly up. If we are unable to be up and running by our RTO limit, we will be in bad shape and business interruption insurance would kick in. Let's say we have a $1 million insurance policy with a $10K deductible, and the policy costs us $50K each year. If we ever have an incident that exceeds our RTO, the insurance company would pay us up to $1 million after taking out the $10K deductible.

We could also justify spending up to $50K on controls to mitigate the risk and not purchase the insurance, as long as we are willing to accept a $10K residual risk. *Residual risk* is the amount of risk left over after we have mitigated a risk. Mitigation does not mean we entirely eliminate risk – it just means we decrease the level of risk so that it is at or less than our risk appetite.

For a given risk, there are usually multiple options that will all mitigate the risk to some extent. However, some will be costlier than others, and so we must be careful to evaluate and choose the lowest cost option that will mitigate the risk to an acceptable level. Arriving at the best decision will usually be an iterative process as we run through various possibilities until the best choice is identified.

The information security manager must understand that technical controls such as firewalls or intrusion detection systems (IDS) are just one dimension that should be considered. Physical, process and procedural controls may actually be more effective and less costly than a technical control. For example, we could use biometric scanners and keycard readers to protect an asset in our local facility that experiences heavy foot traffic, but perhaps simply moving the asset to an off-site location that almost no one visits would achieve the same level of protection. In this case a physical control achieves the same protection as a technical control, but at a much lower cost.

Chapter 5: Analysis of Risk

Risk analysis is the act of identifying the level for a risk, understanding its nature, and determining potential consequences. During this time, we also determine the effectiveness of existing controls and how well each mitigates their assigned risk. The following five actions take place during this activity:

- **Examine all risk sources** identified earlier
- **Determine the exposure** to potential threats each risk has, and the effect on likelihood
- **Determine the consequences** if an attack happens
- **Determine the likelihood** that those consequences will occur and the factors that affect the likelihood
- **Identify all existing controls** that help mitigate the risk

Information used to estimate impact and likelihood usually come from:

- **Past experience** or data and records
- **Reliable practices**, international standards or guidelines
- **Market research** on other organizations and analysis
- **Experiments** and **prototypes**
- Economic, engineering and other **models**
- Specialist and expert **advice**

Risk analysis techniques include:

- **Interviews** with experts and questionnaires
- Use of existing models and **simulations**
- Statistical and other **analysis**

Whatever method is chosen for risk analysis, it must be consistent with the acceptance criteria established earlier when defining the risk management context.

Let's cover the various methods we can use to analyze risk.

Qualitative Analysis

With the _qualitative analysis_ approach, the magnitude of the impact and likelihood of the potential consequences are arranged on a 2-dimensional matrix, with impact on the y-axis and likelihood on the x-axis. Both values increase in severity such that the upper right corner of the matrix represents the greatest severity. Categories are assigned to each risk such as low risk, moderate risk or high risk. **Figure 3** shows an example of a qualitative matrix.

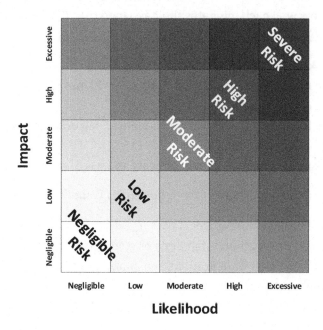

Figure 3: Qualitative Impact Matrix

Semiquantitative Analysis

A *semiquantitative analysis* uses the same approach as a qualitative analysis, but instead of using categories to represent levles of risk, a numerical value is employed. This value is not representative of anything in the real world – it simply represents a relative value among risks, with a higher number representing more risk. If this approach is used, it must be noted that the differences in numerical value may not represent relative severity between each risk. For example, suppose we assigned a value of 4 to risk of fire, and a value of 5 to theft. If the magnitude of the numbers are to be taken at face-value, we might assume that the risk of theft is only slightly higher than the risk of fire, but in reality theft might be three times as likely to happen as fire. So just be careful how you use the results.

Typical minimum and maximum values for impact range from 1 representing no impact to a value of 5 representing a failure or downsizing of the organization. The values for likelihood range from 1 meaning rare to a value of 5 representing frequent, or that the event happens on a regular basis. The risk probability can be calculated using the following formula:

risk = impact x likelihood

For example, if a risk had a major impact of 3 and a likelihood of unlikely or 2, then the resulting risk would be 6. **Figure 4** shows an example of a semiquantitative matrix.

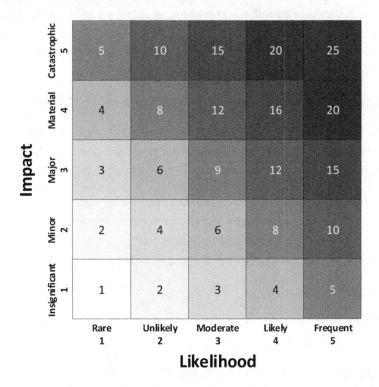

Figure 4: Semiquantitative Matrix

Quantitative Analysis

In a *quantitative analysis* numbers are assigned to both impact and likelihood. Unlike a semiquantitative analysis where a relative value is sufficient, the accuracy of these numbers in a quantitative analysis is very important. Some type of formula is designed to calculate a resulting consequence for each risk, usually expressed in terms of:

- Monetary
- Technical
- Operational
- Human impact

Value at Risk

A different approach that is required in some financial sectors is called *value at risk*, or *VAR*, and has shown some promise for information security management. For this approach to work, we have to a lot of historical data that is very accurate. We won't say much more about this approach. ~~have~~

Operationally Critical Threat Asset and Vulnerability Evaluation (OCTAVE)

Another approach to risk assessment is called the operationally critical threat asset and vulnerability evaluation, or *OCTAVE*. OCTAVE is great when we need a well-established process to identify, prioritize and manage information security risk, and contains three phases.

- Phase 1 locates all assets and builds a threat profile for each.
- Phase 2 locates all network paths and IT components required for each asset, and then figures out how vulnerable those components are.
- Phase 3 assigns risk to each asset and decides what to do about it.

Other Risk Analysis Methods

Some of the more common alternatives to the options we have discussed are the following seven.

- A *Bayesian analysis* looks at historical data and calculates the probability of risk.
- A *bow tie analysis* creates a visual diagram with the cause of an event in the middle, representing the 'knot' of a bow tie, with triggers, controls and consequences branching off of the 'knot'.

- The _Delphi method_ arrives at a consensus by asking a question to a group, tallying and revealing the anonymous results to the entire group, and then repeating until there is agreement.
- An _event tree analysis_ is a bottom-up model that attempts to predict the future by reasoning through various events and calculating the probability of possible outcomes.
- A _fault tree analysis_ is a top-down model where we start with an event and look for possible causes for that event to occur.
- A _Markov analysis_ assumes that future events are not necessarily tied to past events; in this way we can examine systems that can exist in multiple states simultaneously.
- A _Monte-Carlo analysis_ combines known risk with sources of uncertainty and calculates possible outcomes.

Chapter 6: Controlling Threats and Risk

Relationships

When we discuss securing infrastructure or processes, we use terms like vulnerability, threat, threat agent, exploit, risk, and exposure - they are all interrelated. Let's take them one at a time and figure out the relationships between each. Look at **Figure 5** while reading this section to help get a grasp of those relationships.

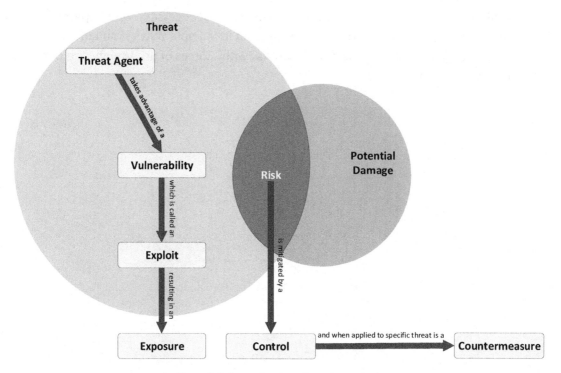

Figure 5: Information Security Relationships

A *vulnerability* is a weakness in a system that allows a threat to compromise security. We normally think of this as a software weakness, but it could also be hardware, a process or even a person. Examples of vulnerabilities are:

- A wireless access point without security enabled
- Too many ports on a firewall being open
- An unneeded service running on a server, such as an FTP server that no one uses

- Not keeping sensitive rooms locked
- Not requiring passwords to be changed periodically
- Not performing background checks on new hires

An *exploit* occurs when a vulnerability is taken advantage of by an attacker. A *threat* is the danger that a vulnerability might be exploited. A person or process that exploits a vulnerability is called a *threat agent*. Examples of a threat agent might be employees not following proper procedure when shredding documents, an attacker gaining access to data through a network connection or even an automated process that deletes the wrong files. Threats can be natural, manmade or technical in nature.

A *risk* is the likelihood that a threat agent will exploit a vulnerability combined with the damage that could result. For example, if an Intrusion Detection System, or IDS, is not implemented on your network, then the risk of an attack going unnoticed goes up.

An *exposure* is a single real-world instance of a vulnerability being exploited by a threat agent. If you are hacked three times in one year, then you have experienced three different exposures within the last year.

A *control* is created or put into place to mitigate the risk of a threat. Note that a control does not usually eliminate the risk altogether – it simply reduces the likelihood of a vulnerability being exploited. Examples of controls might be firewalls, encryption, security guards or requiring strong passwords.

Let's put all the definitions together:

A *threat* is a *vulnerability* that is *exploited* by a *threat agent*. The likelihood of this happening coupled with the resulting damage is called a *risk*, and when it does happen we encounter an *exposure*. The way we reduce *risk* is to implement a *control*. If we target a control to a specific threat, it is called a countermeasure.

One last concept to cover is something called *defense-in-depth*, or a *layered defense*. This is the application of multiple control layers such that if a layer fails, it does not cause the failure of the next layer as well. The number of layers will depend on how critical and sensitive the protected asset is. However, excessive reliance on a single layer is never a good idea. Many organizations install a firewall and feel secure, but in reality, they have not really mitigated any appreciable risks.

Threats

Threats can be both internal and external, and intentional or unintentional. Threats by definition are beyond our control – all we can do is to manage their impact.

There are three types of threats we most often encounter. The first is an **environmental** threat, which includes natural disasters. The actual natural disaster will differ by region, but some may occur for prolonged periods of time such as drought or may occur annually such as flooding during the wet season. Some threats are rare enough or impractical to address, such as a comet strike, and so are generally disregarded or addressed using business continuity insurance.

The second type of threat is **technical** which includes:

- Fire
- Electrical failure
- Heating
- Ventilating
- Air conditioning, or HVAC, failures
- Information system and software issues
- Telecommunication failures
- Gas or water leakage

With proper planning, most of these threats can be managed adequately, with the possible exceptions of advanced persistent threats or zero-day vulnerabilities (we'll discuss both of those in just a moment).

The third type of threat is **man-made** that results from man-made actions. Examples are:

- Damage by disgruntled employees
- Corporate sabotage or espionage
- Political instability
- Embezzlement

Internal Threats

Employees are one of the greatest sources of man-made threats. One way to mitigate this threat is to apply need-to-know and least privilege access to prevent access to assets, but this is not a perfect solution, as *someone* will always have access. The typical malicious insider is a current or former employee, contractor or business partner who has or had authorized access to an organization's network, system or data and intentionally caused harm to the organization. The first step to mitigate internal threats is with the hiring process itself by reviewing references and background checks. When hiring, the employee should be required to sign a nondisclosure agreement (NDA) and be advise of the organization's ethics and policies.

Thereafter, employees should be periodically reminded of those policies. Keeping employees content with their job position goes a long way to mitigating internal risks. An employee who has recently been demoted or bypassed for a promotion may pose an increased risk.

When employment has ended, the employee must return all organizational assets to prevent unauthorized access in the future. Access credentials should be disabled immediately prior to the employee's departure.

External Threats

Anytime a network is present, or an organization has a physical presence of any kind, external threats are real. Some examples are:

- Criminal acts
- Data corruption
- Disease (epidemic)
- Espionage
- Facility flaws, such as burst water pipes
- Fire
- Flooding
- Hardware flaws
- Industrial accidents
- Lost assets
- Mechanical failures
- Power surges
- Utility failures
- Sabotage
- Seismic activity
- Severe storms
- Software errors
- Supply chain interruption

- Terrorism
- Theft

A _zero-day vulnerability_ is a weakness that is so new a fix is not yet available. Many times, the only recourse is to disable the system or process exhibiting the weakness until a fix is available. The 'zero-day' name comes from the risk that an attacker will exploit the vulnerability immediately after discovery before anyone is aware of its existence.

An _advanced persistent threat (APT)_ is a skilled external attacker who is willing to invest considerable time and resources into bypassing an organization's network and system security controls. APTs may be sponsored by governments, organized crime or competitors. Typical APT attacks have the following life cycle:

- The **initial compromise**, where an attacker uses social engineering and spear phishing via email to plant a zero-day virus.
- **Establish foothold**, where the attacker installs a remote administration tool (RAT) or creates backdoors for later use.
- **Escalate privileges** by gaining administrator access to a computer.
- **Internal reconnaissance** is carried out by collecting information about the network and devices.
- **Move laterally** by expanding control to other computers and stealing data from them.
- **Maintain presence** using the channels and credentials already used
- **Complete the mission** by retrieving the stolen data and hiding their tracks

The typical sources for ATP are:

- Intelligence agencies
- Criminal groups
- Terrorist groups
- Activist groups
- Armed forces

An _emerging threat_ consists of mounting evidence that something 'hinky' is going on in the organization's network and systems. This may be unusual system activity, repeated alarms, slow system or network performance, or new activity (or excessive activity) in logs. Often, logs will contain advanced warning of a coming threat, but is overlooked because no one paid attention to it.

Since technology is almost always built with functionality in-mind and rushed to market, it is a core source of vulnerabilities. In fact, it is not too uncommon to discover that new software itself is a threat agent because the authors had malicious intent. Bring your own device (BYOD) where employees are allowed to use their personal devices on the corporate network can be a cost-savings boon to companies, but it brings a substantial increase of risk with it, so be careful with this tempting trend. On the flip side, a security posture that focuses on rejection of new technology will completely fail in short order, so a compromise is essential.

Vulnerabilities

A vulnerability, sometimes called a 'weakness' is not a yes or no proposition – we can't say an asset is vulnerable or not. Pretty much everything is vulnerable to something, it is simply a matter of degree. NIST SP 800-30 provides a list of vulnerabilities to consider as well as _predisposing conditions_ – scenarios which may lead to the rapid or unpredictable emergence of new vulnerabilities.

Estimating the degree of vulnerability can be carried out by testing or by using estimates from subject matter experts. It is important to communicate to management the uncertainty in estimates by using either ranges or distributions – by doing so we can inform management on unlikely maximums and likely values.

Be careful not to overplay weaknesses of a single control if it is part of a very effective mitigation approach when combined with one or more other controls. For example, a legacy system may have a very weak password protection mechanism, but if the system is only accessible from a single physical workstation locked away in a high-security room, it is probably not worth worrying about. Automated scanning of IT systems can serve as a leading indicator of vulnerabilities, but process and performance weaknesses are tougher to uncover.

Vulnerabilities can be grouped into the following categories:

- Network vulnerabilities
- Physical access
- Applications and web-facing services
- Utilities
- Supply chains

- Processes
- Equipment
- Cloud computing
- Internet of Things (IoT)

Some typical examples of vulnerabilities include:

- Defective software
- Improperly configured hardware/software
- Inadequate compliance enforcement
- Poor network design
- Uncontrolled or defective processes
- Inadequate governance or management
- Insufficient staff
- Lack of knowledge to support users or applications
- Lack of security functionality
- Lack of proper maintenance
- Poor choice of passwords
- Transmission of unprotected communications
- Lack of redundancy
- Poor management communications

Vulnerability management is part of the incident management capability, and represents the proactive identification, monitoring and repair of any weakness.

Risk, Likelihood and Impact

We have already defined risk as the likelihood that a threat agent will exploit a vulnerability combined with the damage that could result. If we were to put it into a formula, it would be:

risk = (likelihood of vulnerability exploitation) x (amount of damage)

But *risk* can be expressed as an equation:

risk = threats X vulnerabilities X consequences

If threats, vulnerabilities or consequences increase, then so does risk. We almost always view risk as a negative thing. Believe it or not, there is such as 'positive risk' – we just normally call it an opportunity. The risk in this case is the risk that we might not take advantage of it.

A *risk* is the likelihood that a threat agent will exploit a vulnerability combined with the damage that could result. For example, if an Intrusion Detection System, or IDS, is not implemented on your network, then the risk of an attack going unnoticed goes up

Probability is the likelihood that a threat will exploit a vulnerability, which is itself a measure of frequency – how often an event might occur. When identifying risk, likelihood is used to calculate the level of risk based on the number of events, combined with the impact that may occur in a given time period, usually a year. The likelihood combined with the magnitude of the impact is used to determine ALE (which we will discuss up in a few chapters). The greater the frequency, the greater the likelihood, the and the greater the risk.

For example, on the anniversary of its founding, nation states often experience elevated levels of attacks from foreign countries. Anti-American countries love to launch attacks on July 4th. So, the *probability* of a threat exploiting a vulnerability goes up during this time period. But since ALE is the *annualized* loss expectancy, we spread that increased likelihood over the span of one year.

Determining likelihood requires us to consider the following factors:

- *Volatility* is a measure of how stable the conditions giving rise to risk are. The more volatility there is, the higher the risk will be at times, and we must estimate using the higher value.
- *Velocity* measures two intervals – the amount of time from warning to the actual event, and the time from the actual event and subsequent impact. The greater the velocity, the less time we have to react.
- *Proximity* indicates the time between an event and impact. The greater the velocity, the closer the proximity.
- *Interdependency* measures the correlation of multiple risk events – if they happen concurrently or sequentially impacts interdependency.
- *Motivation* measures the type of motivation the attacker has. For example, a politically motivated attacker will go after different targets than an attacker who is motivated by financial gain.

- *Skill* measures the proficiency of the attacker and informs us of potential targets. The greater the skillset, the greater the likelihood the attacker will go after high-value assets.
- *Visibility* is an attribute attached to the target, as high-visibility targets are more likely to be attacked.

No single model can provide a complete picture of all possible risk, but if we logically group risk areas together, it will help us to focus on the most important decision to be made.

We need to accept that it will be impossible to eliminate all risk, so prioritization of risk is an absolute must. We simply need to be OK with a certain amount of acceptable risk.

Most organizations focus on controlling unauthorized system access, which actually represents a small percentage of losses. More attention should be paid to risks such as outsourced services, electronic backups, lost or stolen laptops and paper records. Some of the best controls are the following:

- Strong access controls
- Limiting access to need-to-know
- Network segmentation
- Effective termination procedures
- Good monitoring

As we stated before, the majority of risks do not come from technology, and can therefore not be solved with technology. The majority will be management and personnel problems.

Risk Register
While identifying risk, a *risk register* should be created and populated. This is a central list of all information security risks including specific threats, vulnerabilities, exposures and assets. It should also include the asset owner, risk owner and other stakeholders.

Evaluation of Risk
When we evaluate risk, we must decide if mitigation is needed, and if so, how we will achieve that. We actually have four options, which are:

- *Accept* the risk as-is
- *Mitigate* the risk until it falls within range

- ***Avoid*** the risk by terminating the activity that encounters the risk
- ***Transfer*** the risk by outsourcing to third party or taking out insurance in case we encounter an incident.

There is one other option, which is a really terrible choice in most cases, and that is to ignore risk. *Accepting* risk is not the same as *ignoring* risk. When we accept risk, it is implied that we have done our due diligence and taken due care to assess the severity of the risk and have made a conscious choice to not mitigate it. On the other hand, when we ignore risk we are aware that it exists but do not bother evaluating it. The only case in which ignoring a risk is a valid choice is when an impact is so small it is not worth measuring, or the impact is so great that no one will be around to care anyway, such as a comet strike or nuclear war.

Note that when transferring risk, we can only transfer the financial impact. The legal responsibility for consequences can almost never be transferred.

So, our rules then are the following:

1) If the level of risk falls at or below our acceptable risk criteria + risk tolerance variance, then we **accept** the risk and do nothing else.
2) If the level of risk is not acceptable, then we will need to **mitigate** the risk using one of the following options:
   a. Modify an existing control or add a new control
   b. Change a business process to lower the risk to an acceptable level
3) If we cannot mitigate the risk, then we have two choices:
   a. If the risk has a low likelihood but high impact, **transfer** (or share) the risk
   b. If we can't transfer the risk, then we must:
      i. **Avoid** the risk by terminating the activity that is causing the risk
      ii. If we can't avoid the risk and the benefits are very high, **accept** the risk
      iii. If we reach this point, we need to start over and choose a valid option!

Risk Ownership and Accountability

Once a risk has been identified and evaluated, an owner must be chosen, who must be either a manager or senior official. A risk owner is expected to accept risk based on the organization's risk appetite and must be someone with the budget, authority and mandate to select the appropriate risk response based on information provided by the information security manager.

The owner also owns any controls used for mitigation and for ensuring proper effectiveness monitoring is carried out.

Residual Risk

A risk prior to mitigation is called an _inherent risk_. The risk that remains after controls have been implemented is called _residual risk_. Risk can never be entirely eliminated, and so there will always be residual risk. An interesting side effect of mitigation is that when we reduce one risk, we will always introduce another risk, but hopefully one that is of a lesser nature. For example, when we require a dual control such that two people are required to carry out a risky operation, we have now introduced risk that the two people will get together and collude to get around our new control.

The bottom line is that we must ensure that residual risk is equal to the organization's criteria for acceptable risk plus risk tolerance. To ensure that residual risk is acceptable, we must perform a follow-on risk assessment after the initial control has been implemented. It is also possible that residual risk is so low that we decide to lessen the original control to save on costs.

Impact

An impact is caused when a threat exploits a vulnerability and causes a loss. Impact is expressed as a financial loss in commercial organizations. Impacts can be qualitative (such as loss of reputation) or quantitative (such as replacement costs for hardware).

Chapter 7: Controls and Countermeasures

Slicing and Dicing Controls

For the upcoming discussions, we will cover three ways to slice and dice controls, and it can get a little confusing if you're not careful. Therefore, we're going to cover all three right now at a high-level to try and prevent confusion.

First, we have the *method* in which a control acts, which can be physical, technical or procedural. A physical control might be a door lock or a gate. A technical control is usually technological in nature, such as a firewall or user credentials. A procedural control reduces risk by providing a step-by-step list of instructions to be followed.

Next, controls can be grouped into *categories*, such as preventative, detective, corrective, compensating, deterrent. We'll wait to describe each of those.

Finally, controls can be grouped into *technological categories*, such as native, supplemental or support. This last grouping only applies to controls using the technical method.

Controls

A *control* can be defined as a policy, procedure, practice, technology and organizational structure designed to provide reasonable assurance that business goals are achieved, and undesirable events are either prevented, or detected and corrected.

Put much more simply, a *control* mitigates a risk. It can be a policy, procedure, practice, technology or a change in organizational structure. Whatever form it might take, a control must help us achieve our business goals by preventing, detecting or correcting an undesirable event. For example, if our Musk-ian spacecraft is going to survive a trip to Mars, then we must shield it from radiation from the sun or it will simply fall apart after a year or two. So, we make the ship's skin out of material that can filter out harmful radiation (maybe *that's* why we need Vibranium). That skin is a *control* that prevents an undesirable event – namely the destruction of our space-faring Roadster.

Standards and procedures that are too restrictive or prevent the business from achieving its goals will be ignored. If we require employees to pass through a turnstile, swipe a card, and then submit to an iris scan every time they need to go to the bathroom, we will very quickly discover that our security devices have been mysteriously sabotaged. Instead, we need to balance the need for controls with the requirements for the business. This means the security manager must have a good business perspective, resulting in controls that are the least restrictive while still delivering acceptable risk mitigation.

Control Categories

Controls can be grouped into five functional categories:

- A _preventative control_ stops attempts to violate a security policy, such as access control, encryption or authentication
- A _detective control_ warns us of attempted or successful violations of a security policy, such as an audit trail, intrusion detection method or the use of checksums
- A _corrective control_ remediates or reverses an impact _after_ it has been felt. An example is a backup restoration process, which will recover a system that has been so damaged it is no longer usable in this current state
- A _compensating control_ makes up for a weakness in another control *
- A _deterrent control_ provides warnings that can deter a potential compromise. Examples might be a warning sign that cameras are monitoring the premises, or login warning banners

* The CISM manual is in conflict with other exams when it comes to defining a compensating control. For example, the CISSP exam defines a compensating control as a secondary control that is selected as an alternative to a primary control, because the first choice is deemed too expensive or impractical. However, if you want to pass the exam, stick with the definition as discussed.

Let's use an example to cover all five of the control categories. Let's say we need to protect a system in mission control from evil alien hackers coming in over the Internet. We put a firewall in place to try and **prevent** unwanted traffic from getting into our network. We require a login as an **access** control to prevent unauthorized access. On the network we have an intrusion detection system, or IDS, that will act as a **detection** control by looking for hackers trying to carry out a brute-force login attack against the system. In case we don't catch the attacker and they compromise a system, we use a backup and restore process as a **corrective** control to bring the system back to a usable state. And finally, we add session timeouts as a **compensating** control so that if credentials are compromised, the damage is limited to 20 minutes.

Figure 6 shows the relationships between controls and their effects.

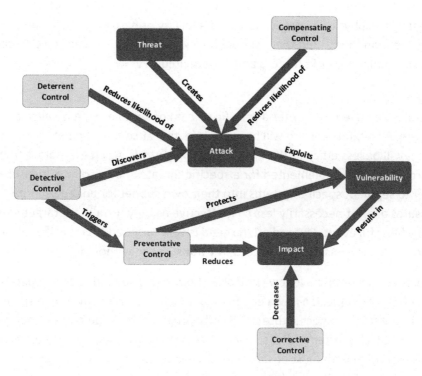

Figure 6: Control Types and Effect

Control Methods

Controls can implement a procedural, technical or physical *method*.

A *procedural control*, sometimes called an *administrative control* or *managerial control*, is anything that oversees or reports on a process and includes the procedures and operations of that process. This includes policies, procedures, balancing accounts, employee development and compliance reporting.

A *technical control*, sometimes called a *logical control*, always contains some type of technology whether it is hardware or software – usually a combination of both. Examples include firewalls, intrusion detection systems, passwords and antivirus software. A technical control requires one or more administrative controls to operate correctly. Most security failures can be attributed to failures of management, and we need to remember that management problems do not have a technical solution. Therefore, we need to be careful about being too reliant on technological controls.

A *physical control* can physically restrict access to a facility or hardware. Such controls require maintenance and monitoring, and there should be a way to react to an alert if the control provides one. Examples are locks, fences and closed-circuit TV.

Countermeasures

When a control is deployed to counter a specific threat known to exist, it is called a *countermeasure*. A countermeasure will be more effective at countering the specific threat, but as a side-effect will be less efficient than more *general controls*. As an example, a firewall is a general control that is not implemented for a specific threat, while a countermeasure might be using a router to segment specific systems into their own subnet for added security. Countermeasures are not necessarily less cost-effective as they usually are targeted to reduce the cost of any harmful event. Our radiation shield is very targeted to a specific threat, and while it is very costly, the mission would certainly not succeed without it.

A countermeasure may often be a new control, but often it is applied as an enhancement to an existing control. For example, if a new version of an email scam is uncovered, a spam filter may be enhanced to detect that specific threat. Security programs must be nimble enough to roll out countermeasures quickly, often with a special process that bypasses the normal procedures. However, this exception path must ensure that all change management and approval processes still take place, even if it is after the fact.

A countermeasure may be preventative, detective or corrective, or any combination of the three, but are not recognized by ISO 27001 (which is discussed later) as they address a specific threat. A countermeasure can be expensive not only in terms of cost, but also because it may distract from core security operations. Their use should be authorized only after careful consideration and justification.

We must keep in mind that controls are not the only way to implement security. In some cases, we can simply reengineer a process or modify an architecture. Something else to be aware of – at times risk mitigation can actually reduce business opportunities and will be counterproductive. Some risks are worth living with when only financial considerations are being looked at. Ultimately, the goal of information security is to assure that business goals are achieved. Security for the sake of security is useless.

As a valid example of ignoring risk, suppose a business decides to expand into manufacturing shoes, where we might encounter the risk of the glue not holding the shoe together. We calculate this would result in a potential loss of $15 per pair due to returned merchandise. But, if we make $20 per pair, it's well worth the risk. Just because some risks cannot be mitigated doesn't mean the business venture is not worthwhile.

Control Design Considerations

With the current regulatory environment, which is heavy on rules and light on forgiveness, the best approach to identifying and selecting controls is a top-down, risk-based approach. Top-down so that we don't leave gaps, and risk-based because control goals will be defined by the amount of acceptable risk the organization has. This means that the overall objective for any control is both its goal and the metrics used to measure how well it has achieved the goal. Normally, reaching the goal of a control will actually involve using a combination of different types of controls, such as physical, technical and administrative. For example, a *technical* firewall will require some *physical* protection and oversight by an *administrative* control.

The cost of the control is one of the most important considerations, but there are others that factor in, such as:

- Impacts on productivity
- Inconvenience to users
- Training costs
- Operation costs
- Maintenance and testing costs
- User acceptance
- Cultural and ethical acceptability
- Legal and regulatory requirements
- Adaptability to changing risk
- Scalability
- Ability to monitor
- Ability to provide notifications
- Robustness
- Resilience
- Reliability
- Ease of testing
- Self-testing capability
- Acceptable failure mode (when it fails, what ode does it default to?)

- Tamper resistance

Control Strategies

An overall strategy to follow when selecting controls is to:

- Determine acceptable risk and risk tolerance
- Determine control objectives based on acceptable risk levels
- Determine requirements for controls based on the objectives

Some security products can act as multiple types of controls simultaneously. For example, a firewall may act as a **deterrent** control by having a proxy service running on the firewall to display a warning banner. It can also act as a **preventative** control by restricting the types of traffic allowed in. At the same time, it can be a **detective** control by examining inbound traffic and generating alerts if suspicious patterns are discovered. The same control can also be a **corrective** control by rerouting traffic to an alternative site if it determines that the systems it is protecting have degraded below a preset threshold.

Of course, none of the features just mentioned have any reliance on the appliance being a firewall. Rather, that appliance just happens to implement multiple control types. It is important for the security manager to be able to distinguish capabilities apart from whatever an appliance may be called. Just because we might call an appliance 'Super-Strong Security Gizmo' does not in fact mean that it can actually secure our network. We need to be able to look at its individual capabilities and make that determination for ourselves.

Controls need to be automated as much as possible to make it harder to bypass. Anytime we introduce a human into the equation, we increase the risk of a critical process or procedure getting missed or intentionally skipped. Let's discuss some various aspects of automation.

Access Control

Before a user is allowed to access information, a system should always identify, authenticate and authorize that user:

- _Identity_ – something that uniquely identifies the user, such as a user name, email address or thumbprint
- _Authenticate_ – something that only the user knows, has or is. Examples might be a password, a security token, or an iris pattern.

- _Authorize_ – based on the identity, decide what level of access and to what resources the user should be allowed

While there are many ways to implement access control, most fall into two categories:

- _Mandatory access control_, or _MAC_, which looks at the classification of the requested resource and compares it to the security clearance of the user. This approach is used in high-security implementations such as a military system but is difficult to administrate.
- _Discretionary access control_, or _DAC_, which uses groups to make security administration easier, and allows anyone with access to a resource to pass that access on to other users at their 'discretion'.

Secure Failure

When a control detects a malfunction, and decides it is no longer effective, it can default to one of two states:

- _Fail unsecure_ (open) – when a failure is encountered, behave as if the control were never in-place to begin with. For example, if the control is an electronic door lock and power is interrupted, a fail unsecure state would be to leave the door unlocked.
- _Fail secure_ – lock down all access, usually resulting in an outage. In our door example, this state would leave the door in a locked position until power is returned.

The initial reaction might be to always desire a 'fail secure' behavior, but we need to be careful. For our door lock example, what if a fire caused the power outage and we fail secure? Everyone would be trapped inside – not a happy ending.

Compartmentalize to Minimize Damage

The _compartmentalize to minimize damage_ approach groups resources into separate 'compartments' that each require a unique authorization control. For example, if you visit the Amazon website, you can often see basic details of your account – such as your name – without having to log in again – your browser has a cookie that remembers who you are. But, if you attempt to look at your order history, you will be forced to authenticate again. Some sites will force a third authentication if you try to access credit card information. This approach can be taken to the extreme by requiring different credentials for each level of access.

Transparency

We achieve _transparency_ when all stakeholders can easily understand how a security mechanism is supposed to work. This allows them to clearly see what effects their activities have on system security. How do we do this? By keeping the technology design as simple as possible to avoid confusion. Each department is free to layer on their domain-specific terminology within their own discussions, but cross-department communication should remain at a level that everyone understands.

Trust

Trust relevant to security means that we trust an external party to tell us if a user's identity has been authenticated and is valid. A common use of this mechanism is with certificates such as SSL or TSL. In this example, a certificate is handed to us from a third party (the certificate authority) that represents the user, and we trust the certificate because we trust the third party.

Trust No One

Trust no one is a design strategy that does not trust any one person to follow the proper procedures when administrating a system. Instead, we rely on one or more oversight controls to monitor and audit their activity. An example might be closed-circuit television that watches activities from a remote station.

Two other important controls are segregation of duties (SOD) and principle of least privilege, both of which were covered in Section 1.

Control Strength

Although we have stated previously that an automated control is favored over a manual control, there are exceptions to this rule. Why? If the effectiveness of a control cannot be measured, then it is useless. In fact, it is usually harmful as it will give us a false sense of security. In this scenario it is far better to rely on a manual process that can be proven to be effective. For example, let's say we implemented a biometric pad that reads fingerprints before unlocking a door. It sounds great, but if we have no way of knowing how many false positives it is giving off then it has failed spectacularly. On the other hand, a person looking at faces and checking badges and recording the results by hand in a log book may be expensive and slow, but it can be proven to work. The automated control in this example is said to possess a very low control strength, while the manual method has a high control strength.

The overall strength of a control is a result of two factors:

- The **inherent** (or design) strength
- The **likelihood** that it will be effective

As an example, a segregation of duty control has an inherent strength simply by the nature of its design – if you require more than one person to carry out a function, the chance of fraud decreases. Now, if you use that control to require two or more people to balance out registers at the end of the day, the control now has been applied in a way that will likely to be effective. Inherent design strength plus the way in which it has been applied results in overall control strength.

When evaluating control strength, the following must also be taken into consideration:

- If it is preventative or detective
- If it is manual or automated
- If it has formal or ad-hoc

A _formal control_ has documentation reflecting its procedures and how well it has been maintained.

Control Recommendations

Beyond determining a control's strength, the following checklist should be used when selecting controls:

- The effectiveness
- Compatibility with other systems, processes and controls
- Relevant regulation and legislation
- Organizational policy and standards
- Organizational structure and culture
- Operational impact
- Safety and reliability

Control recommendations are provided as an input to the **risk treatment process**, which evaluates, prioritizes and implements the controls.

Physical and Environmental Controls

Physical security is of special concern as a violation in this area can render other controls completely useless. For example, suppose we have a great access control mechanism in place to prevent unauthorized individuals from logging into an application and looking at sensitive payroll information. But, if someone can simply walk up to the database server, plug in a USB drive and copy the data off, what good is that access control? Physical security forms the basis for all other security.

Some methods to prevent this scenario are the following:

- Identification badges
- Authentication devices such as smart cards
- Security cameras
- Security guards
- Fences
- Lighting
- Locks
- Sensors

Environmental controls are a specialized type of physical controls dealing with facility capabilities that allow us to host computer equipment. These include:

- Air conditioning
- Water drainage
- Fire suppression

If an organization has facilities dispersed over a large geographical area, it may be necessary for the security manager to delegate on-site responsibilities to local employees.

Control Technology Categories

We have already discussed control categories such as deterrent, detective, corrective, preventative and compensating. But now we are going to discuss different control _technology_ categories. Obviously, this will apply only to controls falling under the technical method, as opposed to administrative and physical methods. So be careful to not get confused between the various ways in which we group controls.

Control technologies will fall in one of three technology categories – native, supplemental or support.

Native control technologies are out-of-the-box capabilities, and we can start using them immediately without any type of additional work beyond configuration. For example, a web server usually comes with the ability to enforce authentication, log access attempts and provide TLS encryption. All of these controls are said to be *native* to the web server. In the spirit of segregation of duties, most native controls are configured and operated by IT, not by information security staff. Some devices that will always have some level of native controls include:

- Servers
- Databases
- Routers
- Switches

While native controls come out-of-the-box, a *supplemental control technology* is added on to an information system after the fact. As a result, supplemental controls tend to be more specialized and are therefore often operated by security specialists. However, it usually is of some benefit to share oversight of these technologies between the information security and IT groups. Some examples of supplemental controls are:

- Federated identity management systems
- Single sign-on (SSO)
- Intrusion prevention systems (IPS)
- Firewalls

Management *support technologies* serve three primary purposes:

- Automate a security-related procedure
- Process management information
- Increase management capabilities

For example, we might want to automate the analysis of event logs or add a device to scan for compliance. Support technologies are usually used exclusively by the security department but are maintained by IT in order to follow a segregation of duties approach. Some common supporting technologies include:

- Security information management, or SIM
- Security information and event management, or SIEM

- Compliance monitoring
- Access management workflow systems
- Vulnerability scanning tools
- Security configuration monitoring tools
- Policy management and distribution systems

Chapter 8: ALE, RTO, RPO, SDO, MTO, MTD and AIW

ALE

Part of calculating risk to a valuable asset is to express that risk in terms of money – there is nothing like dollar signs to get the attention of executives! The most common means to do so is something called _annual loss expectancy_, or _ALE_. This term will popup repeatedly as we go through each domain, so be sure to get this concept down cold.

But, there are several other terms we must understand before we can start generating an ALE.

First, each asset must be assigned a monetary value, called the _asset value_, or **AV**. If a building cost $400,000 to replace, then AV = $400,000.

The _exposure factor_, or _EF_, is the percentage of an asset's value that is likely to be destroyed by a particular risk and is expressed as a percentage. For example, if we are assessing the risk of a building catching fire, and we estimate that one-third of the building will be destroyed in a fire, the EF = 33%.

The _single loss expectancy_, or _SLE_, is the loss we will encounter if we experienced a single instance of a specific risk. In other words, for our building above, SLE would be the replacement cost for the building ($400,000) multiplied by how much of the building would be destroyed (33%). So:

$$
\begin{aligned}
\text{SLE} \quad &= \quad \text{AV x EF} \\
&= \quad \$400,000 \times 33\% \\
&= \quad \$132,000
\end{aligned}
$$

In simple terms, we expect that if the building catches fire, it will cost us $132,000 to repair it.

We have one more term to cover before we can calculate ALE.

The _annualized rate of occurrence_, or _ARO_, is the number of times a threat on a single asset is expected to happen in a single year. This number can be less than 1, which means we expect it to happen every few years instead of multiple times per year. If we expect our building to catch fire once every 10 years, then ARO = 1/10, or .1. If we, for some bizarre reason, expect our building to catch fire 3 times each year, then ARO will be 3. Let's go with the once per 10 years in our example, since that seems to be a bit more reasonable.

So now we finally get down to calculating ALE, which is simply how much money we will lose for each instance of the threat multiplied by how often it will happen each year. This will give us how much money we can expect to lose each year – that is why we call it the *annualized* loss expectancy. The formula is:

ALE   =   SLE x ARO

And calculating it for our example, we would use:

ALE   = $132,000 x .1
        = $13,200

Remember, this is all in relation to performing a quantitative analysis, where the result for each risk will be expressed as either SLE *or* ALE, most commonly ALE.

Recovery Time Objective (RTO)

A good chunk of security management is focused on preventing bad things from happening. However, there is no way to completely prevent an incident from occurring, and in those cases, we must shift our attention to getting compromised facilities and systems back to an acceptable level of operation. The *recovery time objective*, or *RTO*, is the amount of time required to do this. The acceptable level is defined by the service delivery objective, or SDO (more on that in just a bit).

The acceptability of some risks can be quantified by using the approach of RTO, which tells us how much downtime we can absorb without serious consequences. RTO can then be used to quantify the cost of getting back to full recovery. For example, if we decide that our business can survive for only 3 days if our order taking system were to go down, then RTO must be no greater than 3 days. We can then estimate how much it would cost us to always be in a position where we could bring all order systems back to full operation within 3 days. As a result, we now know our risk capacity is 3 days, and our risk appetite must be the same or less. Furthermore, if we decide our risk appetite is 2 days, but our risk tolerance is 75%, something has obviously gone wrong, since we are saying that we cannot survive longer than 3 days without the ordering systems, yet out of the other side of our collective mouths we are claiming we can stomach 3.5 days of downtime. Something doesn't add up!

Recovery Point Objectives (RPO)

The *recovery point objective*, or *RPO*, focuses on data backup and restoration. RPO will tell us how much data we can stand to permanently lose in case of interruption in terms of time, usually hours or days. Backup schemes normally will perform full or partial backups of data systems automatically on a periodic basis. RPO tells us the maximum amount of time we should ever go without performing some type of backup. There is a scenario in which the time to restore exceeds the RPO or RTO. For example, the RPO dictates we can lose only 6 hours of data, but if an interruption occurs, it will take 8 hours to restore that 6 hours' worth of data, in which case we will have exceeded the RPO by 2 hours. Or, perhaps the RPO is 2 days, but RTO may be set at 6 hours, in which case the RTO will be exceeded due to a slow restore. In either case, we are simply unable to meet the RPO or RTO, and if we cannot make them align by using different technologies, we just have to accept the risk.

Service Delivery Objectives (SDO)

The *service delivery objective*, or *SDO*, defines the minimum level of service that must be restored after an event until normal operations can be resumed. Both RTO and RPO affect the value of the SDO. The units of SDO are specific to the system, but some possibilities might be transactions per second (TPS) or the number of concurrent users.

Maximum Tolerable Outage (MTO, or MTD)

The *maximum tolerable outage*, or *MTO*, is the maximum time that an organization can operate in an alternate or recovery mode until normal operations are resumed. Many factors can limit MTO, such as the availability of fuel to operate emergency generators, or the accessibility of a remote backup site. MTO will have a direct impact on the RTO, which in turn impacts the RPO.

Maximum tolerable downtime, or *MTD*, is another name for MTO.

Allowable Interruption Window (AIW)

The *allowable interruption window*, or *AIW*, reflects the amount of time normal operations are down before the organization faces major financial problems that threaten its existence. MTO should never be greater than AIW but can be much shorter. Increasing the gap between MTO and AIW will lessen the impact the organization feels from a given outage.

Bringing It All Together

Let's assume that we work for a company manufacturing rocket engines for gigantic Tesla Roadster spaceships. We have committed to delivering 40 engines each week, and you have been tasked with figuring out how to keep the system up that runs our assembly lines. The primary assembly line runs at 75% capacity, meaning if we need to, we can kick up the speed temporarily to 100% to churn out engines more quickly. The CEO tells you that the company cannot survive if it is down for more than 7 days, so we set **AIW** (allowable interruption window) to 7 days. AIW represents the downtime before the company will be forced to cease operations.

Now, if the main assembly line goes down, our plan is to shift to a backup facility until the primary facility can be repaired. But, the backup facility can only operate at 50% of our normal capacity. So, we can run on the backup facility for only a few days. Without going into the details, we calculate that to be 3 days to get back up to speed before we hit the AIW. Therefore, **RTO** (recovery time objective) would be set to 3 days – that is the maximum amount of time we have until the assembly lines must be back up and running.

But, since our backup facility only operates at 50% relative to our primary facility (which normally runs at 75% of its capability), once we have resumed normal operations the primary assembly line will need to run at 100% for a few days to catch back up. So, we define **SDO** (service delivery objective) to be 100%, and then once we have caught up we can return to 75%. This means in the event of an outage, the primary facility must be ready to run at full speed for a few days.

But we discover that **MTO** (maximum tolerable outage) for the backup facility is only 2 days because it cannot store enough fuel to operate for longer. Since MTO is less than RTO, we have a problem. We solve it by installing an additional fuel tank for the backup facility, bringing MTO to 4 days. MTO >= RTO, so we're good.

Once we solve MTO, we discover that we only backup the system running the assembly line once per week, forcing **RPO** (recovery point objective) to 7 days. Since the entire assembly process depends on tracking progress by the second, an outage would set us back by a week, which exceeds RTO. Obviously, this is unacceptable. So, we decide to start backing the system up once per day, meaning that our RPO is set to 1 day, which is just enough to squeeze by. But, there is another problem – restoring the backup is a lengthy process and will take 2 days. That means we cannot bring the backup facility online for 2 days after the outage starts. Not a good thing, since RTO is 3 days. Therefore, we have to invest some major money into purchasing a system that will allow us to restore data to the backup facility in only a few hours.

Now, how does **ALE** (annual loss expectancy) factor into this? Well, we have a plan that kicks into place if an outage occurs, but we would rather not incur that cost if we can avoid it. We can calculate an ALE for a specific threat to help us understand how much money we should spend to avoid an outage. Let's assume that the most likely reason our primary assembly facility would go down is due to an alien attack trying to take out our Roadster spaceship fleet. In our example, the following is calculated:

- AV (asset value) of the primary facility is $100 million
- EF (exposure factor) is the percentage of the facility destroyed in an attack, which we estimate to be 40%
- The loss from a single attack would be SLE = AV x EF, or ($100 million) * (40%) = $40 million
- We expect an attack every 4 years, so ARO (annualized occurrence rate), would be .25
- Finally, ALE = SLE x ARO = ($40 million) *.25 = $10 million

If ALE = $10 million, that means we can justify spending up to $10 million per year to prevent an alien attack. Obviously, this means that we should spend that $10 million each year on laser satellites to protect Plane Earth.

And all because Elon Musk can't resist launching electric cars into space.

Chapter 9: BCP, DRP and BIA

Business continuity is a strategy that:

1. Allows us to prevent most disasters from happening to our business
2. Tells us how to handle the disasters that slip through
3. Enables us to recover once the disaster has ended

In other words, it is a strategy to prevent, recover and continue from disasters. But normally, most people think that business continuity is about prevention and how to keep functioning after a disaster. That part in the middle – recovering from a disaster – is so important that it gets its own name – _disaster recovery_. That is why disaster recovery, while discussed all by itself, is really a subset of business continuity.

We usually don't call them business continuity and disaster recovery though. When discussing these matters, we will usually talk about the _plan_ that addresses them. So, we have a business continuity plan, or BCP, and a disaster recovery plan, or DRP. DRP is contained within a BCP.

A _disaster recovery plan_, or _DRP_, documents how we will quickly restore data, applications and core services that run our business after a serious event happens.

A _business continuity plan_, or _BCP_, documents how an organization will prevent disruptions and continue operating at a strategical level with minimal or no downtime after a serious event happens.

A DRP is all about boots on the ground getting our systems back up at an operational level after some bad event has happened. A BCP is all about how the organization will function before the event and after we have recovered.

However, it turns out that before we can talk about either a BCP or DRP, we have to perform something called a _business impact analysis_, or _BIA_. The BIA helps us to understand what assets are important, and what their loss will mean to us. After all, if we don't know which assets are important and why, how can we possibly know how to recover from their loss using a DRP or BCP?

A BIA is undertaken so that we can easily see the impact to the organization of losing the availability of any given resource. One of the downsides of a BIA is that all assessments tend to be 'worse-case' and end up being inflated. This leads to management often discounting the estimates. An alternative is to look at a small subset of scenarios, and have key stakeholders analyze each and produce a range of outcomes. Based on these results, we then estimate a minimum, maximum and likely values along with a confidence level. We can then perform some quantitative magic to objectively come up with a final estimate that can be trusted.

RTOs (recovery time objective – how long it will take for us to get operational again) are defined when carrying out a BIA as part of BCP development. Often, there can be two different perspectives on RTO, with each providing a different answer: the individuals who consume information, and senior management who have a broader view of the organization and must consider costs. For example, a lower-level supervisor may believe that specific information is critical to his job, but a vice president may disagree because she is looking at overall organizational risk, and that particular asset is actually much lower in priority. However, the information security manager should take both views into account and try to achieve an RTO that services both views.

The BCP will take RTOs and use them to arrive at a priority order in which assets are restored – those with the shortest RTO first, with assets having the longest RTO being restored last. Of course, it's never that simple as some assets will have dependencies on other assets before they can be declared 'recovered'. For example, a specific generator by itself may have an RTO of 2 weeks, but a system having an RTO of 2 days might depend on that generator being available. Therefore, the generator must jump in priority even though its personal RTO is quite long.

Costs must also be factored in when setting RTO and restoration priority. System owners will always lean toward shorter RTOs, but a shorter RTO usually comes at a cost. Near-instantaneous recovery is almost always technically possible, but not necessarily financially justifiable. For example, we can maintain a backup system that is an exact duplicate of the one we use in production, but if they both must have 20 servers, that can be costly. To justify such an expense, the system must generate significant revenue, or any downtime must be extremely impactful. In general, the longer the RTO, the less cost is involved. There is a break-even point in the time-period where the impact of the disruption begins to be greater than the cost of recovery, and we need to make sure that RTO never exceeds that value. In other words, RTO should be shorter than the point at which the impact loss exceeds the recovery cost.

Now that we've discussed RTO, BCP and DRP at-length, let's go back to the BIA and discuss it a little deeper.

Question: If we don't understand the impact that an undesirable event will have on our business, then how do we plan an appropriate response to it?

Answer: We can't.

We will either wind up protecting ourselves from something that really isn't important, or we will completely neglect some critical aspect of our business that will bring us to our collective knees when it is no longer accessible.

And that is where the BIA comes in - it will tell us about potential incidents and any related business impacts, and it will prioritize them for us. Whereas risk calculates the probability of compromise, the BIA determines the consequences of compromise.

The BIA ultimately creates a report that stakeholders use to understand the business impact that various incidents will cause. Each impact will be expressed in either quantitative terms, such as money, or qualitative values, such as a relative rating. There are three primary goals for any BIA, and they are:

- **Prioritize the criticality** of every business process
- **Estimate the amount of downtime** in terms of the MTO until the business can no longer survive
- Identify **resource requirements** for each critical process

Despite the importance of carrying out a BIA, many organizations fail to do so. And even if they do, some businesses fail to keep the BIA up to date when systems and business functions change.

Chapter 10: Business Continuity and Disaster Recovery

Now that we have looked at the relationships between BCP, DRP and BIA, let's dive a little deeper into each.

Recovery Planning and Business Recovery Processes

Disaster recovery can be described as the recovery of IT systems after a disruption. Business recovery is the recovery of all critical business processes required to resume operations. Since DR is required for us to achieve BR, disaster recovery is said to be a subset of business recovery.

Not all events are actually security incidents. But, planning must include the criteria for declaring a disaster. Planning typically includes the following seven phases:

- Conducting a risk assessment or a BIA
- Defining a response and recovery strategy
- Documenting response and recovery plans
- Training that covers response and recovery procedures
- Updating response and recovery plans
- Testing response and recovery plans
- Auditing response and recovery plans

Recovery Operations

When an organization must fail over to an alternate site, the team that is responsible for that move is also responsible for returning operation to the original site when it is ready. As soon as that secondary move has ready, the team notifies the business continuity leader, who then declares normalcy and gives the OK to move operations back. There are some scenarios in which the original site will never be made operational again within an acceptable timeframe, and so the decision must be made to either make the alternate site the permeant site, or to choose a third site to become the permanent site. Choosing a third site is most often the case when the original site is no longer viable, and the company is using a third-party's facility for backup operations.

During moves such as these, it is important that information assets continue to be protected. If the security manager does not feel the assets can be secure the entire time, he should execute a risk assessment and create a plan to mitigate risk as much as possible. During the crisis, any lessons learned, and gaps identified should be documented and recorded for future actions.

Recovery Strategies

Choosing the correct recovery strategy will be the one that address probable events, and best achieves an acceptable recovery time at a reasonable cost. The total cost of the recovery process is a combination of the following:

- The cost of preparing for possible disruptions before a crisis, such as purchasing, testing and maintaining redundant equipment and facilities
- The cost of putting that equipment and facilities into effect during a crisis
- The cost of business interruption insurance

The implementation of an effective recovery plan will likely take considerable time and cost. Multiple alternatives should be explored and developed, with a single plan being selected by senior management. Outsourcing may help with both time and cost.

Addressing Threats

Part of the incident management plan will be to proactively address threats, which can be three separate strategies as follows.

First, we can **eliminate or neutralize a threat**. While this seems like a no-brainer, if the threat is external we really have limited ability to eliminate it. On the other hand, if the threat is internal *and* specific, we might be able to eliminate it by stopping whatever activity is causing it. As an example, if a threat is a result of a VPN connection to a minor partner, we could simply end the relationship with that partner and close the VPN connection.

Secondly, we might be able to **minimize the likelihood of a threat's occurrence** by reducing vulnerabilities or exposure. This is usually the best option and is normally achieved by rolling out physical, environmental or security controls. For example, adding a layer of firewall controls may degrade the ability for a bad actor to penetrate a sensitive network.

Lastly, we can try to **minimize the effects of a threat if an incident occurs** by implementing effective incident management and response, purchasing insurance, putting in redundant systems with automatic failover, or some other compensating or corrective controls.

Whichever strategy we go with, and we can choose a combination of all three, every sensitive system must be addressed.

Recovery Sites

A recovery site is where we move operations when the original site has been compromised. The recovery site should be a temporary move, but in extreme cases they can become permanent when the original is no longer viable, and the recovery site is acceptable in terms of both capacity and long-term cost. There are seven different types of recovery sites that we can choose from.

A _hot site_ is fully configured and can be ready to operate in a number of hours – the only additional work is to add staff and restore the latest data.

A _warm site_ has the complete infrastructure ready to go, but usually is not able to operate at the capacity of the original site. Additionally, some updating to software may be required. A warm site should be ready to go in a day or less.

A _cold site_ only provides the basic infrastructure with no servers or software, and can take up to multiple weeks to bring online. Normally, backups of software and data are required to configure the environment. Two primary options exist for equipping a cold site during a disruption. The first option is to use vendors or third-parties to provide equipment, particularly if the hardware is not something easily purchased off-the-shelf. The second option is to use equipment that can be easily acquired or purchased when needed. In this case the hardware should be of a common design and not specialized.

A _mobile site_ is a specially designed trailer that can be quickly moved to a business location when needed. It is usually equipped with wireless links that do not require surrounding infrastructure and is particularly useful in areas in which there are no close recovery facilities.

A _duplicate site_ is a site that is configured exactly like the primary site and can be anything from a hot site to a reciprocal agreement with another company. If this route is chosen, the following precautions should be taken.

- It should be located in a separate geographical area so that the same disaster does not take out both the original and duplicate site
- The two sites must remain in-sync with both hardware and software
- The availability and scalability of the duplicate site must be tested and monitored so that it is always ready to go

A *mirror site* is a duplicate site that is always active. Traffic and workload is continuously shared between the two sites, even when a disruption is not taking place. This configuration can result in no downtime in case either site goes offline as use is automatically shifted to the other site. Care must be taken that each site can handle all work by itself if necessary.

A *reciprocal agreement* is an agreement between one or more businesses that promise to share their data centers and systems in the event one of the partners experiences an outage. While this agreement is theoretically the most cost-effective, in reality it has a large number of problems:

- The two companies must align on the same type of infrastructure and coordinate any changes
- There must be a certain degree of trust as each company will have some access into the systems of the other company
- It is unlikely that one company can sustain usage for two companies, as normally companies cannot afford to have double their needed capacity simply sitting around until needed
- Staffing needs will more than likely be overwhelmed at the fail-over company, and when push comes to shove, they will operate their own systems at the expense of the company experiencing the disruption
- It is exceedingly difficult to create a contract that provides adequate protection

Because of these problems, reciprocal agreements are no longer very common.

A company may decide that more than one type of recovery site is needed. For example, business critical systems may require a hot site, while systems running HR applications may be covered by a cold site. After a recovery strategy has been selected, it must be validated to ensure it works for the entire recovery period until all capabilities have been restored. Some strategies to use for this are:

- Do nothing until recovery facilities are ready
- Use manual procedure
- Focus on the most important customers, products or systems with the available resources
- Capture data for later processing or perform a reduced amount of local processing

Basics for Recovery Site Selections

When deciding on the type of site to be used for recovery operations, there are a number of factors to consider.

- AIW, RTO, RPO, SDO and MTO – all concepts we covered in Section 1.
- *Proximity factors* represents the distance a facility is from potential hazards such as flooding risks or hazardous material storage.
- The *location* of an alternate site must be a sufficient distance away so that the same environmental event will not take out both primary and alternate facilities. This distance will vary based on the geographical locations being looked at. For example, the distance should be greater when hurricanes are likely than in an area where only tornadoes are expected.
- The *nature of probable disruptions* needs to be looked at when determining the MTO. For example, earthquakes may render a site unusable for months, while power disruption due to aging infrastructure would be a more frequent but much shorter-lasting risk.

As a rule of thumb, as RTO decreases, the cost of the alternate site will increase but the cost of the recovery process should decrease. As an example, if we RTO is only 2 hours because we cannot afford to be down for more than 2 hours, then will almost certainly require a hot site which is expensive. However, the effort to bring the hot site online will be fairly inexpensive. Alternatively, if a system can be non-functional for up to a week, then we can probably leverage a cold site which is much cheaper than a hot site, but the cot to spin the cold site up to operation will be pretty costly.

Response and Recovery Strategy Implementation

Things to consider while developing a response and recovery plan are:

- How ready we are before incidents happen
- Evacuation procedures
- How to declare a disaster
- How to transition to disaster recovery if we fail to respond to an incident
- Identifying the business processes and IT assets that should be covered
- Identifying individuals with decision authority and responsibilities
- Identifying individuals responsible for each function

- Contact information
- Step-by-step explanation of the recovery options
- What resources will be required for recovery
- Making sure that personnel relocation and temporary housing is covered

The plan should be written in an easy-to-understand language, with copies kept off-site for backups, including at the recovery site, a media storage facility, and at the homes of key decision-makers.

Response and Recovery Plan

The response and recovery plan, also call the incident response plan, or IRP, should include the following elements:

- Mission
- Strategies and goals
- Senior management approval
- The organization's approach to incident response
- Who the key-decision makers are
- How communication will be carried out
- Metrics for measuring incident response capability
- A road map for maturing capabilities
- How the program fits into the overall organizational structure

Supplies

The incident response plan must include provisions to ensure continued delivery of supplies that are essential to continued operations. Easy to follow hard copies of all procedures that can be easily followed by both employees and contract personnel should be stored at the recovery site. A supply of special forms, such as invoice or order forms, should also be secured at an off-site location.

Communication Networks

The plan must contain details of the telecommunication networks required to restore operations, and this should be given a high priority. Telecommunications are not only susceptible to the same disasters as data centers, but also to special events such as cut cables. The local provider is normally not required to provide backup services, so redundant paths must be planned. Uninterruptible power supplies, or UPSs, are useful for providing backup power sources for these networks.

Some telecommunications to consider are:

- Wide-area networks, or WANs
- Local-area networks, or LANs
- Third-party EDI providers
- Satellite and microwave links
- Wireless links

Methods for Providing Continuity of Network Services

There are 6 common methods for ensuring continuity of network services.

Redundancy, or providing fail-over systems, can be achieved in a number of ways:

- Provide extra capacity so that it can be used if the primary capacity becomes unavailable.
- Providing multiple paths between routers
- Using special dynamic routing protocols such as OSPF or EGRP
- Avoid single points of failure by using failover devices with routers, switches and firewalls
- Saving configuration files for the expedited recovery of network devices such as routers and switches

Alternative routing refers to routing information through an alternate medium such as copper cable or fiber optics. Other examples are dial-up circuits, or cellular paths.

Diverse routing is a method in which we route traffic through split or duplicate cables. A split cable is comprised of two cables running through the same conduit, which mitigates the risk of a cable breaking or degrading, but both are still at-risk from the same physical event. A duplicate cable is a separate cable usually run through an entirely different path.

Long-haul network diversity is achieved when we subscribe to two or more network service providers at the same time. This ensures that if the infrastructure of one provider is compromised, we can depend on the second provider's infrastructure.

Last-mile circuit protection protects an organization from a local disaster that takes out the communications infrastructure connected directly to a facility. By having redundant local connections to larger networks, the impact of a local disruption can be mitigated.

Voice recovery is specific to voice networks but is essentially has the same focus – providing redundancy for voice lines.

High-Availability Considerations

The technology used inside of networks can directly impact availability even when expected maintenance actions are being performed. We therefore need to consider some options for keeping services available.

Beyond providing multiple power providers, within our network UPSs can provide decent level of continued operation for a short time in the event of a power outage.

Direct attached storage, or _DAS_, is data storage device that is connected directly to a server or client. The typical hard drive installed within a computer is a great example. With DAS, if we need to reconfigure or increase storage, the entire device must be taken offline, resulting in down time.

Network attached storage, or _NAS_, is a storage device that is actually a self-contained server, usually running some flavor of Linux, and is accessed through a network connection. Reconfiguring or adding storage to a NAS results in no down time.

A _storage area network_, or _SAN_, is a self-contained network that provides mass storage using any number of internal media such as hard drives, optical disks or tape drives. Adding new media is invisible to clients connected to the SAN. SANs typically offer redundant fail safes such as disk mirroring, and backup and restore functions.

A _redundant array of inexpensive disks_, or _RAID_, provides great redundancy and performance improvements by writing data to multiple disks simultaneously. RAID can be used with DAS, NAS or SAN solutions.

The relationship between RPO and RTO will dictate what solution is required, as is shown in **Figure 7**. For example, if RTO is instantaneous with no RPO loss, meaning we can experience no downtime or data loss, then tape backups are not going to work. The only viable solutions are those in which the primary system communicates in real-time with the fail-over system, called _fault-tolerant_ storage solutions. This strategy works well but does result in wasted cost as we have a perfectly functional system do nothing but 'mirroring' the primary system. Instead, we usually employ *load balancing* or *clustering* in which the primary and fail-over system both process load during normal use, and on failure of either system the remaining system takes on all load. Care must be taken that all load can be handled by either system by itself.

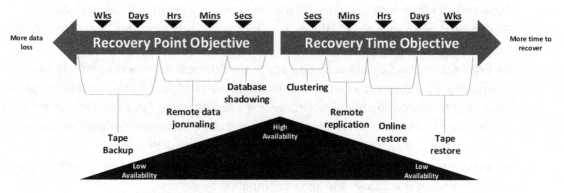

Figure 7:Techniques Implemented in Relation to RTOs and RPOs

While fault-tolerant systems are great at mitigating risk, they are also very costly. If the RPO and RTO can be a little more flexible, we can save quite a bit of money by implementing a *high-availability* storage solution. In this configuration, we still have two systems, but only one is in active use and the second is not necessarily kept up to date in real-time. Instead, when the primary storage system fails, the application is restarted and uses the secondary storage system. This results in some down time, but it can be only a few seconds. It may also result in the loss of a small amount of data – whatever data was collected since the last time the two systems synchronized.

Insurance

The incident response plan should include information about insurance policies the company has taken out regarding general coverage, cyber insurance or IT-related insurance. Insurance covering information systems cover a variety of scenarios and should be customized to an organization's unique environment. Keep in mind that it is very rare to take out a policy against failing to comply with a legal or regulatory requirement, or some other violation of law. Specific coverages include the following ten.

- Policies covering **IT equipment and facilities**, particularly if equipment is leased and the business is responsible for any loss. Care should be taken as many policies hide a clause allowing the insurer to replace equipment with 'like kind and quality' that seldom is.
- Policies to cover **software media reconstruction** costs.
- **Cybersecurity** insurance that covers losses incurred as a result of a cyberattack.
- **Professional and commercial liability** insurance which protects a business from losses experienced as a result of third-party claims.
- An **extra expense** policy which reimburses to the business for expenses incurred in maintaining operations at a facility that experiences damage. This can include net profit losses due to suspension of operations even if a facility is not damaged. For example, if a power loss causes operations to cease for several days, extra expense policies would reimburse the business for profit it would have made during that time.
- **Business interruption** insurance reimburses lost profit as a result of an IT malfunction or security incident that causes the loss of computing resources.
- **Valuable papers and records** policies that covers the actual cash value of papers and records that have been disclosed, or physically damaged or lost.
- **Errors and omissions** insurance that legally protects a business in case it commits an act, error or omission that results in a loss.
- **Fidelity coverage** policies that covers loss from dishonest or fraudulent acts by employees and is most commonly carried by financial institutions.
- **Media transportation** insurance that covers loss or damage to media during transport.

Updating Recovery Plans

The incident response plan needs to be updated whenever one of the following occurs:

- Organizational strategy changes, sometimes altering which applications are critical
- New software applications are created or acquired
- Software or hardware environments change
- Physical and environment circumstance change

Plan maintenance activities include the following:

- Create a schedule for a periodic review
- Call for a revision when significant changes have happened

- Review revisions and update the plan within a reasonable time (30 days) after the review
- Coordinate scheduled and unscheduled tests
- Participate in annual scheduled tests
- Write evaluations of tests and update the plan to address failed tests within a reasonable time (30 days)
- Create a schedule to train personnel in emergency and recovery procedures
- Maintain records of maintenance activities
- Keep the notification directory updated

Chapter 11: Testing Incident Response, Business Continuity Plans and Disaster Recovery Plans

Executing tests on all aspects of the incident response plan is the leading indicator to how successful the plan will be during an emergency. Testing should focus on six areas:

- Identifying gaps
- Verifying assumptions
- Testing timelines
- Determining the effectiveness of strategies
- Evaluating the performance of personnel
- Determining the accuracy and currency of plan information

Testing should be carried out:

- At least once per year
- After major revisions
- After key changes in personnel, technology or the business environment

Prior to each test, the security manager needs to ensure that:

- The risk of disruption is minimized
- The business accepts the risk of testing
- The organization has the ability to restore operation at any point during testing

Periodic Testing of the Response and Recovery Plans

Response and recovery testing should be carried out up to, but not actually execute, the point of declaring a disaster. If a plan is not tested it leaves the business with a false sense of security that it will not fail. Testing should include the following five steps:

- Developing test objectives
- Executing the test
- Evaluating the test
- Create recommendations to improve effectiveness
- Make sure recommendations were implemented

A third-party should be present to monitor and evaluate the test. It is very unlikely that everything will work perfectly with no follow-up recommendations. If a plan does appear to succeed 100%, the business should create a more challenging test.

Types of Tests

There are five types of basic tests, which are:

- A *checklist review test* of all steps to be carried out.
- A *structured walkthrough test* in which team members implement the plan on paper.
- A *simulation test* with team members role-playing a simulated disaster without activating the recovery site.
- A *parallel test* where the recovery site is brought up to a state of operational readiness, but operations at the primary site continue.
- A *full interruption test* that activates the recovery site and shuts down the primary site.

Testing should start minimally and progress as success is reached at each level. At a minimum, a full interruption test should be executed once each year.

Another way of looking at recovery testing is using three categories, of which the five basic tests are a subset. First, we have *paper tests*, which cover checklist reviews and structured walkthroughs. Then we have *preparedness test*, which cover simulation and parallel tests. And finally, we have a *full operational test*, which is the same as a full interruption test. **Table 1** illustrates the mapping between categories and basic tests.

Basic Test	Category
Checklist Review	Paper Test
Structured Walkthrough	Paper Test
Simulation Test	Preparedness Test
Parallel Test	Preparedness Test
Full Interruption test	Full Operational Test

Table 1: Basic Recovery Tests and Categories

It is not uncommon for full-scale tests to be skipped due to the severe interruption of daily operations. However, even if this is the case there is no reason not to execute the precursor tests anyway. Surprise test can be very effective as they best simulate a real-life emergency, but they can cause quite a stir with negative feedback if performed too often. There are many cases in which 'tests' resulted in extended outages due to the inability for the business to roll back to a safe place. As a result, performing disruptive tests are best scheduled during off hours such as nights or weekends.

Test Results

Every test should include three phases – pretest, test and posttest.

The **pretest phase** sets the stage for the actual test. These actions would not happen during an actual emergency but are intended to remove any distractions not necessary for the actual test. Some examples might be putting out tables and chairs or installing backup phone equipment.

The **test phase** is where the emergency is simulated, and people, systems and processes are moved to the recovery site to the extent the test allows.

The **posttest phase** cleans up after the test by returning people and assets toothier correct location, disconnecting test equipment, and deleting company data from all third-party systems. This phase also includes the formal evaluation of the plan and implementing improvements.

Recovery Test Metrics

Just like everything else in information security, the success of recovery tests needs to be based on metrics collected during the phases. These need to be quantitative and used not only to evaluate the test but also to improve it. There are four types of metrics we need to collect during testing.

- The **elapsed time** for completion of each major component of the test should be measured.
- The **amount of work performed at the backup site** by people and by information systems.
- **Percentages or numbers that reflect the number of vital records** successfully carried to the backup site vs. the required number, and the number of supplies and equipment delivered vs. actually received.
- The **accuracy of data entry** and processing cycles at the recovery site vs. normal accuracy, recorded as a percentage

Executing Response and Recovery Plans

To make sure that response and recovery plans are properly executed, a facilitator or director needs to be identified. The security manager may take on this role, but at a minimum the manager must make sure the role is assigned to a single individual.

Chapter 12: Roles, Responsibilities, RACI and Skills

A _role_ is a title given to someone based on their job function. A _responsibility_ is a description of something that a person with that role is expected to accomplish. Roles are important to information security because we can assign responsibilities and needed access rights to a role, instead of assigning them to a specific individual. This greatly simplifies administration. For example, let's say we have three responsibilities – Create Widget, Update Widget, Delete Widget. If we do not use roles, each time we want an employee to be able to work with widgets, we must give them all three responsibilities. Alternatively, we can create a role called 'Widgets' and assign the responsibilities to that role. Now, when we need to give someone the ability to do widget work, we simply assign the role to that employee. Later, we discover we completely forgot about the Decorate Widget responsibility. If we use roles, we simply add the missing responsibility to the 'Widgets' role, and all employees already assigned the 'Widgets' role get the Decorate Widget responsibility automatically. That makes management tons easier.

A _RACI chart_ is a great tool to use when defining roles. Essentially, RACI is a 2-dimensional matrix that lists roles on one axis, and responsibilities on another axis. If the intersection of a role/responsibility is marked with an R, A, C or I, then that responsibility is assigned to that role according to the abbreviated letter. RACI stands for:

- **R**esponsible – the person is responsible for executing the action
- **A**ccountable – the person makes sure the action is executed, but does not do it themselves
- **C**onsulted – the person optionally takes part in the execution
- **I**nformed – the person stays informed about the status of execution

RACI is useful to ensure there are no gaps and to ensure clear understanding of who does what. **Table 2** shows a rather silly, but effective, example for RACI. If you don't know who Phineas and Ferb are, I offer my condolences for your sheltered social life.

Activity	Phineas	Ferb	Doofenshmirtz
Identify something to do today	R	A	I
Provide one-liners	A	R	I
Make it all disappear	I	I	R

Table 2: A RACI Example

A *skill* represents the training, expertise and experience an individual has for a given role and must be considered when populating a RACI matrix. Consultants possessing the needed skills are often a very effective solution for short-term projects.

Why do we even bother defining this? Because it is important to be able to map a person's ability to carry out a responsibility in a clear way. This will allow us to identify training that needs to happen before the person is allowed to take on a given responsibility. If a particular skill is difficult to acquire and the need for that skill is temporary, then we have just stumbled upon a prime candidate for relying on an external provider.

When we have identified specific responsibilities for a given position, the required skills should be reflected in formal employment agreements, which should then be heavily referenced when screening applicants.

Chapter 13: Due Diligence and Due Care

Due diligence and due care are two closely related concepts, but we need to understand the difference between them. In short:

Due diligence is shown when we purposefully try and discover things that can go wrong

Due care is shown when we act to ensure those things don't go wrong

Just keep this in-mind: due diligence (discovery) always comes first, because we can't show due care (act) if we don't know what to do.

The opposite of due diligence is 'lazy', 'haphazard' or 'being careless'. By not taking the time to discover if something can go wrong, when it should be obvious to anyone with half a brain that there is some level of risk, we are guilty of not exercising due diligence.

The opposite of due care is 'being negligent'. In this case we _know_ there is risk, but we refuse to do anything about it.

Some people can easily get confused by the concept of 'accepting' risk. "Isn't that the same thing as being negligent, or not exercising due care?" they might ask. The answer is 'no', and here is why – instead of ignoring a risk as we do when not exercising due care, we have _purposefully and intentionally_ decided not to act and to accept the consequences if that risk is exploited. Now, if that risk does wind up being exploited, it may turn out that we get sued because we made a terrible decision not to mitigate that risk, but you cannot claim that we did not exercise due care.

In summary – we carry out due diligence by discovering risks, and then we exercise due care by either avoiding, accepting, transferring or mitigating those risks.

Companies will often take out insurance to protect board members in case of a breach, but those policies will almost always contain a clause that requires senior management to have exercised due care, or the breach will not be covered. Beyond that, federal regulations such as the Sarbanes-Oxley Act (SOX) state that if a company is listed on a US stock exchange, it must maintain an audit committee with an acceptable level of experience and competence – often made up of the board's own members. In this case, the goal is to ensure that financial statements are kept up-to-date and are factual. Security is enforced through both technical and procedural controls, and the security manager must stay in close contact with this committee.

As security governance is being increasingly recognized as a necessary burden for any company, a number of corporate rating organizations have been formed. A grade is assigned to each company based on the impacts and consequences of past security compromises. This in effect forces businesses to carry out *due care* in order to avoid a low rating, which almost always is associated with a loss in company value.

Chapter 14: Security Principles

When a security expert mentions CIA, they are not talking about some shadowy government agency. CIA is an acronym for confidentiality, integrity and availability.

Confidentiality prevents unauthorized disclosure of information. Loss of confidentiality can result from both intentional and accidental events. The resulting damage can result in fines, loss of reputation, loss of security, law suits and other negative impacts. For example, if word gets out that SpaceX has launched secret spaceships to Mars, we have lost confidentiality.

Integrity refers to the ability to protect information from improper modification. If unauthorized or accidental changes are made to data or an IT system, then we have lost integrity. If this is not corrected, and the data or system remains in use, the impact could get even worse. Integrity could also be the first step of an attack that then compromises confidentiality or availability. As an example, if we send encrypted communication packets to Martian colonists, but Facebook intercepts them and replaces the contents with 'fake news', then we have lost integrity.

Availability is a measure of how accessible an IT system or process is to its end users. If users are not able to get to data or applications when needed, it will almost always result in loss of productivity as well. For example (yes, again!), if we lose radio contact with our intrepid colonists because of a power outage, then we no longer have availability of those systems.

In addition to those three, there are two others that are closely related – authentication and nonrepudiation.

Authentication is the action of proving who we claim we are, usually by the three classic methods:

- Something we know, such as a password
- Something we have, such as a key card
- Something we are, such as a fingerprint

Nonrepudiation is a situation in which we cannot deny having sent a message. For example, if I write a nasty letter and sign it using a secret name that only you and I know, I cannot later claim it wasn't me who sent the letter, because we are the only ones who know the secret name.

There are three more terms that fall in this area.

Access control is the act of controlling who has access to sensitive information based on their identity, which we assume has been authenticated.

Privacy is freedom from unwanted intrusion or disclosure of information.

Compliance is the act of measuring policies, procedures and controls to ensure they are being enacted and effective.

Chapter 15: KGIs, KPIs, KRIs and CSFs

A _key goal indicator_, or _KGI_, tells us after the fact if an IT process has achieved its goal. For example, if we want to achieve compliance with a regulatory law, a KGI will measure how close we are to meeting the law's requirements. A KGI for reaching Mars might be that a 'space Roadster' is ready to launch.

A _critical success factor_, or _CSF_, is an element or event that must occur if we are to reach a KGI. For example, to achieve our KGI of 'ready to launch', a CSF might be that we successfully pass a safety inspection of the rocket engines.

A _key performance indicator_, or _KPI_, tells us how well a process is performing relative to reaching a goal. KPIs provide a real-time measurement while a process is in-progress, whereas a KGI can only tell us how things went once the process has completed. One KPI measuring the progress of launching the space Roadster might be the percentage of onboard computers installed.

A _key risk indicator,_ or _KRI_, is some type of behavior, activity or event that usually is accompanied by a rise in risk levels. By watching the KRIs, we can tap into advanced warning of pending risk. The KRIs chosen to be monitored are usually selected based on experience within a business. Examples might be increasing employee absenteeism, turnover in key employees or rising levels of security incidents. A more interesting example would be the number of failed Roadster engine tests per week. Whichever direction you wish to go, KRIs will change over time as the organization changes and must always align with the organization's risk appetite.

Chapter 16: Technologies

This section will provide a brief overview on the various technologies referenced in the CISM material.

Adware is unwanted software that is annoying but normally harmless, as it continuously pops up ads while a computer is being used. In some cases, it will slow underpowered computers down to the point of un-usability.

An *antispam device* is a server component designed to detect and delete email SPAM.

Antivirus is software that runs on a computer and detects malicious software either attempting to install or that have already been installed.

Command and control (*C&C*) is a term used to describe a central command point from which all other activities are directed.

A *firewall* is a network device that limits traffic to certain IP addresses and ports.

A *gateway* is like a firewall that links two networks together.

An *intrusion detection system*, or *IDS* is a network device that looks for patterns indicative of an attack and sends out alerts.

An *intrusion prevention system*, or *IPS*, is an IDS that will actively try and stop an attack that is underway.

Network and internet protocols are things such as TCP, IP, OSPF or any number of acronyms that represent the standards on how networks communicate, even across the Internet.

A *one-way hash* is used primarily to encrypt passwords in a way that is unencryptable – but each time the original password is encrypted it will always result in the same 'hash'. This means we can store the password in an encrypted form but still be able to see if the correct password was entered.

PKI stands for 'public key infrastructure' and is how SSL and TLS certificates work invisibly.

Malware is malicious software that a user installs without knowing its true evil purpose.

A *router* allows separate networks to talk to each other by 'routing' the traffic between them.

Spyware is a form of malware but specifically watches whatever the user does, usually to steal credentials.

Virtualization is a way to create a computer in-memory, such that multiple virtual computers are running simultaneously on one physical computer. It is a great way to do two things:

1) Save money
2) Allow a server farm to grow or shrink in real-time as needed

VoIP stands for voice over IP, the protocol that soft phones use. A soft phone is a software phone that runs on a computer.

Wireless security is represented by network protocols such as WEP, WPA and WPA2, and is specifically designed to protect computer traffic traveling through the air.

Chapter 17: Standards and Frameworks

Throughout this book you will encounter a number of external standards and frameworks with exotic-sounding names. The CISM makes frequent references to these things, often without really describing what they are. We will cover each very briefly in this section.

First of all, let's discuss some organizations that keep showing up across the four domains.

- The _Committee of Sponsoring Organizations of the Treadway Commission_, or _COSO_, provides a framework called the 'COSO Framework'.
- The _International Organization for Standardization_, or _ISO_, has authored the ISO 2000 series, of which ISO 278001 and ISO 27002 are ones the most frequently used.
- _ISACA_, which uses to be an abbreviation for something but is now just a name, is the owner of the CISM certification, and who has created the Risk IT Framework.
- The _International Information Systems Security Certification Consortium, Inc._, or _(ISC)²_, is the owner of multiple other security certifications (such as the CISSP).
- The _US National Institute of Standards and Technology_, or _NIST_, provides quite a number of standards and frameworks, most notably NIST 800-30 and NIST 800-39.
- The _Sarbanes-Oxley Act_ (_SOX_) is a US federal law passed in 2002 that puts requirements on all publicly traded businesses to encourage transparency.
- The _Health Insurance Portability and Accountability Act_, or _HIPAA_, is a US federal law passed in 1996 to protect the privacy of a patient's medical information.
- The _Federal Information Security Modernization Act_, or _FISMA_, is a federal law passed in 2002 that provides a framework to protect federal agencies from security breaches.

Now let's dive into the standards and frameworks.

COBIT

The _Control Objectives for Information and Related Technologies_, or _COBIT_, is currently at version 5, and so we simply call it COBIT 5. The framework was created by ISACA and is geared specifically to IT, as opposed to other frameworks that are more general in nature. COBIT 5 offers sample IT metrics for 17 suggested enterprise goals, for a grand total of 150 metrics. However, there is a lack of guidance on how to actually develop and implement the listed metrics – some people see this as a positive while others view it as a drawback. _COBIT 5 for Information Security_ is based on COBIT but focuses on guidance for providing CIA (Confidentiality, Integrity and Availability) for information across the entire organization.

Principles

COBIT 5 is based on five key principles, as shown in **Figure 8**.

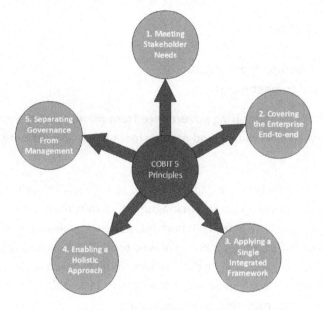

Figure 8: COBIT 5 Principles

The first principle – **meeting stakeholder needs** – illustrates the need for the organization to balance achieving business goals while managing risk and resources.

The second principle – **covering the enterprise end-to-end** – highlights that governance from the top must include all parts of the business, including IT. COBIT 5 does not focus only on IT, but looks at information and technologies as assets right along with tangible assets such as warehouses or inventory.

The third principle – **applying a single, integrated framework** – recognizes that a successful framework must play nicely with other frameworks and standards. For example, COBIT 5 aligns well with the ISO 27000 series.

The fourth principle – **enabling a holistic approach** – reveals the fact that an effective and efficient governance of enterprise IT requires a holistic approach, meaning it must consider multiple components interacting with each other. To help with this, COBIT 5 defines seven *enablers* – 'things' that help us reach our goals. They are:

- Principles, policies and frameworks
- Processes
- Organizational structures
- Culture, ethics and behavior
- Information
- Services, infrastructure and applications
- People, skills and competencies

The fifth and final principle – **separating governance from management** – ensures we can make a clear distinction between governance and management by clearly defining each.

Enablers

COBIT 5 defines _enablers_ as factors that individually or collectively influence whether something will work – in our case the governance and management of information security. Enablers are driven by the _goals cascade_ – an approach where higher-level goals define what the different enablers should achieve. For example, if our goal is to protect our incoming supply chain, then the goals cascade might call out the willingness of our shipper to add security guards at their facilities, which is an enabler. If the shipper is not willing to incur this cost, it directly influences how successful we will be at protecting our supply chain.

COBIT 5 describes seven categories of enablers:

- **Principles, policies and frameworks** translate a desired behavior into guidelines for day-to-day management.
- **Processes** are activities that achieve a goal and produce an expected output.
- **Organizational structures** are the people or group that make decisions.
- **Culture, ethics and behavior** of individuals and the entire organization are key to success.
- **Information** is required by an organization to continue running but is also a key product of the organization.
- **Services, infrastructure and applications** provide the organization with information technology processing and services.
- **People, skills and competencies** complete activities, make correct decisions and take corrective actions.

It is important to remember that enablers can function as both resources and constraints. **Figure 9** illustrates the relationships between all seven enabler categories.

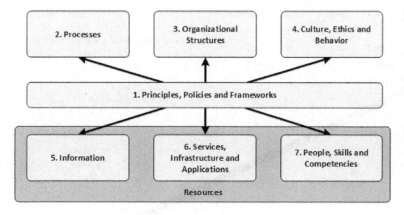

Figure 9: COBIT 5 Enterprise Enablers

COBIT 5 Process Assessment Model

The _COBIT 5 Process Assessment Model_ _(PAM)_ is a tool used to capture both the current and future desired state for information security. We do this by assessing the capability of each COBIT 5 process by assigning a maturity level from 0 to 5 (see **Figure 10**). The process dimension uses COBIT 5 as the _process reference model_, which defines 37 different processes in a life cycle.

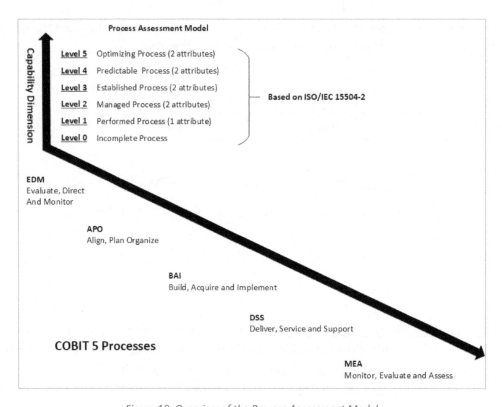

Figure 10: Overview of the Process Assessment Model

ISO/IEC 27000 Series

The ISO 27000 Series is a set of standards to help organizations create and implement a valid security plan by providing a framework containing 14 security areas, which can be mostly mapped to COBIT. It is the standard to which many organizations choose to be assessed and certified against. The 'series' part of the name reflects the standard's layout containing multiple sections, all named 'ISO 27XXX' where 27XXX is some number ranging from 27001 to 27799. There are actually only 24 different standards, so most of these numbers are skipped. By far the most well-known are:

- ISO 27001, which lays out requirements for an information security management system, or ISMS
- ISO 27002, which provides best practices for information security controls

ISO 27002 provides implementation help for ISO 27001, and is used to comply with the standards contained in 27001.

Note that while ISO 27001 refers to 114 'controls', those are simply sections in ISO 27002. ISO 27002 does not mandate specific controls but leaves it to each organization to choose the ones that best fit their needs. A risk assessment should be used to help make these decisions. ISO 27002 is used as a cafeteria plan – organizations simply pick and choose the ones that fit best. Organizations are also free to select controls not listed in this standard as long as the control goals are satisfied.

TOGAF

The *Open Group Architecture Framework*, or *TOGAF*, is a framework for enterprise architecture that covers four areas, called architecture domains. They are:

- **Business architecture**, which defines the business strategy, governance, organization and key business processes
- **Applications architecture**, which provides a blueprint for the systems to be deployed, and describes their interaction and how they relate to business processes
- **Data architecture**, which describes the structure of logical and physical data, and management resources
- **Technical architecture**, which describes the hardware, software and networks needed to implement applications

TOGAF uses something called the *Architecture Development Method*, or *ADM*, to drive progress. ADM contains 9 phases and a central block to which eight directly connect. Let's dig into the phases for a few minutes, which are shown in **Figure 11**.

- The *preliminary phase* deals mainly with the definition of the architecture framework. Here is where we identify scope, constraints, goals and assumptions.
- The *architecture vision phase* defines the vision and scope of the architecture, along with the segments of work to be performed.
- The *business architecture phase* figures out where we are (as-is), where we want to be (to-be), and the gap in-between for the business domain.

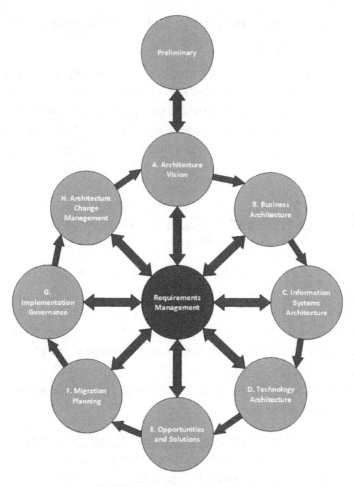

Figure 11: TOGAF Architecture Development Cycle

- The *information systems phase* describes the as-is and to-be for data and applications, and conducts a gap analysis
- The *technology architecture phase* describes the as-is and to-be for technology, and conducts a gap analysis
- The *opportunities and solutions phase* creates the strategy to go from as-is all the way through to-be
- The *migration planning phase* creates an implementation road map, which includes costs, benefits and risks

- The *implementation governance phase* makes sure that the implementation matches the architecture
- The *architecture change management phase* ensures the architecture remains current and responds to needs as they arise, which feeds back into the architecture vision phase
- The central *requirements management block* makes sure that all projects are based on business requirements, and that requirements are validated against the architecture

Capability Maturity Model Integration

Capability Maturity Model Integration, or *CMMI*, is a framework that helps organizations reach an elevated level of performance. This is done by benchmarking current capability performance, comparing those results with best practices, and then identifying gaps. CMMI has five maturity levels, and by assigning a maturity level to existing capabilities, a road map can be created to get the organization to higher levels and achieve more effective processes. **Figure 12** shows all maturity levels along with a short description of the effectiveness an organization is when that level is reached.

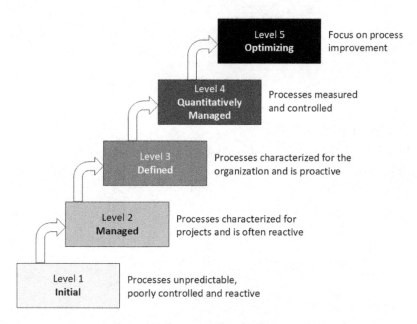

Figure 12: Characteristics of CMMI Maturity Levels

Balanced Scorecard

The _balanced scorecard_ is a management system that helps organizations to create clear goals and translate them into action. It provides feedback around both internal processes and external outcomes, thereby moving from an academic exercise into something real and actionable.

This approach uses four perspectives:

- Learning and growth
- Business process
- Customer
- Financial

For each perspective, metrics are developed, data is collected, and the information is analyzed. **Figure 13** illustrates how the approach works.

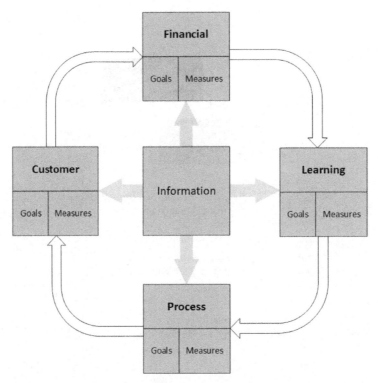

Figure 13: Balanced Scorecard Dimensions

OCTAVE

The *Operationally Critical Threat Asset and Vulnerability Evaluation*, or *OCTAVE*, is another approach to risk assessment. OCTAVE is great when we need a well-established process to identify, prioritize and manage information security risk, and contains three phases:

- *Phase 1* locates all assets and builds a threat profile for each.
- *Phase 2* locates all network paths and IT components required for each asset, and then figures out how vulnerable those components are.
- *Phase 3* assigns risk to each asset and decides what to do about it.

ITIL

The *Information Technology Infrastructure Library*, or *ITIL*, is a set of detailed practices for managing IT services with a special focus on aligning those services with the needs of business.

Chapter 18: Culture

Every company has a unique *culture*, even if no one recognizes it, and it can be defined as the beliefs and resulting behaviors that are expected and are viewed as normal within the company. Cultures will emerge, either accidentally or purposefully – but you can't avoid having one. Creating a security-aware culture is only possible if individuals perform their jobs in a way that protects information assets. Everyone – from the top to the bottom - should be able to quickly articulate how information security relates to their role(s). For this to happen, the security manager must actively foster communications, participate in committees and projects, and make sure that end user needs are met. This requires 'soft skills' above and beyond those required by security. In other words, an effective security manager must be able to build relationships and foster collaborative attitudes with other employees and departments. If done properly, the security department can quickly answer questions such as "What's in it for me?" and "Why should I care?".

How do you know if your organization has a successful security culture? That's easy – look for these four clues:

1) Other departments routinely **include information security representatives** in their internal projects *without* you having to prod them
2) **Users know how** to **identify and report** incidents
3) People **know who the security manager** is
4) People can **tell you their role** in protecting information security

Culture is comprised of seven things:

- Organizational behavior
- How people influence the organization's structure so that work can get done
- Attitudes
- Norms
- How well teams work together
- The existence or lack of turf wars
- Geographic dispersion

The single most element that impacts culture is the experience and belief of each person in an organization. Every organization has a culture whether it has been purposefully defined or simply emerged as the reflection of leadership. It is absolutely critical that an information security manager not focus solely on the technical and administrative aspects, but also foster a desire in the entire department for softer skills such as relationship management.

There is a predictable pattern to the creation of culture, consisting of five steps as shown in **Figure 14**:

1. A group **experiences** something in common
2. The group **responds** to the experience
3. The response is now the **expected behavior** when a similar experience happens in the future
4. That behavior becomes an **unwritten rule**
5. That unwritten rule becomes what is considered **normal**

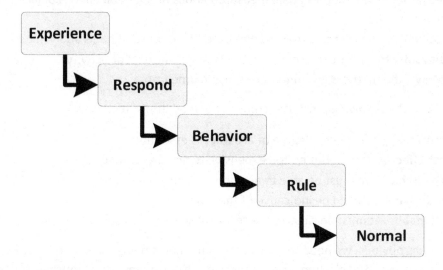

Figure 14: How Cultures are Created

Chapter 19: Metrics

The term *metric* simply means that we have two data points and are comparing them to each other – a reference point and a measured point. The *reference point* represents some type of a baseline – a known value taken at some point in the past. The *measured point* is taken later and is compared to the reference point to see how far off we are, or how far we have come.

The key to effective metrics is to use a set of criteria in determining which are the most suitable. One method for ensuring a given metrics is of value is if it meets all the following attributes in the *SMART* acronym:

- **Specific** – the metric is based on an understood goal, and is clear and concise
- **Measurable** – the metric can be measured and is quantifiable, and is objective instead of being subjective
- **Attainable** – the metric is realistic and based on important goals and values
- **Relevant** – the metric is directly related to a specific goal or activity
- **Timely** – the metric is grounded in a specific time frame

Beyond SMART, the following attributes comprise a good litmus test as well:

- **Accurate** – a reasonable degree of accuracy is essential
- **Cost-Effective** – it cannot be too expensive to acquire or maintain
- **Repeatable** – we must be able to acquire it reliably over time
- **Predictive** – it should be indicative of the outcome
- **Actionable** – it must be clear to the recipient what action should be taken

Though it seems obvious, we need to make sure that what is being measured is actually relevant. Many times, organizations use metrics not because they are of much value, but rather because they are easily available. Metrics serve one purpose only – to provide information necessary to make decisions.

Metrics will fall into one of three categories – strategic, tactical and operational – and each category will be valuable to different audiences. For example, senior management won't care too much about tactical metrics such as the number of password resets, but the IT security manager might. But senior management will be keenly interested in strategic metrics such as emerging risks that may impact business goals.

Chapter 20: Current State, Desired State and the Gap In-Between

Overview

To make progress, we must figure out where we are, where we want to be, and what it will take to get there. A lot of CISM is dedicated to this process – so much so, in fact that we have our very own language around it:

- Where we are now being called the *current state*
- Where we want to be is called the *desired state*
- The work to be done to get from the current state to the desired state is identified by carrying out a *gap analysis*

While the desired state takes a good bit of work to nail down, it is considerably harder to identify and document the current state. So, let's look at the desired state first, then the current state, followed by the gap analysis.

The Desired State

The term *desired state* represents what we would like something to look like at a specific point in the future. To get a high degree of precision, the desired state would be expressed in a *quantitative* value, such as a number with well-known units – for example, US dollars or a percentage of achieving a target goal. Such a quantitative target is seldom possible in the security world, and so we have to settle for a *qualitative* definition in terms of attributes and outcomes. Even though we have to deal with qualitative assessments, that does not mean we should not be as precise as possible, particularly with the desired outcomes. For example, if a desired outcome is to be in compliance with a specific regulatory requirement, there are a host of technical and process requirements that become instantly visible, and we can be precise with those. For example, if we have to comply with 34 different compliance mandates and we have only completed 7, we can estimate the percentage of completion with a high degree of precision at 20.6%.

The Current State

When drawing a picture of the desired state we use a combination of methodologies such as COBIT, CMMI or the balanced scorecard. It turns out that to create a valid picture of where we are today (the current state), we must use the exact same approach we use for creating the desired state of tomorrow. If we use COBIT only for the desired state, then we need to use only COBIT to capture a picture of the current state. If we don't do this, then the subsequent gap analysis will be completely meaningless, since we will not be comparing apples-to-apples. This approach also gives us a leg-up when it comes time to capture metrics, since we can use the same approach to generate those values. Bottom line – choose the approach or approaches and stick to them all the way. A mid-stream changeup is your worst governance nightmare.

When we measure the current state of security, we must also measure the current state of risk. A full risk assessment includes a threat, vulnerability and impact analyses. Many organizations encounter resistance to the cost of carrying this out before mitigation steps are executed, but it is an absolute necessity and will allow us to choose the most cost-effective strategy. Additionally, existing controls must be inventoried and tested so we can know how much they help in getting us to the desired state. Some of the most common methods used to assess risk are the following:

- COBIT 5 for Risk
- NIST SP 800-30
- ISO 27005
- Operationally Critical Threat, Asset and Vulnerability Evaluation (OCTAVE)

A final piece in creating the current state is to carry out a BIA, which does two things for us at this stage:

1) Allows us to **develop an effective strategy** by understanding how effective current controls are and the exposure various risks put us at
2) Provides an input for **information classification** based on business value

After we have ascertained the current state, created a view of the desired state, and performed a gap analysis to show the delta between the two, we are free to create the strategy to move us to the desired state.

When we measure the current state of security, we must also measure the current state of risk. A full risk assessment includes a threat, vulnerability and impact analyses. Many organizations encounter resistance to the cost of carrying this out before mitigation steps are executed, but it is an absolute necessity and will allow us to choose the most cost-effective strategy. Additionally, existing controls must be inventoried and tested so we can know how much they help in getting us to the desired state. Some of the most common methods used to assess risk are the following:

- COBIT 5 for Risk
- NIST SP 800-30
- ISO 27005
- Operationally Critical Threat, Asset and Vulnerability Evaluation (OCTAVE)

A final piece in creating the current state is to carry out a BIA, which does two things for us at this stage:

3) Allows us to **develop an effective strategy** by understanding how effective current controls are and the exposure various risks put us at
4) Provides an input for **information classification** based on business value

Gap Analysis

A _gap analysis_ is simply a recognition of where we are and where we want to be – basically the delta between the two conditions. This needs to be performed for each control goal, each risk, and each impact goal. This exercise needs to be repeated at a minimum once per year – perhaps more – so that changes can be made to reflect the environment the organization operates. A typical approach is to work backward, starting with the desired state and going back to the current state, and determine the series of steps required to reach our goal. CMMI or other methods can be used to assess the gap.

Chapter 21: Information Security Infrastructure and Architecture

Infrastructure can be defined as the foundation upon which information systems are deployed. This would include computing platforms, networks and middleware layers. Applications are built on top of this infrastructure. Security infrastructure is essentially infrastructure that is secure.

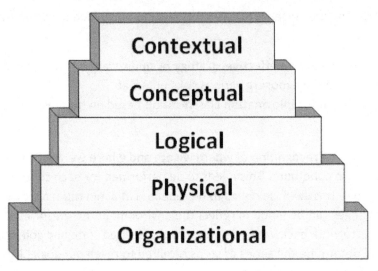

Figure 15: Common Framework Layers

Enterprise information security architecture (EISA) was designed to prevent ad-hoc, haphazard network architectures that are incredibly difficult to secure. The goals of information architecture are the following ten:

- Provide **structure**
- Serve as a **road map**
- Ensure strategic **alignment**
- Support the business **strategy**
- **Implement** security policies and strategies
- Ensure **traceability** back to business requirements and goals
- Provide a level of **abstraction** over technologies
- Establish a **common language** for information security
- Allow many contributors to **work together**

There are several architectural approaches that have been developed over the years, and they can be grouped into three categories:

- **Process models**, which dictate the processes used for each element.
- **Frameworks**, such as COIT, Zachman, SABSA and TOGAF, are very flexible and open. They describe architectural elements and how they relate to each other.
- **Reference models**, which are actually small-scale representations of the actual implementation.

There are four commonly accepted sections within enterprise architecture, as shown in **Figure 16**, and are:

- A business architecture that defines high-level strategies and processes
- A data architecture covering logical and physical assets
- An applications architecture representing deployed applications and their relationships to each other
- A technology architecture describing the infrastructure on top of which applications will be deployed

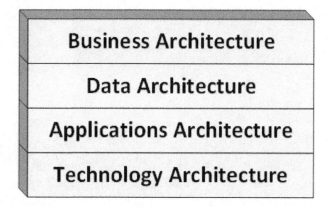

Figure 16: Enterprise Architecture Domains

Unfortunately, the complexity of some frameworks prevents wide-spread adoption. For example, both the SABSA and Zachman frameworks uses a multi-layer approach to try and help with definition. **Figure 15** provides a brief overview. From top to bottom the layers are:

- **Contextual** – who, what, when, where and how

- **Conceptual** – combines architectural design with business concepts
- **Logical** – describes relationships between elements
- **Physical** – describes relationships between the security mechanisms
- **Organizational** – describes the security organization

Many organizations who have attempted to implement SABSA or Zachman have found it difficult to maintain as rapid changes are experienced by the organization.

Chapter 22: Cloud Computing

The concept of cloud computing has been around since the 1960s, but really came into its own when the Internet became a full-fledged force in the early 2000s. The idea behind _cloud computing_ is that processing and data are somewhere in "the cloud" as opposed to being in a known location. However, the cloud does not have to be accessible across the Internet – many companies host their own cloud that is restricted to an intranet – only systems and people within the company's own network can get to it.

Cloud computing has five essential characteristics:

1) It provides **on-demand self-service** by provisioning computing capabilities without any type of human interaction.
2) It is accessible over a **broad network** and can be used with diverse client platforms.
3) Computer **resources are pooled** and reusable so that multiple tenants can use it simultaneously. A tenant can be anything from a single user to an entire company.
4) Resource can rapidly scale up or down, called **elasticity**, in response to real-time business needs. In most cases this happens automatically without any reconfiguration needed.
5) Customers are charged-per-use, so they only pay for what they use. This is called a **measured service**.

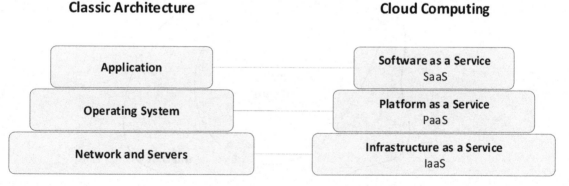

Figure 17: Classic Architecture vs. Cloud Computing

The cloud model is comprised of three service models, all having a corresponding cousin in classic computer architecture, as shown in **Figure 17**.

Infrastructure as a Service, or *IaaS*, provides the customer with a ready-made network, storage and servers, ready for the operating systems to be installed and configured.

Platform as a Service, or *PaaS*, takes it one step further and manages the operating systems, middleware and other run-time components. PaaS is ready for a custom application to be deployed.

Software as a Service, or *SaaS*, is essentially an application that someone hosts and maintains. The customer simply manages user accounts, and employees log in and use the application.

There are four types of cloud deployment models, as shown in **Figure 18**.

A *private cloud* is entirely hosted inside of a company's intranet and is not accessible externally. Employee-only applications, such as an HR website, are hosted in a private cloud.

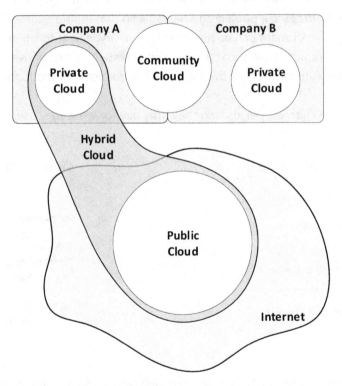

Figure 18: Cloud Computing Deployment Models

If you take a private cloud and allow a select few other companies to access it, it becomes a *community cloud*. Private networks between multiple companies are examples of this model.

If an application is hosted across the Internet and is publicly accessible, it is in the *public cloud*. This represents the majority of SaaS applications.

The last model, a *hybrid model*, is achieved when a private cloud connects across the public Internet into another application. This is the model normally chosen when companies want to host their custom applications in the public cloud but need to maintain a constant connection between employees and the application.

Overtime, new classes of services have evolved using the 'as a Service' model. These are shown in **Figure 19**.

Figure 19: 'as a Service' Offerings

Security as a Service, or *SecaaS*, provides a way to outsource security processes. For example, a cloud service provider, or CSP, can provide managed services such as antivirus scanning and email security. Or, the CSP can actually host CPU and memory-intensive processes onto hardware managed in the cloud. This has the advantage of reducing the need for the customer to apply patches or updates to those systems as the CSP will take care of it.

When a company offers *Disaster Recovery as a Service*, or *DRaaS*, it takes on the responsibility of hosting and maintaining a disaster recovery solution in the cloud. In addition to backup equipment, the CSP will usually offer services for a business continuity plan, or BCP. The benefits include the following:

- The **cost** over an in-house DR **is much less**. Since DR is not a core business function, the ROI can often be considerable.
- Although it is hosted in the cloud, the servers must be physically located *somewhere*, and if those backup servers are not in the same general area as the company's primary servers, then a **disaster is less likely to affect both**.

Identity as a Service, or *IDaaS*, has two different interpretations:

- The management of identities used by the company internally is hosted in the cloud, but the company still implements its own identity and access management (IAM) solution.
- The IAM itself is hosted in the cloud. This is called a *federated identity*.

Data Storage and Data Analytics as a Service, or *big data*, is delivered when the storage and analysis of huge amounts of data is performed in the cloud. The primary advantage of big data is that it delivers an almost unlimited amount of storage capacity so that any amount of data can be mined for patterns.

Cloud access security brokers, or *CASBs*, provide an easy and comprehensive way to secure the path between a company and hosted cloud services. CASBs provide the following services:

- Authentication
- Authorization
- Single Sign-On (SSO)
- Tokenization
- Logging
- Notification and alerts
- Malware detection and prevention

Information as a Service, or *IaaS* – not to be confused with Infrastructure as a Service – builds on big data and takes it one step further. Whereas big data provides the processing power to sift through data and answer a question, IaaS only requires you to ask the question – it takes care of the analysis itself.

Integration Platform as a Service, or *IPaaS*, comes into play when a hybrid cloud model is used. Because systems in a hybrid model are accessed across company boundaries and into the public cloud, connecting systems and applications together while maintaining a cohesive IT approach can be daunting. IPaaS by providing a virtual environment on which to host all of these systems.

Computer forensics can be a tricky proposition unless you have the right tools, which are often very expensive, and the experience needed to analyze and store evidence that will hold up in court. _Forensics as a Service_, or _FRaaS_, provides those tools and optionally the needed expertise.

Advantages of Cloud Computing

Some have compared the advent of cloud computing to the introduction of the personal computer or even the Internet. However, there is one big difference – personal computers and the Internet took decades to develop, but cloud computing has popped up and made its way into everyday use over the course of just a few years. Let's discuss a few of the reasons why that is so.

First of all, by using cloud-based resources that can scale up or down at a moment's notice, we have a virtually unlimited resource pool to draw from whenever we need to. Add to that the ability to pay for only what we use, and the value proposition goes through the roof.

Secondly, companies operate on two types of expenditures – capital and operational. Capital expenditures are not favored for a variety of reasons, but that is how money spent on hardware and software is categorized. On the other hand, if we take that same money and pay for cloud-hosted solutions, then we can claim it is an operational expenditure since we are not actually purchasing anything. Not only that, but we can 'dip our toes in the water' and try out new capabilities without having to spend huge amounts of money. Add to that the ability to quickly implement new solutions, and we have the makings of a major win-win.

Next, because we can scale up at any time, our applications become that much more performant, responsive and scalable basically for free. All of those adjectives – performant, responsive, scalable and most of all, _free_ - are things IT managers love to hear.

Another advantage is the ease with which we can upgrade software versions and apply patches. Without going into a lot of explanation, virtualization and virtual images are behind that.

And finally, cloud services such as Amazon's AWS or Microsoft's Azure are famously redundant with fail-over data centers located around the globe. This takes resiliency to a whole new level.

Unfortunately, all of this high-praise does come at a cost in terms of increased risk. Due to the inherent nature of intentionally hiding the complexity of hosting cloud services, we also have to deal with a lack of transparency on the CSP's side. If we were to host data in our own data center, the data owner would have full access to and knowledge about that data. When we store this data in the cloud, we rarely have any type of knowledge of where the data is stored and in what manner. As a result, certain types of data and processes should not be stored in the cloud regardless of the economics due to increased security risks.

Another factor to consider when dealing with global cloud providers is that our data may now cross jurisdictional boundaries without us even knowing it. That could get us in real trouble if regulatory offices hear about it and decide to enforce some rather stiff penalties.

One last negative note about security and CSPs. The availability of audit logs will almost certainly be a challenge to overcome, and the actual level of secure controls being implemented will more than likely be completely invisible to the customer.

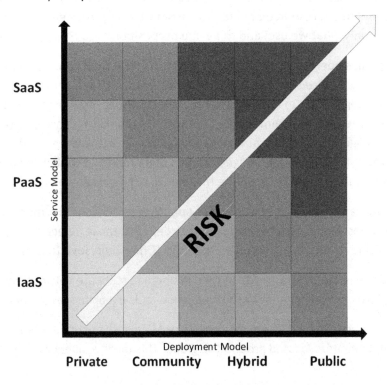

Figure 20: Cloud Computing Risk Map

115

If you take all of the above advantages and disadvantages together along with both the cloud and deployment models, we can come up with a two-dimensional matrix to help us map and describe the risk/benefit discussion. This is shown in **Figure 20**.

To help with the selection of a CSP, there are a number of frameworks available for us to use that are built specifically for cloud providers, such as the CSA Cloud Control Matrix and the Jericho Forum Self-Assessment Scheme.

Chapter 23: Metrics Development

When it comes down to it, we can ask three simple questions to help us design meaningful metrics:

- Who needs to know what?
- What do they need to know?
- When do they need to know it?

In short, we need to define the who, what, and when. Beyond that, there are three levels at which metrics can inform us – strategic, management and operational. Let's take a look at each.

Strategic metrics provide the information necessary to guide decisions at the senior management level. While often comprised of multiple management metrics, strategic metrics let us know if the security program is headed in the right direction.

Management metrics, sometimes called tactical metrics, is used by the security manager to determine if the security program is remaining in compliance, tackling emerging risk and is in alignment with business goals. There is also a need at the management level to look at technical metrics to ensure the various mechanisms are operating at the right level. For example, while driving a car we need to keep an eye on the gas gauge, because while the level of fuel says nothing about where we are headed, if we run out of gas we are sure to never get there.

Operational metrics are comprised of technical and procedural metrics such as existing vulnerabilities and the progress of our patch management processes. There are a number of attributes that a useful metric should contain. We are going to use the fuel gauge in a car to illustrate each attribute.

- **Manageable** – the data should be readily collected and understood; the fuel gauge must reflect the gas level in real-time, and we should not be wondering what the little pointer means.
- **Meaningful** – the data should be relevant to our goals; if the car is turned off the fuel gauge is useless – it only applies when the car is running.
- **Actionable** – the data should indicate what actions to take without requiring further investigation; it does no good for the fuel gauge to say, 'fuel may be low – you should calculate how much fuel you have left based on the number of miles driven' – instead it simply show the level of fuel!

- **Unambiguous** – the data must be clear; we should not have to wonder if the bottom of the scale is full or empty.
- **Reliable** – the data must provide the same information each time the same set of circumstances is reached; it does no good for a fuel gauge to read ¼ full sometimes or completely empty at other times when it is actually 1/8 full.
- **Accurate** – the data represents the actual situation; it is far worse for a fuel gauge to show half full when it is nearly empty, than it is to simply be broken.
- **Timely** – the data is delivered when needed; it does us no good to run out of gas and *then* the gauge dips to empty.
- **Predictive** – the data must predict where we are heading; cars that show the number of miles till empty based on historical fuel usage are very handy indeed.
- **Genuine** – the data must not have been manipulated and represent actual measurements; sometimes cars will hide the number of miles till empty starting at 50 miles or so instead of showing us the real value – we need metrics to give us the real information instead of trying to 'help'.

If we measure how well a specific metric meets each attribute just mentioned, then we could theoretically calculate an overall value and prioritize metrics based on how well they meet the attributes. This is called using *metametrics*. Unfortunately, just because a metric scores well using the metametrics approach does not guarantee it will be useful. Instead, we can choose two different metrics that measure the same thing, and then see how well they track with each other. In our example, if we fill a 20-gallon gas tank, and drive a number of miles until it should be half-full, we would expect our fuel gauge to show half-full. In this case the two metrics are miles driven and fuel gauge readout. If they agree, then we can be reasonable certain they are both accurate.

Chapter 24: Business Model for Information Security (BMIS)

The *business model for information security*, or *BMIS,* takes a business-oriented approach to information security by modeling complex relationships in businesses using *system theory*. The classic definition of *system theory* is...

> *...a complex network of events, relationships, reactions, consequences, technologies, processes and people that interact in often unseen and unexpected ways.*

In simpler terms, system theory views a system as a complete functioning unit – not simply the sum of its parts. This means that we can use one part of a system to understand other parts, since they all function together. *Systems thinking* is the term for this approach, and it explains why 'the whole is more than the sum of its parts'. Systems thinking drives us to study the results of interactions within a system, and we therefore get a better understanding of the system itself.

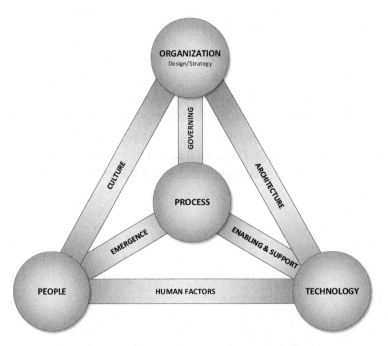

Figure 21: Business Model for Information Security

Why is this important? Well, if you look at how organizations have historically approached security, you see a lot of spectacular failures resulting from the inability to define security in a way that stakeholders can comprehend it. If you can't understand a problem, then you really have no hope of solving it. Systems theory and systems thinking allows us to cut through the fog, so we can clearly view the actions needed to manage security effectively. In this way, both internal and external changes are considered.

Because of its value, BMIS provides the basis for frameworks such as COBIT. As can be seen in **Figure 21**, COBIT contains four primary elements – Organization, People, Process and Technology, and each element is connected to all other elements by dynamic relationships. If any one relationship changes and is not managed, the overall equilibrium becomes unstable. Let's dig into each element a little further.

Organization Design and Strategy

The first element in BMIS is *organization design and strategy*. A good definition of an <u>organization</u> is…

> …*a network of people, assets and processes interacting with each other in defined roles and working toward a common goal.*

An organization's <u>*strategy*</u> is made up of a list of goals to be reached, and the values that will be adhered to along the way. Another way of putting it is that strategy is the basic direction in which we will be heading. <u>*Design*</u> is how an organization implements the strategy and includes processes, culture and architecture. Design tells us what the 'boots on the ground' are going to be doing.

So, how do we get from strategy to design? That's where <u>*resources*</u> come into play – people, equipment and know-how. In summary, a strategy is created, and resources take that strategy and create a design.

People

The second element is people, which represents the humans in the equation along with all of the security problems they bring with them. The value of this element is that it tells us *who* will implement each part of the strategy using our design. Because humans are involved, the information security manager must work closely with the Human Resources and Legal departments to address three things:

1. **Recruitment issues** such as background checks, interviews, access rights after hire, and roles and responsibilities.
2. **Employment issues** such as office location, access to the proper tools, and training.
3. **Termination issues** such as knowing the reason for leaving, timing of exit, and removing access to systems.

Process

The third element is called *processes*. If design results from strategy, then processes result from design and is where the actual work happens. Put simply, *processes* are how we implement the design of our strategy. But, not all processes are created equal – to be of value a process must:

- **Meet** some type of **business requirements** and align with policy.
- **Be adaptable** to changing requirements.
- **Be well documented** and communicated to the right people.
- **Be reviewed periodically** to make sure they are effective.

Technology

The last major element in BMIS is called *technology* and represents all the tools, applications and infrastructure at our disposal. While technology is a fantastic tool to solve many security issues, management teams often over-rotate on this view and think it can be used to address all threats and risks. While technical controls are very handy, technology by itself is *not* an information security solution. Security managers must understand that people will always try and sidestep technical controls, and so other non-technical controls must be used as well.

Dynamic Interactions

So, we've covered the four primary elements in BMIS – organization, people, process and technology. Now let's take a look at the six dynamic interactions between each of those elements. There are four elements, and each element has a relationship with the other three. That results in six unique relationships.

Governance is the relationship between Organization and Process. The *organization governs* by using *processes*. This is successful only when processes can adapt to changing requirements and their performance is effectively measured.

Culture is the relationship between Organization and People – *people* within an *organization* will always create a *culture*. This can be defined as a pattern of beliefs, assumptions and attitudes that drive the way we do things.

Culture exists on many levels, such as national, organizational and social. It is created by both internal and external influences. Most importantly, culture is simultaneously driven by organizational patterns and is itself influenced by organizational patterns.

Enabling and Support is the relationship between Process and Technology. *Processes* and *technologies* by themselves are mostly useless, but when we combine them, we find ourselves *enabling and supporting* business goals. But, when applying those processes and tools to information security, we have to be careful. There is always a certain amount of tension between effective security and ease of use. If security places too much of a burden on people, they will attempt to go around it. On the other hand, if security focuses too much on ease of use, then it can easily become ineffective. Being transparent with planned security measures can go a long way to make users feel that their concerns are being considered.

Emergence is the relationship between Process and People. *People* will always cause new issues to *emerge*, and we use *processes* to handle those issues. Put another way, when people are involved, the unexpected will happen. That is why it is important that processes are created that can accommodate emerging trends and needs in a quick manner. Feedback loops are often useful within this dynamic interaction.

Human Factors is the relationship between People and Technology. When you combine people with technology, we encounter *human factors*, or the ease with which *people* interact with *technology*. This interaction represents the gap between technology that is being used, and the adoption of that technology by people it touches. If people do not understand how to use it, do not like it or do not follow the appropriate policies, effective security will not happen. Some reasons for these gaps are varying experience levels, and cultural or generational differences. Security risks that result are data leakage, theft and misuse.

Architecture is the relationship between Organization and Technology. An *organization* creates an *architecture* to roll out *technology*. When applied to information security, a key term to remember within this dynamic is _defense in-depth_, meaning the organization's security architecture should be comprised of multiple layers of risk controls. If defense in-depth has been applied, the failure of any one control does not result in a security breach because there is always a secondary control that should kick in. Often companies have 4 or 5 different layers. An example of securing a database with a defense-in-depth approach might be the following layers:

1. A **firewall** watching all Internet traffic
2. A **secondary firewall** behind the first
3. The **database is encrypted** and requires a decryption key
4. The unencrypted database will not operate without a **username and password**
5. All passwords are stored as **one-way hashes** instead of clear text, requiring a brute force attack to be read

In this example, we have 5 layers of defense, and a successful breach would require all 5 layers to be defeated.

Section 2: The Four Domains

Now that we've covered the basics, it's time to dive into each domain. When we run across a concept or term that has already been covered, we're not going to rehash it – if you have already forgotten, just look back in Section 1 and do a quick review. Now, let's take a quick look at each domain so you can see how they fit together.

First, the **Information Security Governance Domain** introduces what a proper governance structure looks like, and how to use one to ensure security goals are aligned with business goals.

Then, the **Information Risk Management Domain** explains how to identify risk and keep it an acceptable level under the watchful eye of governance.

This is followed by the **Information Security Program Development and Management Domain**, which covers how to create and run a security program that prevents a business from having to experience events such as security breaches or sabotage. Well, that prevents *most* of them from happening anyway.

And finally, the **Information Security Incident Management Domain** discusses what to do when security events occur in spite of our security program. In this domain we cover the detection, investigation, response to and recovery from those events.

To make it easier to understand, each domain is presented in the same format and flow, with the content being tailored for the specific area. You will encounter the following sections, in order, for each domain:

1) **Overview** – a high-level view of the domain's content and purpose
2) **The Goal** – the goals we want to achieve within the domain
3) **The Strategy** – the strategy on how we will achieve our goals
4) **Who Does What** – the roles, responsibilities and skills required for to be successful
5) **Resources That Help** – people, mechanisms, processes and systems that we will need to take advantage of
6) **Constraints That Hinder** – factors that will work against our success if we don't stay vigilant
7) **The Action Plan** – a plan on how to take the theoretical strategy and implement it in the real world
8) **Metrics and Monitoring** – how we will measure our action plan along the way to see if we are being successful

9) **What Success Looks Like** – what the outcome will look like when we successfully define the goal, develop a strategy to reach the goal, create a plan based on the strategy, implement the plan, and measure success of the plan. In short, what we hope to see if we carry out the domain properly.

Let's get started!

Chapter 25: Information Security Governance – Overview

What is Information?

Information is 'data having meaning and purpose'. In today's world, generating or handling information is often the whole point of why many companies exist. For the rest of the companies, information almost always plays a crucial part in their survival. Information is important!

But the sad truth is that most organizations do next to nothing to protect that vital resource. Whether it is keeping it out of a competitor's hands or simply making sure it doesn't get lost due to some hard drive failure, the clear majority of businesses simply play Russian Roulette and hope nothing bad happens. But here is the truth we all need to accept – it is not a matter of 'if', but 'when', something bad happens. And that is why we need to take _information security_ seriously and secure our precious information against theft and loss.

Sounds simple, right? Oh, but the devil in the details can be overwhelming. So much so that business after business gives up on securing their data, simply because it is so complex and hard to secure that information. The only way a company can reliably make sure it protects its own information is to implement some type of _governance_ that has the authority to make it happen. And that is why we have something called – wait for it - information security governance. In a nutshell, _information security governance_ is the act of creating a plan on how a company will protect information and then making sure everyone executes that plan.

Let's revisit our definition of information – we previously said that it is 'data having meaning and purpose'. But if information just sits there without being consumed, it is pretty much useless. The moment we absorb some of that information, it becomes _knowledge._ Turning that around, we can also say that knowledge is persisted as information.

To recap, _data_ is nothing but facts. But when data means something to us, it becomes _information_. When we absorb that information, it becomes _knowledge_. And when a company has knowledge, it can do some pretty amazing things with it. Information security governance is all about protecting the entire path of 'data to information to knowledge', and the reverse of that path.

Interestingly enough, in recent years businesses have slowly become aware of a benefit of proper information security governance besides the obvious protection against theft and loss. As security breaches have become more public, a company that proves it has a high-level of security hygiene might very well enjoy an improved perception in the marketplace, often resulting in an increased monetary value for the company. So, while the cost of proper information security can be quite expensive, we are approaching the point at which intangible benefits often help underwrite that cost. In fact, many companies today consider those costs to be an investment with a rather sizeable return. The world is slowly arriving at a point where a company can actually *increase* its value by investing in proper information security! Just a sign of the times.

Lots of Governance

In Section 1 we described governance as someone having the authority and responsibility to make sure something happens. Within the typical business, there are four different areas of governance we will encounter – enterprise, corporate, IT and information security. **Figure 22** illustrates the various relationships.

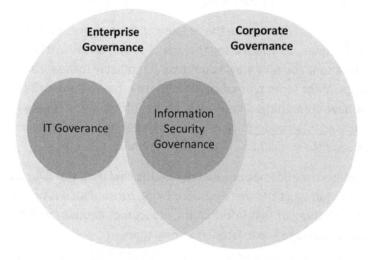

Figure 22: Governance Relationships

Starting at the top, *enterprise governance* watches over the entire organization or business, commonly referred to as the *enterprise*. Sitting right beside it is *corporate* governance, which sets the strategic direction of a business by defining goals. Enterprise governance and corporate governance overlap slightly, and this is right where *information security governance* lives since it is concerned with both business goals and how a business operates internally. Finally, IT governance, which is concerned with all things IT, resides wholly inside of enterprise governance.

127

GRC, the Trifecta

In addition to governance, there are two other concepts that are important to this topic - risk management and compliance. Collectively, the three - governance, risk management and compliance - are considered to be a trifecta in the information security world because of the advantage of integrating those three different areas into a single approach. In fact, the acronym _GRC_ is used to describe this business activity. Let's quickly describe these two new terms.

Risk management is the action of addressing known risks until they are at acceptable levels, identifying potential risks and associated impacts, and prioritizing both against our business goals. Reducing risk is called _mitigation_, and the way we mitigate risks is by implementing one or more _controls_. A control can be anything from setting up a firewall to making sure doors are locked after business hours. We have already covered the meaning of compliance in Section 1, but we'll repeat it here anyway. _Compliance_ is the act of measuring policies, procedures and controls to ensure they are being enacted and effective.

GRC pulls them all three together – governance, risk management and compliance - but there is a dependence on the order in which we can address each. Governance must be put into place _before_ risk can be mitigated or compliance enforced. GRC was originally created in response to SOX but has evolved over time to be a valid approach to risk management. The primary difficulty with GRC is that each of the three terms can mean different things to different organizations. In spite of this, the security industry has pretty much settled on using GRC in the following three areas:

1. Finance and audit
2. IT management
3. Enterprise risk management

Chapter 26: Information Security Governance – The Goal

Bad Assumptions

Before we can develop a successful information security strategy, the very first question to answer is pretty simple – "What is our goal?" While the question is straightforward, getting to the answer is surprisingly difficult. Many companies assume the answer is obvious – we want to protect the organization's information assets. The problem here is that we are assuming two things:

1) Information assets are known to any degree of precision
2) We understand what 'protect' means

The problem is that it is hard to state *which* assets need *how much* protection and against *what*. Rather than go to the trouble of answering that question, most organizations simply take the view that storage is cheap, people are intrinsically nice, and humans don't make really bad mistakes. A seriously bad move, because now it is almost impossible to justify spending resources on something that is not a real risk in our mind. We ignore the amount of dangerous data floating around our servers. Dangerous data in this context refers to information that might be used against the organization but could have been destroyed if we had simply taken the time to put in a proper retention policy.

There is a saying that goes something like "If you don't know where you're going, you won't know when you get there." Without clearly-defined goals we cannot create a strategy. Without a security strategy we have no hope of increasing security, and in fact we will probably make things worse by spending money with no return. Unfortunately, the reality is that most organizations do not spend resources on security until *after* the first major incident, which winds up being way costlier than if proper measures had been taken upfront. The problem is that it is nigh impossible to prove that we have avoided a bad thing if the bad thing never happened because we took steps to avoid it. You just can't prove a negative like "We avoided a car accident because we chose to drive down a different street."

Good Goals

This is why it is so crucial to state security goals in business terms, so that senior management can clearly see the link between 'avoiding bad things' and the resulting positive revenue impact. Another approach is to use security to enable activities that would otherwise be too risky. For example, if we use public key infrastructure (PKI) to enable real-time communication between high-value partners, or we implement a virtual private network (VPN) to allow employees to work remotely, our security capabilities have just allowed us to reach business goals that would have been otherwise impossible due to the risks involved.

Yet another approach is to examine business linkages and to couch security goals in terms of facilitating those linkages. For example, let's say that one of our operations unit churns out blue widgets 24 hours a day, and relies on the raw materials to arrive on-time based on automated supply orders. Furthermore, shipping of the completed blue widgets depends on an automated system to contact trucking companies and arrange for pickup. This represents two separate linkages. All of this infrastructure relies on confidentiality (don't let competitors know), integrity (the data needs to be accurate) and availability (the connections need to always be available) – core tenants for information security. Information security now has the task of ensuring uninterrupted manufacturing of blue widgets, and an interruption in the entire supply chain can be easily quantified in terms of lost sales or idle employees. We have now tied our security value proposition to business linkages.

Chapter 27: Information Security Governance – The Strategy

Who's Creating this Strategy, Anyway?

When developing a strategy, there are a number of participants that must be accounted for, as shown by **Figure 23.**

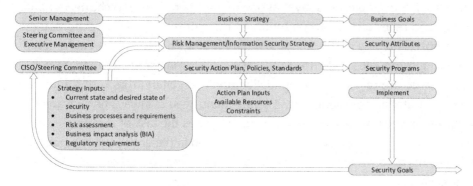

Figure 23: Information Security Strategy Development Participants

The most important thing to note here is how security goals align with business goals. The business strategy not only leads to business goals but provides an input into the risk management and information security strategy block as well. Note also how both the current and desired state of security feeds into that block as well. While not clearly shown here, the organization's appetite for risk acts as a constant constraint over the entire process. Be sure to note all 'Strategy Inputs' which are:

- Current state and desired state of security
- Business processes and requirements
- Risk assessment
- BIA
- Regulatory requirements

Putting Data in Buckets

Let's assume that we are smarter than the organizations we described at the beginning of this chapter, and we are going to invest in information security. The first thing we need to do is to classify information by its criticality and sensitivity. By doing this, we can apply protective measures in proportion to the information's business value instead of making wild guesses. If done properly, most organizations discover that the vast majority of data is neither critical or sensitive, meaning we have just saved ourselves a huge amount of money by not protecting those assets. Keep that in mind when people complain about the time and effort required for proper classification!

The protection of information assets must be prioritized if the organization is budget constrained, which is almost always the case. By attaching value to the various assets, it becomes much easier to figure out which should be protected if we can only cover a portion of all valued assets. Arriving at a value can be difficult though – we can choose to use the cost of creating or replacing the information, or how much damage would result if the information were to be leaked. In some case there simply is no way to arrive at a value since the loss would completely devastate the company, such as trade secrets. A useful approach is to create levels of value, with the lowest being very little value and the highest level representing those assets that are priceless. Assets that have no discernable owner, and there is no evidence of the information being used for a period of time would be assigned the lowest value.

A second approach that might be much easier to execute is to define critical business processes and figure out what information and physical assets are required for those processes. By tying assets to revenue generation, it becomes clear what is important and what is not.

But, those two approaches are designed to identify value, or *criticality*. The other attribute that is important is the *sensitivity* of information. Whereas criticality is concerned with the impact if we lose control of information, sensitivity is concerned with the impact if we accidentally disclose information - in this case we have not lost control of the information, but others are now aware of facts that can then be used to damage the organization. In this case the data owner is the best person to identify the classification level.

Data classification is an absolute necessity if we are going to be serious about security governance, because it prevents us from over-protecting low-value assets and under-protecting high-value assets. The longer we wait, the harder it becomes over time. However, we must be sure not to over rotate and declare that everything is of high-value – this often happens in a high-blame environment where no one wants to be charged with not protecting information properly. A useful way to combat this is for IT to charge business units for storage of higher-classified information – hitting the pocketbook always makes people think twice. One last item that must be addressed if we hope to become a security-conscious organization is to ensure that all assets have a defined owner and accountability – a RACI matrix is a great tool for making this happen.

A strategy will give us the needed framework on which to create a road map, which are the series of steps to be executed to implement our strategy. A good security strategy will mitigate risk while supporting business goals, as well as showing us how we will embed good security practices into every area of the business.

Staying Cheap

We can classify data all day long, and come up with sorts of great strategies, but if the cost of implementing a given strategy is too high, it will never see the light of day. That is why keeping a tight view on the costs of a strategy the entire time it is under development is very important. We need to ensure the following statements are true if we hope to have a cost-effective security strategy:

- **Business requirements have been defined** for information security.
- **Goals have been defined** for information security that will meet business requirements.
- **Information assets** and resources have been identified.
- **Value has been assigned** to information assets and resources.
- **Information has been classified** for both criticality and sensitivity.
- All assets have a **defined owner**.

Avoiding the Reinvention of the Wheel

The chances are that 80% of our strategy work has already been done by some other organization, business or entity. While our business is bound to have some unique aspects to it, we should be able to leverage one or more standards or frameworks. However, the various options for this are not all created equal – some are targeted for general use while others are more specific in their intended use. **Figure 24** illustrates this by listing our options in the following four categories:

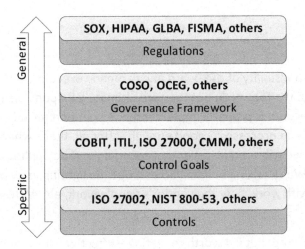

Figure 24: Prevalent Standards and Frameworks

1) SOX, HIPPA, GLBA and FISMA are designed for federal agencies, although some have seen extensive use in the private sector.
2) COSO and OCEG provide a governance framework only.
3) COBIT, ITIL, ISO 27000 series and CMMI provide goals for controls.
4) ISO 27002 and NIST 800-53 provide a list of very specific controls.

Chapter 28: Information Security Governance – Who Does What

Who Does Governance?

Governance is the responsibility of the board and company executives. These folks at the top might delegate a lot of the footwork, but they are ultimately responsible (and legally liable) to ensure information security is properly implemented. A common mistake is to assume that protecting IT systems and processes is good enough. After all, that's where the data is stored, right? Unfortunately, we will soon discover that security must be applied at a much larger scope than just IT systems. We're talking building access, outside lighting, how people work, how the vendors we interact with work, how the vendor's people work, etc. MUCH bigger than IT systems.

We've mentioned it before, but it's worth repeating – effective information security governance only happens when the most senior levels of management are involved. If those at the very top aren't behind it, *it will fail*. Along the same lines, if those at the top can't tell if their actions are being effective, *it will also fail*. That is why those in charge must periodically be provided a report on how well information security policies and procedures are doing in the form of a BIA. It should go without saying that senior management must abide by the policies they demand everyone else follow.

We have already covered roles, responsibilities, RACI and skills in Section 1. We just need to note here that employment agreements should reference those roles, responsibilities and skills, and should be considered when screening applicants for new hires.

Working with the Top Dogs (the Executive Team)

Let's now discuss how the information security manager works with the executive team. As stated before, the executive team is ultimately responsible for ensuring proper security, but that team relies heavily on the information security manager to provide direction in the form of an advisor. Essentially, the manager will make recommendations to senior leadership, who will consider all options and make decisions, which are then carried out by the manager. It is crucial that senior management remains visibly engaged throughout the entire process, as this will set the 'tone at the top' and will directly influence how engaged the rest of the organization remains. If this is done properly, the entire organization will be on-board with a healthy view of security.

Another method for ensuring that the entire organization remains engaged with security is to form a _steering committee_ that is made up of senior representatives from all impacted groups. This makes it much easier to arrive at a consensus on priorities and tradeoffs and is a great method for establishing communication channels. Some common topics this committee addresses are:

- How to **integrate security** with business activities
- How to get business units to **support** the security goals
- **Emerging risks** and compliance issues

It is up to the security manager to clearly define the purpose of the steering committee and how it should operate. The biggest obstacle to overcome is to make sure the committee does not get sidetracked on unimportant subjects. Another hurdle to overcome is to ensure members review material and subjects for upcoming meetings _before_ each meeting actually takes place.

While we're on the subject of working with executives, we need to recognize that all organizations have a _chief information security officer_, or _CISO_, or a _chief security officer_, or _CSO_, even if the organization doesn't know or acknowledge the fact. Whoever is responsible for ensuring information security is the CISO, even if they also hold another title such as CEO, CFO, etc. But it _must_ be a C-level officer. If a business tries to pretend such a position does not exist, the responsibility will fall to the CEO, who will become the default CISO in the eyes of the law – there is just no way of getting around it. In 2006 only about 20% of organizations officially recognized the title of CISO or CSO. By 2011, more than 80% did so.

The Never-Ending Battle Between IT and Information Security

There is an interesting dynamic at-play when it comes to IT that we should discuss as part of senior management responsibilities. The classic IT responsibility has always been about performance – how fast features operate, how much up-time the business experiences with those features, how much they cost to maintain and how easy it is for people to access services. IT has always been about making technology and people work smoothly. But security is often directly at-odds with that view. Security is more concerned about keeping data and capabilities out of the hands of unauthorized people and making sure we have redundant stores so that data is not lost, even at the expense of speed or usability. A rule of thumb says that as security increases, ease of use decreases. It is very difficult to achieve a nice balance between the two.

Now, just imagine you have two people trying to carry out each viewpoint – one whose job it is to make technology easy to use, and one whose job it is to make data safe. They will be forever getting in each other's way. But there is a much more concerning scenario – what if one person was tasked to do both jobs? Talk about a conflicted person! When that happens, that individual will always choose the path that will be the least painful, which will be ease of use. After all, employees will always gripe when things are hard, but when is the last time you heard a hacker call up IT and say 'You know, you should really put in a firewall. You're making my life way too easy.' That is why it is so crucial that you have separate people assigned to each role.

But even if you assign the roles to different people, it can still get complicated. Imagine both of these people reporting to the same boss. Guess what direction the boss is going to give? You got it – whatever will make the most people happy. Therefore, not only must you give each role to different people, they must also each report up through different C-level executives. *Never* have a security manager report up to the same executive that the IT manager reports to. In fact, it is not uncommon for a security manager to report directly to the CEO or the board, instead of up through the _chief information officer_, or _CIO_. Alternatively, we are seeing more CISOs than ever before existing right alongside the _chief technology officer_, or _CTO_.

The primary goal for information security governance is to manage risks effectively at an acceptable cost. A balance between risk mitigation and how much it costs to carry that out must be discovered over time, and this can be achieved only if everyone is involved. When carried out properly, risk management activities are integrated together and fall under a clear set of rules and goals. This in turn prevents gaps in coverage, redundant effort and departments working against each other.

Roles – Top to Bottom

NIST has created a number of publications, one of which is particularly relevant to risk assessments – _NIST 800-30: Guide for Conducting Risk Assessments_. This special publication describes the key roles that support the risk management process. While each organization is unique, the defined roles map fairly well to just about any company. Let's go over them and describe the responsibilities of each.

- The **Governing Board and Senior Management** must exercise due care and is ultimately responsible for ensuring sufficient resources are made available to address security risk. Ongoing risk assessments must be part of their decision making.

- The **Chief Risk Officer**, or CRO, is in charge of enterprise risk management (ERM), which may include information security, but certainly includes operational risk, environmental risk and credit risk.
- The **Chief Information Officer**, or CIO, handles IT planning, budgeting and performance, and often includes information security as defined by the policies and standards of the CISO or the security manager.
- The **Chief Information Security Officer** or CISO, performs the same functions as the security manager, but holds greater authority and reports to the CEO, COO or the board of directors. This position includes more strategic and management aspects than a security manager might have.
- The **Information Security Manager** is responsible for security programs that create a methodology to identify and manage risk, usually including IT systems. Security managers also act as consultants to senior management and the board.
- **System and Information Owners** ensure controls are in place to address CIA (confidentiality, integrity and availability), and who must approve changes to IT systems.
- **Business and Functional Managers** are managers responsible for business operations and the IT procurement processes.
- **IT Security Practitioners** interact with IT systems on a daily basis and enact changes as needed. Security practitioners use the risk management process to identify and triage new risks, and make sure that new security controls are implemented properly.
- **Security Awareness Trainers** understand risk management goals and processes and create training materials and programs to spread this knowledge to the appropriate employees.

To summarize some of the information we just covered, take a look at a RACI chart showing roles and responsibilities in **Table 3**.

	Information Security Manager	Board of Directors	Chief Information Security Officer	Chief Executive Officer	Business Process Owner
Define the target IT capabilities	C		R	A	I
Conduct a gap analysis	R		A		R

Define the strategic plan and roadmap	C		A	C	
Communicate the IT strategy/direction	I	I	R	R	I

Table 3: Roles and Responsibilities RACI Matrix

Getting Buy-In from the Top

Once the information security manager has created the security strategy, it is time to get approval. Since it can be a rather complex subject, the manager may need to educate the board while presenting the solution, sometimes with associated workshops. Since the true value of a solution is often not recognized until information systems security fails, we want to make every effort to get leadership on-board with the plan *before* we experience those nasty failures.

If the information security manager is not able to get effective buy-in, it is sometimes useful to resort to educating senior management on regulatory compliance, the sanctions they may face, and how dependent the company is on the informational assets. Documenting the potential impacts of various scenarios may also help. A reminder that senior management will be held liable for failure to exercise due care is always a good fallback. If senior management needs help in understanding what actions would constitute an appropriate level of support, the following list may help (some are repeated from earlier for completeness):

- **Clear approval** and support for formal security strategies and policies
- The ability to **measure performance** in implementing those policies
- Supporting security **awareness and training** for all staff
- Sufficient **resources and authority** to implement security activities
- Treating information security as a **critical business issue**
- Demonstrating to third-parties that information **security is taken seriously**
- Providing high-level **oversight and control**
- Periodically **reviewing security effectiveness**
- **Setting the example** themselves by following policies and procedures
- Addressing information security issues at **board meetings**

At times, full support from senior management may simply be a matter of insufficient resources. In these cases, the information security manager must simply recognize the reality and do his or her best to implement proper information security within the constraints of their budget.

Tying Paychecks to Security Roles

We need to recognize the importance of providing full descriptions for each as part of the security strategy. If employees are compensated in-part based on their adherence to their job responsibilities, there is a much better chance of achieving our security governance roles. Therefore, the information security manager should work with the personnel director to define security roles and responsibilities.

Do We Have the Skills?

Any effective security strategy must consider the skills that the organization has access to within its employees. If the strategy requires internal skills that are non-existent, it is doomed to failure. Choosing a strategy that uses already available skills can be a cost-effective approach, but at times we must be OK with having to acquire new skills either by training existing employees or by hiring new employees with the required skills. A skills inventory is important to know where we stand today and what changes, if any, we will need to make before reaching the desired state. This can be done through proficiency testing.

Chapter 29: Information Security Governance – Resources That Help

Assurance Process Integration, or Convergence, or Making Security Actually Work

Security needs are almost always found in every department and business unit. Unless the company is very purposeful about creating an integrated security approach across these areas, a big 'mess' usually results. Some of the areas contributing to this mess are risk management, the HR department, and the legal department.

Three efforts to prevent those 'messes' are:

- **GRC**, which we have already discussed (governance, risk management and compliance).
- **BMIS**, which we just discussed in detail (Business Model for Information Security).
- **ISO 27001**, which describes how to implement an Information Security Management System (ISMS).

These approaches work well for information security, but not so much for physical security. It might seem strange at first to discuss physical security on an exam for information security, but there is a great reason for doing so. The planning around physical security – such as door locking mechanisms to server rooms – are fairly routine these days, and it is not difficult to integrate physical security into information security. The other way around is much harder, though - trying to address information security *without* including physical security is just about impossible. This combination of the two security aspects – physical and information - is called _assurance integration_, or _convergence_.

Convergence is becoming more important each year. In fact, the _alliance for enterprise security risk management_, or _AESRM_, has authored a document called *Security Convergence: Current Corporate Practices and Future Trends*. This study concludes that there are five factors driving convergence, or the combination of physical and information security. They are:

- Rapid **expansion** of the enterprise
- The **increasing value** of information and intangible assets above physical assets
- **New technologies** blurring functional boundaries
- **New compliance** and regulatory requirements
- The pressure to **reduce cost**

The study also delivers three recommendations:

1. We must **improve the value of the entire business**, not just physical or information areas
2. Security needs to move from a centralized mindset to a **decentralized model** in which people have the power
3. Security needs to develop an **enterprise view of risk** instead of an asset-based view

A prime example of the above needed changes is to adopt something like a BMIS view, where we look at people, process and technology across the organization. You didn't think we discussed that model just for fun, did you? It has real-world value!

A recent example highlights the need to join physical and information security. A bank had a very sophisticated information security program in-place, but thieves posing as janitors were able to sneak in key loggers (a hardware device that captures keystrokes as they are entered into a keyboard). With valid credentials in the hands of thieves, all of that fancy information security was completely useless. A converged approach between physical and information security would have stopped this simple attack approach.

Good Presentations

A crucial aspect to the security manager's job is to educate senior management. Often security information systems are not taken seriously until they fail. Therefore, the security manager must be vigilant on making sure senior management understands applicable regulations and how critical it is to properly secure IT systems and information. What does it look like when a security manager has achieved these goals? Some signs are:

- There is a **clear support** and approval for security strategies
- There are effective **ways to measure** security effectiveness in-place
- Security **effectiveness is routinely reviewed** by executives
- Security awareness and **training is not considered optional**
- Management has **provided adequate resources** (people and money) to implement security
- Information security is treated as **a critical business component**
- It is abundantly clear to third-parties that **security is a big deal**
- Information security is discussed at **board meetings**

So, as a security manager, just how do you get senior management's attention and support? Well, the most widely used tool is a formal presentation in which you present one or more business cases. Things to emphasize are in a formal presentation are:

- **Aligning security goals** with business goals, by showing how security will actually help the company achieve its business goals
- Illustrate the **consequences of failing** to properly secure company assets or meet regulatory compliance requirements
- **Highlight budget items** so the cost can be clearly seen
- Use tools such as the total cost of ownership, or **TCO**, or return on investment, or ROI, to cut through the noise
- Be clear on how success will be **measured**

Even though we have already stated it, it is worth repeating: employees *must* see senior management abiding by the security policies. The example starts at the top.

Once you, as the security manager, have senior management's full support, you must periodically report to that group on how implementation is going. Ideally, you will use the same format and talking points you used in the original presentation that won their support in the first place. Some things that should be covered are:

- **How far along** implementation is based on the approved strategy
- A before-and-now **BIA comparison**
- Statistics on the threats that have already been mitigated as **proof it is working**
- Identifying the **weakest links** and recommendations on how to address them
- Any on-going **required approvals**

In addition to formal presentations, continuous communication should also be happening between the following groups:

- Senior Management
- Business Process Owners
- Other Management (such as line supervisors, department heads, and supervisors)
- Employees

Making the Business Case

A business case presents the value a project can deliver in terms of a cost-benefit analysis. In other words, it shows what the company will gain if it chooses to invest in the project. This is often the first step in a project, but at times may be presented directly before the project commences.

The initial business case is usually based on a feasibility study – an activity to figure out if a project will meet a specific need at a reasonable cost and within an acceptable time frame. It consists of the following 6 elements:

1) The **project scope** defines the business problem or opportunity to be addressed. It should be clear, concise and to the point.
2) The **current analysis** describes our current understanding of the problem or opportunity, and its strengths and weaknesses will determine our goal(s).
3) **Requirements** are defined based on needs and constraints. Note that software requirements are quite different than system requirements.
4) The **approach** is the recommended system or software solution that will satisfy our requirements. Included is a description of alternatives and why each was not chosen. The 'build vs. buy' question is answered here if both are options.
5) An **evaluation** brings together all the previous elements to produce a feasibility study report telling us how cost-effective the proposition will be.
6) A formal **review** of the feasibility study report is carried out with all stakeholders, and a final approval or rejection for the project is provided. If rejected, the rational should be attached to aid in future project proposals.

The business case is not just a one-time deal, however. It should be referenced throughout the project whenever increased costs or reduced benefits are encountered. Additionally, well-planned projects have built-in decision points, called _stage gates_ or _kill points_, that force a review to make sure the business case is still valid.

A formal presentation by the information security manager is the most common technique to obtain approval and can be used to both educate and gain acceptance simultaneously.

Communicating Up and Down the Food Chain

After a project has been approved by senior management, the information security manager must establish reliable reporting and communication channels downward throughout the organization. Both reporting from and communication to various parts of the organization are essential if we are going to recognize emerging security issues. Effective communication is needed to broadcast changes in policies, standards or procedures, and to notify employees of emerging threats. Upward reporting from the information security manager to senior management must happen on a recurring basis to make sure that the top decision makers are kept in the loop.

There are four groups that need communications tailored to that specific audience. The first is **senior management**. It is important that the information security manager attend business strategy meetings to stay on top of business strategies and goals. One-to-one meetings with individuals are important to gain an understanding of business goals from their perspective.

The second are **business process owners**. The information security manager should join operation review meetings to gain an understanding of the daily struggles this group deals with. Monthly one-to-one meetings are important to gain their continued support with security initiatives.

The third group are **other management personnel**, including line managers, supervisors and department heads charged with carrying out security and risk management-related activities. It is important that the information security manager inform them of their individual security-related responsibilities.

The final, and fourth group are the **remaining employees**, which need the following:

- Timely **training programs**
- An on-boarding **program for new hires**
- Updated **strategies and policies communicated** using appropriate materials
- An information security governance **coordinator assigned to each business unit** to retrieve accurate feedback of daily practices in a timely manner

Some Great Ways to Kick-start Governance

A Few Architectural Frameworks

An _architecture framework_ is a foundation on top of which multiple architectures can be built. The architecture should describe a method for designing a desired state using a set of building blocks, and then show how those blocks fit together. The target architecture is called the _reference architecture_.

An _enterprise architecture_ represents the foundation on top of which the entire company is built. _Enterprise information security architecture_, or _EISA_, is a subset of enterprise architecture, and is designed to give a jump-start on designing an information security program. Unfortunately, EISA is not something we can find in-use in most organizations for multiple reasons:

- EISA projects are **expensive** and time-consuming

- There is **little appreciation** for the potential benefits
- There are very few security architects who can **implement** EISA effectively
- It must be an **integral** part of the enterprise architecture (EA) to be really effective

In the early days of IT, architectures focused on IT systems only was found to be lacking because it did not consider business and security concerns. Today, we have a number of architectural frameworks that consider IT, security and business concerns together – some of these are:

- The Zachman Enterprise Architecture Framework
- Sherwood Applied Business Security Architecture (SABSA)
- The Extended Enterprise Architecture Framework (E2AF)
- The Open Group Architecture Framework (TOGAF)
- COBIT 5

The Zachman framework that uses a who, what, why, where, when and why matrix, which is then used by both SABSA and E2AF. However, TOGAF has gained a lot of ground in the last decade.

Regardless of the approach, all architecture frameworks seek to do the same three things:

1) Detail the **roles, entities and relationships** that exist
2) Provide a **taxonomy** (naming conventions) for all processes that describes how they are executed and secured
3) Deliver a set of **artifacts** describing how a business operates and what security controls are required

COBIT 5 does a great job of the above and has enjoyed widespread acceptance globally. The reason for this success is two-fold. First, we need to describe information security in an enterprise context, and COBIT 5 does this well. Secondly, there is an ever-increasing need for the enterprise to execute the following four areas, which COBIT 5 also excels at:

1) **Protect** information systems
2) Ensure continuous **availability** of those systems
3) **Comply** with a growing number of laws
4) Do those all while **keeping costs down**

Regardless of the chosen approach, if an existing organizational standard does not dictate the choice, it should be based on form, fit and function. In other words, one approach may be better aligned with existing practices or situations.

As we mentioned before, effective use of a security architecture absolutely requires that it be tightly integrated with the overall enterprise architecture. Using an enterprise architecture such as TOGAF will almost force that to happen, since TOGAF includes security as an essential component of the overall design.

ISO 27000 Series (NOT an architecture framework)

Instead of an architectural framework, a business might elect to use the ISO 27000 Series. This is a set of standards to help organizations create and implement a valid security plan. ISO 27001 provides a framework containing 14 security areas and is the standard to which many organizations choose to be assessed and certified against. ISO 27002 provides implementation help for ISO 27001, and is used to comply with the standards.

The 14 security control areas of ISO 27001 are:

- A.5. Information security policies
- A.6. Organization of information security
- A.7. Human resource security
- A.8. Asset management
- A.9. Access control
- A.10. Cryptography
- A.11. Physical and environmental security
- A.12. Operations security
- A.13. Communications security
- A.14. System acquisition, development and maintenance
- A.15. Supplier relationships
- A.16. Information security incident management
- A.17. Information security aspects of business continuity
- A.18. Compliance

Other Approaches (also NOT Architecture Frameworks)

Some other approaches may be useful for developing and implementing a strategy, such as:

- ISO 9001
- Six Sigma
- NIST publications
- Information Security Forum (ISF) publications
- US Federal Information Security Modernization Act (FISMA)

It may be useful to use a combination of different approaches as a way to cross-check goals and make sure that all elements have been considered.

Policies, Standards and Guidelines

We have already discussed procedures, standards and guidelines in Section 1, but there are a couple of points we need to point out that will help us be successful.

First, a standard dictate how we measure procedures, processes or systems to see if they meet requirements. We can use three types of measurements:

- **Metrics**, which provide a yes/no answer
- **Boundaries**, which provide outside limits that must not be passed
- **Processes**, which use a more complex method to determine acceptance

Secondly, let's quickly go over a few examples of guidelines specific to information security:

- Clarification of policies and standards
- Dependencies of a procedure
- Suggestions and examples
- A narrative clarifying the purpose for procedures
- Background information that might be useful
- Tools that can be used

Using Controls

When developing an information security strategy, controls are the primary components we deal with. If you recall, a control mitigates a risk, and can be technical, physical or procedural. COBIT focuses on IT controls, which represents most controls required in organizations. But information security managers must be aware that controls must be developed for non-IT processes as well. This includes physical information (such as hardcopies) in terms of marking, handling and storage. Environmental issues such as physical security are important so that systems are not simply stolen as opposed to being compromised.

Using Technologies

Technologies are the cornerstone of an effective security strategy. However, there is no technology that can compensate for management, cultural or operational problems, and the information security manager should never rely on technology to overcome those deficiencies. An effective defense requires a combination of policies, standards and procedures to be properly melded with technology.

People Are Expensive

The majority of security incidents are not technological in nature - they are the result of people. The most costly and damaging compromises are usually caused by insider activities, whether intentional or accidental. That is why the first defense in this area is to try and ensure the trustworthiness and integrity of new and existing employees. Limited background checks can provide some insight into a person's negative characteristics, but laws (particularly in Europe) put a limit on how deep these checks can go. The extent of background checks should be proportional to the criticality and sensitivity of the roles an individual will be expected to perform. Policies and standards should be developed to ensure background checks are properly carried out.

Attention must be paid to theft not only to reduce loss, but because small occurrences may be an indicator of something much larger going on. Monitoring of email can be a great tool for detecting malicious or dangerous behavior, but the information security manager must be sure to remain in compliance with laws by providing sufficient notice of these activities to employees and ensuring the notice has been acknowledged.

The Org Chart

When developing a security strategy in organizations with an inflexible structure, you can expect to encounter resistance as various factions perceive the changes to be a threat to their authority or autonomy. If senior management can foster a more flexible attitude to organizational changes, security management becomes much easier.

We have already mentioned previously that there is an inherent conflict between IT and security in terms of priority. In other words, the goals of availability are sometimes at odds with the goals of security. This is an organizational issue, so we bring it up here as a reminder.

When an organization is spread across multiple geographical locations, we can choose two different approaches – centralized or decentralized. A centralized approach will require all locations to fall under a single organization-wide security umbrella, while a decentralized approach allows each location to manage their own security as each see fit. There are pros and cons for each.

A centralized approach is the preferred method, because it provides the best alignment across all business units and ensures the same quality of training and responsibilities.

A decentralized approach works well for multinational companies with locations in different countries or legal jurisdictions. Because the various local laws will be different, allowing each location to manage its own security overcomes this. For example, some countries may not allow business data to be stored or processed outside of their national boundaries. Additionally, some countries will collect taxes for software or hardware used within their jurisdiction, regardless of where it physically exists.

A decentralized method also works well for companies who have grown by acquisition of other entities over time, with each acquisition still operating fairly independently. For this scenario, it is not unusual for each entity to have its own IT group and hardware and software infrastructure. Separate policies and procedures may also be in-place for each entity. However, there may be an advantage to creating a single set of enterprise-wide security policies, but let each entity implement its own standards and procedures as it sees fit.

A final advantage with a decentralized approach is that security administrators are usually closer to the users and understand local issues better. They can often react quicker to access change requests or security incidents.

The Human Factor

Training, education and awareness is vital to a security strategy because it addresses one of the most fundamental weaknesses – the human factor. A recurring security awareness program reinforces the importance of information security to employees and is required by law in some jurisdictions. In most organizations, most personnel are not aware of security policies and standards unless a robust awareness program is put into place.

Broadening and deepening the skills of security personnel through training can greatly improve security effectiveness. The hard part is figuring out *what* skills need to be taught. Finding good security people is difficult and is getting harder. Some companies attempt to compensate by hiring overqualified people, but this only results in a high turnover rate or substandard performance due to boredom. Instead, training existing employees is a much more cost-effective approach. However, that training must be targeted to the organization's unique way of doing business.

Audits

An *audit*, which may be internal or external, is used to determine information security deficiencies in terms of controls and compliancy and is one of the essential resources in development of a strategy. The focus is usually on people, processes and technology.

Internal audits in larger companies are usually carried out by an internal auditing committee, reporting to either an executive or the board. In smaller organizations the information security manager or an information security officer may perform the audit.

External audits are usually conducted by the finance department, and often the results do not make it back to information security. That is why it is important for the information security manager to maintain a good working relationship with finance.

Because of increasing regulation, many companies are required to periodically file various audit reports to regulatory agencies. These reports are sometimes a goldmine when it comes to informing us on the performance of information security, and so making the results available to the information security manager should be part of security strategy considerations.

Compliance Enforcement

It is important to develop procedures for handling security violations as part of the security strategy. The biggest problem with enforcement is lack of buy-in from management, so that must be a priority for the information security manager. If management buy-in is achieved, and the organization values openness and trust, the simplest approach to compliance is that of self-reporting. For this to happen, everyone must understand that security is in their own best interest.

Prioritization of compliance issues must be executed, as some issues must experience 100% compliance while others may not be as important. For example, keeping unauthorized people out of the control room at a nuclear reactor facility is probably much more important than making sure office computers are always locked before you walk away.

Threat and Vulnerability Assessments

For the next few paragraphs, keep in mind that threats are constant and always with us, while vulnerabilities come and go as policies and technology change. For example, on the California coast the threat from earthquakes is a given, but if we move offices to a building that has been constructed to be particularly resistant to earthquake damage, the vulnerability could be mitigated enough that we no longer have to worry about it.

Threat assessments are routinely implemented as part of an overall risk assessments. However, those threat assessments have real value by themselves as part of strategy development because we need to understand the various options and related costs to make good decisions. The best cost-effective choice will be made when we analyze threat and vulnerabilities separately.

Additionally, strategy should consider viable threats even if we are not aware of a specific vulnerability, whereas risk assessments will discard those threats because testing does not reveal a current vulnerability. For example, espionage by a competitor is always a threat. But, if we do not have competitors known to be overly unethical, a risk assessment will decide espionage is so unlikely that we do not need to address it. However, our strategy should probably take that into account in case we have a low-cost opportunity to mitigate it. The bottom line is that policy development should map to a threat profile, instead of specific vulnerabilities.

When hearing the term 'vulnerability assessment', people often think of an automated scan against existing IT infrastructure. However, for strategy development that approach is not even close to being thorough enough. Instead we must also test elements such as procedures, practices, technologies, facilities, service level agreements, and legal and contractual requirements. Processes and facilities are the most vulnerable components but are usually the ones seldom looked at due to the difficulty in performing assessments. The development of a security strategy is a great reason to perform these vulnerability assessments.

Risk Assessment and Management

Both threat and vulnerability assessments are extremely useful in developing a security strategy, but an overall risk assessment is really needed if we are to do a comprehensive job. A formal assessment of risk starts with listing the viable threats facing us, including environmental and physical threats, along with technological. Examples of physical and environmental threats might be flood, fire, earthquake or a health pandemic. Examples of technological threats might be malicious software, system failures or attacks (internal and external).

The second step is the risk identification phase, where we estimate the likelihood each threat will occur and how big of an impact each might make. The third step is to determine the extent of organizational weaknesses and exposure to threats. Here we take three things – threat frequency, threat magnitude and organization vulnerability – and determine the level of that risk. Then we can calculate the ALE, or annualized loss expectancy.

To arrive at the frequency and magnitude for a given threat, we can use both our own organization's experience as well as the experiences of like organizations. Special attention must be paid to frequency, even if magnitude is not that large, because small numbers can add up quickly.

Insurance

Insurance is a viable resource to consider during strategy development for risks such as rare, high-impact events. Examples are floods, hurricanes, fire, embezzlement and lawsuits. There are three types of insurance:

- *First-Party insurance* covers the organization from most sources and includes business interruption, direct loss and recovery costs.
- *Third-Party insurance* covers liability with third-parties such as defense against lawsuits and damages.
- *Fidelity insurance* (or bonding) protects against employee or agent theft and embezzlement.

Resource Dependency Analysis

Resource dependency is somewhat similar to DRP in that it looks at systems, hardware and software. In some cases, it can be used instead of a BIA to ensure the strategy looks at all resources critical to the business.

Outsourced Services

Both offshore and onshore outsourcing is common as more companies focus on their core expertise and attempt to cut costs in other areas. These arrangements can be particularly risky since it is very difficult to quantify and mitigate risks. When outsourcing, skills and functions are no longer possessed by the organization, and the loss of control can present problems. Additionally, providers may operate on different standards. If security services are outsourced, it is important that they not become a single point of failure and there is a viable backup in place if needed. Using hosted cloud services can be very cost-effective but opens up new risks. Mergers

153

and acquisitions can become problematic due to different cultures, systems, technology and operations.

Other Organizational Support and Assurance Providers

There are usually a number of support and assurance service providers within an organization that should be part of information security resources. These can include the following departments:

- Legal
- Compliance
- Audit
- Procurement
- Insurance
- Disaster recovery
- Physical security
- Training
- Project office
- Human resources

These departments are usually not very well integrated in terms of assurance functions, and any strategy must include preventing gaps or overlaps between them.

Chapter 30: Information Security Governance – Constraints That Hurt

Governance of Third-Party Relationships

Third-parties may include the following entities:

- Service providers
- Outsourced operations
- Trading partners
- Merged or acquired organizations

Some of the challenges include the following four:

1. **Cultural differences** resulting in unacceptable attitudes toward security
2. **Technology incompatibilities**
3. **How incidences are responded to** in terms of speed, documentation and prosecution
4. The **level of acceptable** business continuity and disaster recovery

To overcome these challenges, the information security manager must ensure that all responsibilities for both the company and third-parties are clearly documented *prior* to the relationship being approved. This allows risk to be identified and either accepted or mitigated. Additionally, there should be a formalized engagement model describing and controlling the relationship.

Legal and Regulatory Requirements

Any effort to design and implement a good security strategy must be built on a solid grasp of applicable legal requirements. For example, privacy rules can change drastically between jurisdictions. Some countries prohibit many background checks that are legal in other countries. We can choose to allow different strategies based on geographical locations or apply the most restrictive requirements across the entire enterprise. There are also a number of legal and regulatory issues related to Internet businesses, global transmissions and transborder data flows. Regulatory compliance should be treated just like any other risk, with the risk being that we might not achieve full compliance.

Let's discuss information retention issues. There are two primary aspects to consider when deciding how long to keep business records:

1. Business requirements
2. Legal and regulatory requirements

Legal and regulatory requirements represent the minimum amount of time to keep records. Business requirements may extend that time but can never shorten it. Regulations such as Sarbanes-Oxley, or SOX, requires us to retain information for a certain amount of time, but doesn't really care how we store it. Additionally, specific legal requests from law enforcement may require that records be kept even longer. Regardless of the retention length, archived information must be properly indexed so that relevant data can be quickly located and retrieved.

E-discovery is the term used to describe locating and delivering information in response to a request in which the company is legally bound to comply with. If information has been archived without indexing, the cost for e-discovery can be extensive. On the flip side, an organization may want to intentionally destroy information after a set time period to limit liability, but great care must be made to not violate regulatory or legal laws when doing so. The best option is to have a policy requiring destruction of any data not required to be retained by law or for a specific business purpose.

Physical Constraints
With regards to physical constraints, storage capacity, physical space, environmental hazards and availability of infrastructure must all be considered during strategy planning. Personnel and resource safety must also remain a consideration.

Company Image
Any organization must take care to cultivate a good image among its customers and the public at-large. If care is not taken, it can have a negative impact on a company's value. These perceptions are often influenced by location and culture. Both the internal business culture and the external culture in which a business operates must be taken into consideration when developing a security strategy. If the strategy is at odds with culture, a successful implementation will be very difficult unless that culture is changed.

Organizational Structure
At times various assurance functions within an organization live in a silo that have different reporting structures and authority. In these cases, the successful development of a security strategy will require senior management buy-in and involvement. For example, two different

departments may have completely opposite attitudes toward security. One thinks very highly of securing information assets, while the other views security as just another way to prevent them from making more profit. The only way to get both departments on-board with a security strategy is to appeal to the senior management that oversees both – if management is bought-in, then both departments will get on-board as well.

Costs

The actual implementation of a successful strategy will consume resources, time and money. Obviously, we need to find the most cost-effective way to get there. With normal projects, we can point to the project's value to justify cost. But with security projects, there is not a direct line to value. Instead, we must point to the control of specific risks or compliance with regulations. A cost-benefit or some other financial analysis is usually the best approach. A traditional approach is to calculate the annual loss expectancy (ALE) and use that dollar amount as the upper limit on the cost of controls – basically an ROI.

However, another school of thought thinks that an ROI approach is not very helpful, particularly when dealing with programs designed to meet some type of regulatory compliance. For example, under SOX some penalties consist of long sentences in federal prison for senior executives. It is a given that senior management will have a great interest in executing a project to mitigate such a risk - regardless of the ROI.

People, Budget and Time

Additional constraints we need to look at are people, budget, time and capabilities. People will always present some constraints since we humans dislike change and additional rules – this must be accounted for when developing the security strategy.

The available budget is also a key constraint that must be taken into consideration. This includes two things:

1. The **total cost of ownership** (TCO) of new or additional technologies
2. The **manpower requirements** of design, implementation, operation, maintenance and eventual decommissioning

Time is a major constraint with any effort, and a security strategy is no exception. There might be compliance deadlines or limited-time merger opportunities that must be aligned with. Or, windows of opportunity may exist representing business activities that might expire quickly. Just as important as time, however, are our capabilities. Any strategy that is based on known and demonstrated capabilities – such as expertise and skills – is much more likely to be successful.

Risk Acceptance and Tolerance

Risk appetite and risk tolerance are important constraints that must be considered, and the challenge here is to measure those values. One method is to develop RTO for critical systems by performing a BIA. The shorter the RTO, the greater the cost and the lower the risk appetite – this translates into a more compelling case to expend resources on mitigating the risk. If the organization has business continuity insurance, the deductible is a good quantifiable number of acceptable risk. Just keep in mind that the cost of protection should never exceed the benefit delivered.

Chapter 31: Information Security Governance – The Action Plan

Gap Analysis – The Start for an Action Plan

If your recall, a gap analysis is simply a recognition of where we are and where we want to be – basically the delta between the two conditions. This needs to be performed for each control goal, each risk, and each impact goal. This exercise needs to be repeated at a minimum once per year – perhaps more – so that changes can be made to reflect the environment the organization operates. A typical approach is to work backward, starting with the desired state and going back to the current state, and determine the series of steps required to reach our goal. CMMI or other methods can be used to assess the gap.

Policy Development

After performing a gap analysis, we now need to create an action plan to execute the strategy. One of the most important aspects of the action plan is to create or modify policies and standards.

Standards Development

Though we have already talked quite a bit about standards, let's list some ways in which they help us specific to governance:

- **Interpret** policies for us
- Provide a way to **measure** policy compliance
- Are a great basis for **audits**
- Set **bounds** for procedures and practices
- **Govern** the creation of procedures and guidelines
- Set the security **baselines**
- **Reflect** acceptable risk and control goals
- Provide the **criteria** for evaluating if risk is acceptable
- Provide **boundaries** for procedures without restricting options
- Must be **owned** by the information security manager

Remember, when we encounter a standard for which there is not a readily available technology, or there is some other reason for which we cannot create a process to meet the standard, we must create an exception process.

Using a Governance Framework

To properly govern, we use something called a *governance framework*, which consists of six components:

1. A **strategy** linked with goals
2. **Policies** that cover strategy, controls and regulations
3. For each policy, a set of **standards** to ensure that procedures and guidelines line up with the policy
4. A **security organization** that has sufficient authority and resources, and that does not have conflicts of interest
5. Defined **workflows and structures** so we can assign responsibilities and hold people accountable
6. A way to **measure** compliance and effectiveness that is useful when making management decisions

Using such a framework allows us to develop a cost-effective information security program that lines up nicely with the company's business goals and makes sure that information is protected according to its value to the company.

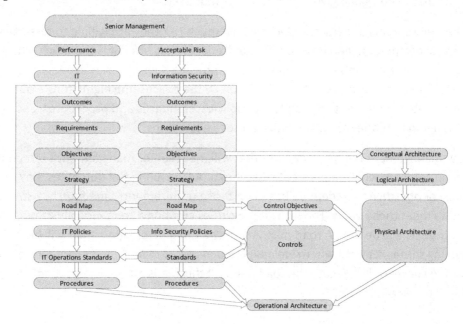

Figure 25: Relationship of Governance Elements

Let's discuss the differences between IT security and information security for a second. IT security is all about how to keep information secure using technology. Information security is concerned not only with that, but also with information that might be overhead in an elevator conversation, or perhaps that is faxed to the wrong number. IT security is a subset of information security, but governance of each is completely separate – this will become clearer as we go.

Figure 25 illustrates the relationships between IT, information security, controls, architecture and other components of a governance framework.

Let's walk through how governance elements interact with each other, and what dependencies exists.

First, senior management must set the goals for both IT and information security separately, meaning that they are governed independently. We're going to discuss why in a few minutes, but just know that those are two very different roles with competing priorities. IT goals almost always center around *performance* – how much up-time systems have, how fast they work, how responsive IT staff are to trouble tickets, etc. So, senior management defines high-level performance-based goals and gives them to the IT manager.

Meanwhile, senior management also decides how much risk they are willing to tolerate with the organization's information, and how to mitigate (reduce) that *risk* if it is too much. Those goals are given to the information security manager. So now we have two tracks operating in parallel – IT and information security. Both tracks now follow the exact same eight steps – outcomes, requirements, objectives, strategy, road map, policies, standards and procedures. Each track at this point is a mirror of the other. Let's follow those eight steps.

First, lower management defines *outcomes* that will meet senior management's direction. Second, then come up with *requirements* that if met, will result in the outcomes they desire. Third, goals, or *objectives*, are defined based on those requirements, and fourth, a *strategy* is developed to meet those goals. The fifth step includes creating a *road map* illustrating when and how specific goals will be met. A road map is simply a timeline of when goals will be delivered. The remaining three steps are where we develop *policies, standards* and *procedures* that will allow them to successfully execute the road map. All this feeds into an *operational architecture* across the entire organization.

We should note that information security *strategy*, *road map*, *policies* and *standards* all flow into their IT counterpart steps. For example, the information security road map is used as an input into the IT road map, and information security policies are used as an input for IT policies. As a result, the information security strategy will have a direct impact on IT strategy, because IT systems fall under the information security umbrella, even though they must act independently to some extent.

It's also important to note that an output of the information security *road map*, *policies* and *standards* steps feed into defining what *controls* will be used. The controls feed into the *physical architecture*, which also feeds into the *operational architecture* right along with *procedures*.

If you may recall, we previously listed the six outcomes for security governance. As a refresher, they were:

- Strategic alignment
- Effective risk management
- Value delivery
- Resource optimization
- Performance measurement
- Assurance process integration (convergence)

Near-Term Goals for the Action Plan

Once the overall strategy has been finalized, it is fairly simple to define very specific near-term goals. Based on critical resources as determined by the BIA, and the current state of security according to CMMI gap analysis, prioritization of these activities should be simple. It is important that the strategy and long-term plan all integrate near-term activities. This will temper the desire to implement point solutions that are thought of when in crisis mode. Numerous unintegrated solutions, formed over the years while fighting in crisis mode, become increasingly costly and difficult to manage.

Chapter 32: Information Security Governance – Metrics and Monitoring

What the Action Plan Needs

The plan of action will always require the ability to monitor and measure progress, as well as tell us when we have achieved a milestone. Costs must also be monitored to allow mid-course corrections to be made if necessary. There are a number of approaches we can use to gather these metrics, including whatever method we used to measure the current state. Among those options we will find the balanced scorecard, CMMI and PAM.

Often organizations will focus on automated scanning results without knowing if a real threat exists. This can result in mountains of data that is extremely difficult to sift through, and the big picture is lost. To get around this problem, we need to create processes that will distill the information down to something that is usable. We can also analyze the available metrics to determine their relevancy and select only those that deliver value. So, what exactly is considered to be a 'valuable metric'? If it has true value, a metric will do four things:

- Deliver whatever is important to manage **information security operations**
- Meet **IT security management** requirements
- Meet the needs of **business process owners**
- Provide what **senior management** wants to know

In general, metrics must be both predictive and actionable.

The resulting strategy and action plans must contain provisions for monitoring and the capture of metrics – otherwise we will never be able to determine if we have been successful or not.

Do Security Metrics Really Help?

Security metrics simply tell us the degree of safety we currently enjoy compared to some point measured in the past. Well, that is the idea, anyway. In reality, metrics gathered from technology devices can tell us all about how much data a firewall is filtering, or how much up-time a server is delivering, or even the percentage of traffic we *think* is malicious. But security metrics cannot tell us how safe we really are, or if our security programs are being effective, or if those programs even align with our business goals. To get answers to those questions, we have to develop metrics that represent management's requirements, as opposed to metrics simply taken from some device. One source for these metrics can be obtained by executing full audits and comprehensive risk assessments. Unfortunately, these only provide a historical view, or at best a snapshot in time – not enough to provide us what is needed to guide day-to-day security management decisions. So, let's talk about how to get metrics that are usable.

How to Get Security Metrics That Help

As examples of security metrics that do _not_ meet all of the criteria we just mentioned, consider some standard metrics organizations often collect:

- Downtime due to viruses
- Number of system penetrations
- Penetration impacts and resulting losses
- Recovery times
- Number of vulnerabilities that network scans reveal
- Percentage of servers patched

While these metrics are useful to IT operations, they really say nothing about how secure an organization is. In fact, none meet the predictive or actionable criteria. What does a useful security metric look like? Some decent examples are:

- Probabilities of penetration
- A list of exposures that must be mitigated
- Value at Risk (VAR)
- Return on Security Investment (ROSI)
- Annual Loss Expectancy (ALE)

The last three – VAR, ROSI and ALE – are the most useful as they can be employed as justification for expending resources and carrying out certain activities.

It has become apparent over the past decade that the lack of useful metrics in information security has really held back effective management. Four major efforts have been carried out to provide guidance in this are:

- **ISO 27004** is a standard that has not seen wide-spread acceptance and is currently being rewritten.
- **COBIT 5** is a standard offering sample IT metrics for 17 suggested enterprise goals, for a grand total of 150 metrics. Unfortunately, there is a lack of guidance on how to actually develop and implement the listed metrics.

- **The Center for Internet Security (CIS)** released a document in 2010 called The CIS Security Metrics based on the consensus of 150 industry professionals, and includes 28 metrics.
- **NIST SP 800-55** is a standard that aligns with the security controls listed in NIST SP 800-53, and offers a comprehensive approach to the selection, development and implementation of metrics. It is primarily targeted to support FISMA, which is useful for the private sector even though it is designed for federal agencies.

Often companies will try and measure security effectiveness by estimating the maximum impact that an adverse event might have. Unfortunately, this is a little like estimating how tall a tree is, and then validating that estimate by cutting the tree down and using a tape measure – you get the answer but only after destroying what you were measuring. Likewise, impact estimates can only be validated after a negative incident has occurred – we get to feel great that we estimated correctly, right up until the impact of the attack sinks in. Simulated attacks, such as penetration testing, can help, but to be valid a very large number of simulations must be carried out to provide any real value.

In the end, all we can say with confidence are two things:

1. **Some organizations are attacked more frequently** or suffer greater losses than others.
2. There is a **strong correlation** between good security management, and fewer incidents and losses.

Because solid security metrics are hard to come by, there is a tendency to settle with whatever we have at-hand, regardless of the relevancy. For example, many companies vet their security posture based on vulnerability scans alone. The trap here is the belief that we can measure risk by simply measuring technical vulnerabilities. One of the most important steps we can take to arrive at true measurability is to properly define clear goals for information security. After all, if you don't know what you should be measuring, then how can you possibly measure it? Once we have clear goals, any measure we come up with is valid as long as it tells us if we are making progress (of any kind) towards our goals. We should note that a given metric will be useful only at a single level – strategic, tactical or operational. For example, strategic metrics will help us measure high-level outcomes, but the number of DDoS attacks we experienced yesterday won't help us with this. However, the DDoS metric is of extreme value at the tactical level.

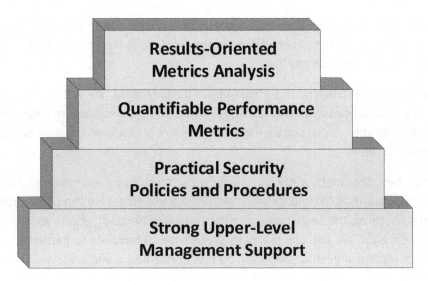

Figure 26: Components of Security Metrics

So, how exactly do we capture usable security metrics? It turns out that there four steps – each building on the one before – that we can climb and wind up with great metrics. **Figure 26** shows the four components in a stacked model.

Starting at the bottom, we have **Strong Upper-Level Management Support**. Without this, the rest of the organization will not see security as valuable and will therefore not buy into it. Additionally, funding and other resources will be extremely difficult to obtain if the drive for better security does not come directly from upper management.

Once we have senior management support, we can move to the second block, **Practical Security Policies and Procedures**. This stresses the need for realistic policies and procedures along with the authority needed to enforce them. Those policies and procedures must be reachable and provide useful security by using the correct controls. Without procedures, there is little hope of collecting useful metrics.

Once policies and procedures are in-place, we can execute the third block, **Quantifiable Performance Metrics**. This represents IT security performance goals, which should be easy to capture. Repeatability over time is a key attribute of these metrics.

The final block, **Results-Oriented Metrics Analysis**, means that we must consistently perform a periodic analysis of the metrics data collected in the third block. Accurate data must be a priority with all stakeholders for this to succeed.

In summary, if we have strong support from upper management, we will be able to implement the right policies and procedures., which will give us the right quantifiable metrics. All we have to do then is to analyze the results, but we have to make sure to perform this analysis on a recurring basis for it to be of value.

It is very important that metrics are put in-place *during* the implementation of a governance program, not afterwards. KGIs and KPIs are metrics we use to decide if our milestones or goals are being met. Because the implementation of various aspects of governance will usually be carried out in projects, we can use standard project measurements to gather our governance metrics, such as slipping milestones or goals, budget performance and achieving the agreed upon timeline.

Measuring How Well We align with Strategic Goals

We have already stressed how important it is that security goals align with business goals. As a result, it would be very difficult to measure success if we don't keep those business goals in mind at all times. And if we are going to be cost-conscious, which all organizations *should* be, we cannot accurately keep tabs on our security cost performance without measuring it against our business goal cost performance. In other words, we shouldn't be spending more money on security than the goals they protect are worth.

The best way we can ensure that security and business goals are aligned is to make sure our security goals are defined in business terms. For example, we could have a security goal that states, "We must provide a three-layer defense-in-depth solution on all database servers." That leaves a lot of questions, such as "Why would we do that? Does it really matter? Can I justify the cost?". Instead, couch the goal in business terms of "We must provide reasonable protection against competitors obtaining our core list of customers." Now the conversation becomes "Oh, let's put in a three-layer defense-in-depth protocol in order to meet that goal."

Not only does such an approach make it so much easier to understand, but it also allows us to ensure that what we build can be tracked back to a real need. Let's say that we purchase a series of firewalls as a technical control to meet our requirement above. It goes something like:

- **Goal** - don't let competitors steal our customer list

- **Requirement** – implement a 3-layer defense-in-depth control
- **Control** – roll out 3 firewalls

Now, if anyone asks, "Why the heck did we just buy 3 firewalls?", we can just point to the requirement, which points to the goal. This makes life easier for everyone.

Some indicators of good alignment between security and the business are the following six:

- The security program **enables specific business activities**
- Business activities exist that **have not been undertaken** because they cannot manage risk sufficiently
- The security organization **listens to business owners**
- Both business and security **goals are well-defined and clearly understood** as measured by awareness testing
- A very high percentage of **security program activities can be mapped** to business goals
- There is a security **steering committee consisting of key executives**

How Are We Doing at Risk Management?

The whole point of information security is to manage risk, but it is almost impossible to measure the effectiveness of this goal. We can define a successful risk management program as one that consistently keeps risk to an acceptable level, but exactly how do you measure 'risk'? It's kind of like trying to watch a football game from outside of the stadium in the parking lot. We really can't see the game, but we can probably figure out if something important is happening based on the sound of the crowd's roar. Likewise, when it comes to measuring risk we have to settle for measuring some 'indicator' that correlates the risk level. Here are seven useful indicators:

- How well-defined the organization's **risk appetite** is in terms that means something
- How complete the **overall security strategy** is
- The number of **defined mitigation goals** for significant risk
- There are **processes for reducing adverse impacts**
- A continuous risk management process **covers all business-critical systems**
- **Risk is assessed periodically** and shows progress to the defined goals
- The **ratio of security incidents** from known risks vs. unknown risks is healthy

The *best* indicator is how much the negative impact of incidents experienced over a year exceed acceptable risk levels. For example, if only 5% of the incidents we experienced over the past year exceeded what we considered to be acceptable risks, then we're probably doing pretty good. Additionally, a good security program should result in a trend where both the frequency and impact of incidents go down. Note that the best units to express quantitative numbers in is in financial terms. That always catches the attention of senior management.

Are We Delivering Value?

Value delivery occurs when the investment in security provides the greatest support for business goals. If the two align very closely, then we have achieved delivery of value. Speaking from a financial point of view, value is greatest when an acceptable level of risk is reached at the lowest cost. Some KGIs and KPIs showing value delivery include the following six:

- Security **activities are purposefully designed** to reach their goal at the lowest cost
- The **cost of security is proportional** to the asset value (there's no use in paying $10K per year to protect a $300 lawn mower)
- Security **resources are assigned** based both on the degree of risk and potential impact
- **Controls are designed** based on clear goals
- There are enough **controls in-place** to reach the desired level of risk and impact levels
- Control cost-effectiveness is determined by **periodic testing**

How to Know When We Are Managing Resources Well

Information security resources are almost always people, processes or technology. *Information security resource management* describes the processes to plan, allocate and control those resources. Here are eight indicators that tell us when we are effectively managing security resources:

- We don't keep **rediscovering** the same problem
- We efficiently **capture knowledge** and disseminate it
- Security processes are **standardized**
- We have **clearly-defined roles** and responsibilities for security functions
- Every project plan **incorporates information security**
- Security activities address a **high percentage of information assets** and related threats
- Information security has the **appropriate authority**, organizational level and people
- The **per-seat cost** of security services is kept low

Are We Performant Yet?

As we previously discussed, being able to measure reasonable metrics is key to being successful. The effectiveness of our security machinery must be measured in terms of performance. Indicators of excellent performance measurement include the following twelve:

- There is a **short time** required to detect and report security-related incidents
- The **number and frequency** of subsequently discovered unreported incidents trends down
- We **compare favorably** to other organizations when using benchmarks
- We **can determine** the effectiveness and efficiency of controls
- There are **clear indications** that security goals are being met
- We do not have **unexpected or undetected** security events
- We have **knowledge of evolving** and impending threats
- We have **effective means** of determining vulnerabilities
- Our **log review practices** are consistent
- The result of BC and DR tests **are good**
- Key controls are **being monitored**
- We have a high percentage of metrics that show we are **achieving defined criteria**

Measuring Physical and Information Security Fusion

Recall that convergence, also called assurance process integration, is where we combine physical and information security together. Since KGIs tell us *after* the fact if an IT process has achieved its goal, KGIs for convergence include the following six:

- There are **no gaps** in information asset protection
- There are **no unnecessary security overlaps**
- Assurance activities are **seamlessly integrated**
- We have **well-defined roles** and responsibilities
- Assurance providers **understand their relationship** to other assurance functions
- There is **effective communication** and cooperation between assurance functions

Chapter 33: Information Security Governance – What Success Looks Like

Six Outcomes

Now, how can we, as a business, know if our information security governance is working? It turns out that there are six basic outcomes we can look for – if we can check off all six items, we're good to go.

First, we are **_strategically aligned_** when information security lines up with our business strategy. Or, when our security goals match our business goals. This is true when we have accomplished three things:

1. Enterprise requirements drives our security requirements by describing what it looks like when 'done' has been reached. In other words, *the enterprise defines what good security looks like.*
2. Our enterprise processes are protected by security solutions that account for culture, governance style, technology and how our organization is structured. Put another way, *security matches the company's DNA instead of trying to rewrite it.*
3. Our investment in information security lines up with the enterprise strategy and operations, and how the company views security threats. In other words, *the amount of money we spend on security accurately reflects how important security is to us.*

The second outcome that lets us know if information security governance is working, is that we are doing a good job of **managing risk** when we consciously decide to act - and in some cases decide *not* to act - so that potential security impacts are lessened to a level we can live with.

The third outcome is that we have **delivered value** when security investments support business goals.

The fourth outcome is that we have **optimized resources**, meaning that information security knowledge and infrastructure are being effectively used as-designed.

Next, when information security processes are monitored and measured to make sure they achieve their goals, then we are **measuring performance**, which is the fifth outcome. Performance measurement allows us to ensure resource optimization, which is the previous item.

And the final outcome we reach when information security governance is working, is that we have achieved **integration**, meaning that all of our processes work as intended from end-to-end.

Training People and Making Them Aware

Any successful action plan must include some type of security awareness and training. We know we have achieved this goal when employees are able to see the connection between their daily tasks, and standards and policies. Training presentations should be geared to individual groups and be clear and understood by that audience. For example, presenting information on how to configure firewalls will not excite the sales department (unless maybe the company happens to sell firewalls!)

Employees who will participate in implementing the security strategy must be properly trained. This means that they will need to understand the following four things:

- Strategy goals, or KGIs
- Processes that will be used
- KPIs
- Critical success factors (CSFs)*

* CSFs are the elements or events that must occur to achieve the KGIs

Chapter 34: Information Risk Management – Overview

At this point you should know everything there is to know about information security governance – at least as far as the CISM exam is concerned! This next domain, Information Risk Management, will build on that expertise as we learn how to identify risk and keep it at an acceptable level under the watchful eye of governance.

An Intro to Managing and Assessing Risk

From a technical point of view, _risk management_ is the act of striking the right balance between taking advantage of opportunities for gain while minimizing the chances of loss. From a business perspective, it means that we ensure risk does not impact business processes in a negative manner. For example, when playing the stock market, you want to invest just enough cash to make money if things go right, but not so much that it will ruin you if things go wrong. Typically, higher risk means potentially higher rewards _if_ we can figure out how to bring that risk down to a level we can live with.

At the core of risk management is a risk assessment process, were we seek to understand the nature of the risk we are facing and the potential impact. Organizations can manage risk centrally using a single _enterprise risk management_ group of people or take a decentralized approach by distributing the work among multiple business units. The decentralized approach requires less commitment up-front but takes more effort to make sure that risk management activities are properly carried out.

Looking into risk assessment a little deeper, we discover that it includes three phases – identification, analysis and evaluation. For the _risk identification phase_, we create a list of vulnerabilities and take inventory of current threats. By combining the results of the two lists of vulnerabilities and threats, we can create a set of plausible scenarios, and figure out probable ways in which a compromise might happen. In the _risk analysis phase_, we take each risk identified in the first phase and perform a BIA to come up with the possible impact. Finally, in the _risk evaluation phase_, we look at the impact from each risk and decide if it falls within an acceptable range based on our risk appetite, tolerance and capacity. In short, we list things that can go wrong, then figure out how bad it would be if they did go wrong, and finally decide if we should do something about each.

After we have assessed risk using the three phases, we then need to execute a _risk response_ for each risk that falls outside of our ranges. We can take one of four actions that we discussed in Section 1. If you recall, they are:

- **Accept** the risk as-is
- **Mitigate** the risk until it falls within range
- **Avoid** the risk by terminating the activity that encounters the risk
- **Transfer** the risk by outsourcing to a third party or by taking out insurance in case we encounter an incident

How we implement the risk management process will be influenced by several things. Culture can either negatively or positively impact the process depending on the nature of the culture – whether it is risk averse or aggressive. A risk averse culture will place a priority identifying and mitigating risk, while a more aggressive culture will tend to focus less and hope for the best.

The organization's core mission and goals can detract from or add focus to risk management, along with how the organization is structured. Risk management will become more important as the ability of a business to absorb loss goes down – conversely if a business is able to absorb a large amount of loss, risk management simply won't be that important. The industry in which a business operates may have a large impact on how important risk management is. For example, if we are building garden hoses the worst-case scenario is that some of our customers might get wet from leaky hoses. But if we are in the business of building airplanes, a mistake can easily cost lives.

How well we implement risk management processes will depend on how mature other processes are, such as management and operation, as well as the maturity of our practices at the enterprise level. Physical, environmental and regulatory conditions may also force us to implement certain risk management capabilities that we might otherwise have chosen to ignore. *We* may not really care about encrypting customer information, but if we're dealing with patient data, then HIPAA will *force* us to encrypt some data whether we like it or not.

Regardless of any of those factors, when faced with the choice between a complex, but more capable risk management process or a simpler, less capable one, always choose the simpler option. Why? Because the simple option will always have a greater chance of success, and we can always add complexity to the process later if desired.

The Circle of Life

The *life cycle* is the process of introducing new information or technology into an organization, managing changes to those assets, and finally retiring them. The 'managing change' part of that cycle is, amazingly enough, called *change management*. The reason change management is a thing is revealed by what happens if we don't track changes – our assets will degrade over time or get lost, and we lose knowledge of their state, location and ownership.

However, security will never be a part of change management unless the information security manager actively promotes it. The best way to do this is for the information security manager to become a member of the change management committee, which should oversee information, IT systems and physical facilities.

Some common areas that often are not updated to reflect changes are the following seven:

- Blueprints for facility updates
- Network documentation
- The BCP
- Remote access configurations
- Physical security
- Contracts and SLAs with providers
- Knowledge of internal or external facility management personnel

Risk and the IT Circle of Life

According to NIST SP 800-30, the reasons an organization will implement some sort of risk management process are two-fold:

1) To minimize negative impacts
2) To provide a sound basis for decision making

The *system development life cycle*, or *SDLC*, describes the life cycle of any system and contains five phases, with risk management playing an important part in all phases.

First, we have the **initiation** phase, where the need, purpose and scope of an IT system is described. Risk management identifies risk, which will then impact the stated requirements for the IT system.

Then we carry out the **development and acquisition** phase, where the system is designed, and purchased or built. Risk management ensures that all risks identified during the initiation phase are addressed or noted for later mitigation.

This is followed by the **implementation** phase in which the system is configured, enabled, tested and verified for use. Risk management ensures that all risks have been addressed prior to the system entering operation, or they at least have been *accepted*.

Next, the **operation or maintenance** phase begins, where the system operates and is updated periodically or as-needed. Risk management performs reauthorization of the continued use of the system whenever major changes are made. Additionally, periodic assessments are carried out to ensure new risks have not been accidentally introduced.

And finally, we execute the **disposal** phase where we move, archive, discard or destroy the hardware, software and data. Risk management ensures that disposal or replacement of hardware and software is carried out properly and that residual data is handled in the right manner.

Risk Management is Alive!

We just discussed how risk management should be plugged into the life cycle of systems, but we need to recognize that risk management has a life cycle itself. It is a continuous process and the life cycle feeds back into itself, as shown in **Figure 27**. It is comprised of the following four steps, that operate in a non-ending circle:

1) IT Risk Identification
2) IT Risk Assessment
3) Risk Response and Mitigation
4) Risk and Control Monitoring and Reporting

In summary, we identify risk, assess the impact, implement controls to mitigate the risk, and monitor the effectiveness of the control, which leads us back to the first step where we identify residual risk. The loop is repeated as long as we are interested in managing risk.

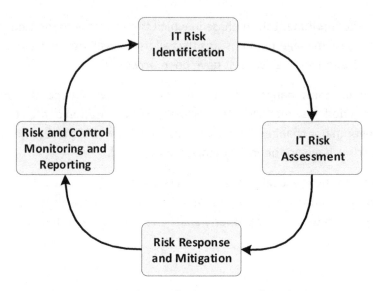

Figure 27: The IT Risk Management Life Cycle

Creating the Baseline

A *baseline* is an initial set of observations that can be used for comparison at a later time. With security controls, we usually take a series of measurements to establish the baseline. The purpose of a security baseline is to set the minimum security requirements throughout the organization so that they are consistent with acceptable risk levels. In other words, we can't have business units being held to different security standards unless we actually *meant* to do that. A secondary benefit to baselines is that we can now easily measure change to our security stance. For example, if we have a biometric system that uses thumbprints to grant access to a secure area, our baseline might be the number of false positives the system falls victim to when we first set it up. Six months later, we might want to make sure the system is still working correctly, so we take the same measurement again, and compare the new set of data against the baseline.

Note that for each classification level we need to set a different baseline. Low classification data will probably not need to meet the more stringent requirements for highly classified data. If we do not have classifications defined, it will be very difficult for the information security manager to develop a rational basis for baselines, and we will find ourselves under-protecting some assets and over-protecting others. While there are a considerable number of sources that we can use for help with setting baselines, such as NIST, COBIT and ISO, each organization is unique due to the combination of technologies and processes used within a given business. For biometric systems, we would need to have a unique baseline for each classification level. It might be perfectly acceptable for low-security class scanners to have a false positive rate of 10%, but for higher-security areas, we may need to establish the baseline at 2%. Ultimately, the goal of baselines and a standard approach is to ensure that the level of residual risk is consistent across the entire organization.

Is It Secure?

When creating an information security program, it can be very helpful to have a consistent method for reviewing the various aspects of a program. A good security review process will have the following five components:

- An objective
- A scope
- A list of constraints
- An approach
- A result

Let's walk through those components and describe each.

The review **objective** is what the security manager hopes to get out of the review. For example, a useful objective might be to determine if an Internet-facing application can really be exploited using a known vulnerability.

Scope ties the objective to the systems or processes being looked at. In the example above, scope would tell us which infrastructure, people and processes are fair game. If we find it hard to define scope, then perhaps we need to revisit the objective.

A **constraint** is a boundary restricting what the reviewer can do or have access to. In our example, perhaps the reviewer is only able to access the system at night to prevent downtime during business hours. Or perhaps, the reviewer is not allowed to have internal knowledge of the network. In either case, the constraint might render the review meaningless, so they are important to call out.

There might very well be multiple ways in which we can achieve the objective. In our example, we might choose to assume an attacker is unable to login, which means they will have to find alternative ways to steal data – the lack of credentials would be listed as a constraint. Or, we can provide credentials to a penetration testing team, so they can focus on other areas once logged in – in this case scope would include the credentials. Each option is considered a different **approach**, with a specific set of activities to be carried out. Regardless of the selected approach, it must achieve the *objective* while remaining within *scope* and obeying the identified *constraints*.

Finally, the **result** lets us know if the review objective was reached. Or, another way of putting it is to simply answer the question 'Is it secure?' If we can't answer that question with a high degree of confidence, then we have no choice but to declare the review incomplete. Suppose the tester could not login using the provided credentials – in this case we would not have been able to test functionality that is only accessible after logging in.

Just How Secure Is it?

Just like a security review, an audit has the same five components – objective, scope, approach, constraints and a result. However, with an audit the result is expressed as a level of 'effectiveness' that measures how well a given control meets the stated objectives. For example, whereas a security review might result in a pass/fail score, an audit result might be categorized as low effectiveness, medium effectiveness or high effectiveness. Or, it might even give it a numerical score.

An audit will result in documentation called 'work papers', that does three things:

- **Maps** controls to objectives
- **Describes** what the team did to test those controls
- **Links** the test results to the final assessment of effectiveness

Work papers may or may not be included in the final report, but often they are more useful than the final report itself.

If an information security program is mature and has established policies and procedures, an audit helps to tell us if those policies and procedures have been fully implemented. On the other hand, if we have an immature program that is still being developed, an audit will normally measure the program's level of compliance against an external set of standards. Examples of external standards or frameworks might be the following, listed in order of a wide scope, down to a scope specific to certain technologies:

- COBIT

- The Standard of Good practice for information Security
- ISO 27001 and 27002, which are specific to IT security

For example, COBIT has a very wide scope, while the ISO 27000 series is specific to IT security only.

While some security managers view auditors as a necessary evil, they can in fact be a great ally. Aside from the fact that an auditor can provide an objective assessment of security, audit results can often be used to emphasize much-needed actions to senior management. However, this will never be effective unless the security manager ensures that the necessary time and resources are dedicated to audit activities.

Technology Needs Some Special Love

Security programs will usually leverage multiple technologies, with newer organizations using more modern solutions. The technologies that older organizations employ will usually be constrained by their legacy architectures, but there should still be multiple sets of alternatives available. The age of a system should never be a reason to not implement a security program – it just changes what that program looks like. For example, it may not be worthwhile to implement strong passwords on a 40-year old system, since we will probably have a tough time finding someone who knows how to program it. Instead, we should restrict access to that system using physical controls. But not protecting that system is simply not OK.

Though information security is comprised of technical, operational and managerial domains, the technical aspect will most often be the majority of the work. In fact, the information security manager and security personnel are usually considered to be the subject matter experts in the entire organization when it comes to technical security. But, there is a wide range of opinions in the wild regarding the scope of the information security department as a whole. For example, on one end of the spectrum we find organizations that view the information security program as simply setting high-level policies. At the other end, an organization may expect the information security program to take complete ownership of specific pieces of the infrastructure. As a result, the technology skills that a security manager is expected to possess will differ based on how the organization views the information security program's responsibilities.

Regardless of the expected technology skills, the security manager must understand security architecture, control implementation principles and the security processes and mechanisms that are most commonly implemented. Additionally, a successful security manager needs to be able to address the following four security areas:

- Perimeter, network and systems
- Application, such as coding practices or data access mechanisms
- Database, such as integration with applications and encryption
- Physical, operational and environmental

Enterprise resource planning, or _ERP_, systems deserve special mention because the compromise of a single element can disrupt the operations across the entire organization. For example, if a system dedicated to creating shipments goes down, we might experience a lag in getting orders out the door. But if an ERP system goes down, it could also impact incoming raw materials, manufacturing, customer relations, automated orders – you name it. The more complex a system is, the more it hurts when it goes down.

What Due Diligence Looks Like

Let's take a look at what due diligence looks like in terms of a security program. In this example, exercising due diligence means that the following twelve components must be in-place:

- We have full senior management support
- Comprehensive policies, standards and procedures exist
- There is security education, training and awareness
- Risk assessments are carried out periodically
- There are effective backup and restore processes
- Security controls have been adequately implemented
- We monitor and measure metrics
- We are in-compliance with relative standards
- We have tested our BRP and DRP
- Data at-rest and in-transit is protected
- Outsourced contracts possess appropriate security language
- Periodic review of the infrastructure by external parties

Industry Standards Come First

Many companies are subject to regulatory standards that control access to information. For example, hospitals must closely monitor who has access to patient health information, or PHI, because the Health Insurance Portability and Accountability Act, or HIPPA, requires very stringent access to certain types of information. However, the danger here is to assume that a regulatory standard should dictate all of our access mechanisms. Instead, a company needs to first use a standard by a non-industry specific organization, and *then* layer on any regulatory standards as needed. In our example above, we could first implement a standard provided by ISO, and then make changes to ensure we are in compliance with HIPAA.

The following is a list of organizations providing some common standards:

- American Institute of Certified Public Accountants, or AICPA
- Canadian Institute of Chartered Accountants, or CICA
- The Committee of Sponsoring Organizations of the Treadway Commission, or COSO
- German Federal Office for Information Security, or BSI
- International Organization for Standardization, or ISO
- ISACA
- International Information Systems Security Certification Consortium, Inc., or (ISC)[2]
- IT Governance Institute
- National Fire Protection Association, or NFPA
- Organization for Economic Co-operation and Development, or OECD
- US Federal Energy Regulatory Commission, or FERC
- US Federal Financial Institution Examination Council, or FFIEC
- US National Institute of Standards and Technology, or NIST
- US Office of the Comptroller of the Currency, or OCC

Staying on Top of Vulnerabilities

Because of the pressure to bring products to market as soon as possible, hardware and software vulnerabilities are rampant. That is why we need to stay on top of new vulnerabilities and react as fast as possible. Fortunately, there are a number of organizations dedicated to finding and reporting vulnerabilities that any organization can take advantage of. Some of these are:

- US Computer Emergency Readiness Team, or CERT
- MITRE's Common Vulnerabilities and Exposures database
- Security Focus's BUGTRAQ mailing list
- The SANS Institute
- OEMS

How to Make Sure We Remain in Compliance

Compliance enforcement is the act of making sure that an organization's security policies, standards and procedures are being followed. There are several different ways that we can enforce compliance – using enforcement procedures, policy exceptions and standards.

When implementing any procedural control, we need to consider how we will be able to monitor for compliance, and then how to enforce compliance to that procedure if it is not being followed. If we cannot do both of those – monitor and enforce – then the control will be of no value and may actually _increase_ our overall risk.

Enforcement procedures are designed to enforce compliance with existing procedures. That can be a little confusing, so let's state it another way. To make sure that a given procedure is being followed, we can create a different procedure to carry out that enforcement, and we call those _enforcement procedures_. For example, suppose we have a procedure that help desk employees should follow when resetting a password over the phone. To make sure the help desk employees are following the password reset procedure, we design an enforcement procedure that requires a supervisor to randomly listen in on phone calls to see if those help desk employees are following the procedure. Now, how do we make sure that supervisors are carrying out the enforcement procedure? Well, there comes a point at which additional procedures introduce too much overhead and we simply have to trust our key employees.

Remember that procedures and processes should always derive from a high-level policy. That policy must be comprehensive enough to cover all information that needs to be secured, but still remain flexible enough for the procedures and processes to choose their own technologies and still remain in-compliance with the policy.

However, there are always exceptions to every rule, and a good policy must take this into account. When writing a policy, the organization should try as much as possible to cover all foreseen scenarios, but in the end a _**policy exception**_ _process_ will need to be allowed. This provides a means for business units or departments to request an exception to an existing policy. This request is reviewed and weighed based on a risk/reward decision and then a final answer is given back to the requesting department. Ideally, the policy will reference this exception process as a means to accommodate exceptional or unforeseen conditions.

A **standard** provides the options that a system, process or action can select from and still remain in compliance with a policy. Procedures can then simply reference a standard, and in this way, we can ensure that we remain in compliance. Additionally, standards provide an economy of scale – we can map a policy to a standard only once, and therefore we do not have to repeat those details in each procedure and process. Just like policy exceptions, there must exist a way to request and approve an exception to a standard as well.

So, we have discussed three ways to enforce compliance. But how do we detect when we're still not in compliance? It turns out that we have a number of detection tools including the following five:

- Normal monitoring
- Audit reports
- Security reviews
- Vulnerability scans
- Due diligence work

Because of the tight relationship between policies and standards, compliance is concerned that processes and procedures fully align with both unless an exception has been made. While an audit simply provides a snapshot of compliance in time, compliance enforcement is a never-ending activity, and is normally shared across the entire organization.

Because the information security program is concerned with compliance enforcement across the organization, it should be audited itself to determine compliance with applicable standards and regulations. The results of this audit should be expressed in terms of risk, mitigating factors and acceptable control objectives.

Assessment of Risk and Impact

Vulnerability Assessment

All information systems should be continuously monitored using automated means to detect vulnerabilities. Part of this activity should be to look for unexpected changes to technical systems. For example, a change to the registry of a Windows server outside of a maintenance window might indicate that the server has been compromised. Furthermore, any changes to systems must be scheduled through a change management system to ensure unauthorized changes do not take place. Ad-hoc changes by a well-meaning technician have been the source of many vulnerabilities that have magically 'appeared'.

Threat Assessment

The best approach to detect and mitigate vulnerabilities is to use a continuous-assessment model. Unfortunately, this approach can be quite costly and beyond the means of most smaller organizations. In such cases, it is important that a *periodic* reassessment of attacker capabilities and exposed vulnerabilities be executed. Carried out at least once per year, the information security manager must evaluate all technical and organizational changes, particularly where an external party is involved. The ability of existing controls is evaluated against this comprehensive list of vulnerabilities. Threat sources can include the following five examples:

- Technical
- Human
- Facility-based
- Natural and environmental
- Pandemic events

For each threat evaluated, the following four aspects should be considered:

- If it is real
- How likely it is to happen
- How large the impact might be
- Which systems, operations, personnel and facilities will be affected

Risk Assessment and Business Impact Analysis

When discussing risk, a BIA does four things:

1. It determines the **impact** of losing the availability of any resource
2. It establishes the **escalation** of that loss over time
3. It identifies the **resources** needed to recover
4. It **prioritizes** the recovery of processes and supporting systems

A risk assessment is primarily concerned with step 1 of the BIA. While a risk assessment is not always associated with a BIA, a BIA cannot be created without a risk assessment. From a risk viewpoint, the key term in step 1 is the word 'impact' – the level of impact is at the heart of any risk assessment. This is why a risk with a high probability of occurring but with little impact is usually accepted, whereas a risk with little chance of happening but would result in a huge impact – such as an earthquake - will usually undergo mitigation to some extent.

If you recall, residual risk is the amount of risk left over after a control has attempted to mitigate a risk. It is interesting to note that most disasters do not result from a single catastrophic event, but rather from a number of smaller incidents and events that contribute to the major event. The take-away from this nugget of wisdom is that while individual residual risks might be acceptable, they tend to aggregate to a level that can be disastrous.

The ultimate decision on whether to apply some type of mitigation controls around a given risk must consider the cost/benefit ratio that a control would provide. Unfortunately, mapping a specific control's benefit to a security business goal is not always easy. In these cases, it will probably be necessary to create a business case before approval will be given. One of the key points a business case can make is to state that while there will always be residual risk, and all residual risk tends to aggregate, the control in question will reduce the overall amount of residual risk. This will tend to overcome the lack of direct correlation a risk has with a security goal and redirect the conversation to look at overall residual risk.

The information security manager must take care to continuously communicate the effect of emerging risk to security stakeholders. This can be done all at once each year or it can be broken up into sections to be carried out each month or quarter.

Resource Dependency Assessment

If an organization cannot carry out a comprehensive BIA, a _business resource dependency assessment_ might be a better option. This activity looks at all business functions, and for the most important figures out what resources (such as database and servers) are critical for that function to continue operating. However, one thing this approach does not provide is the impact if those resources were no longer available, which a BIA does provide.

Outsourcing and Service Providers

There are two types of outsourcing that a security manager will have to deal with:

- Third-parties providing security services
- Outsourced IT or business processes that must be integrated into the information security program

While the security requirements for both are the same, each option will have a different owner. The most significant risk introduced by outsourcing - and it is a large amount of risk - will be the fact that an external organization now has a direct connection with our own internal network.

So, if the risk is that great, then why even bother with outsourcing? The number one reason is economics – it is often cheaper to have someone else take care of systems or processes that do not fall within a company's core expertise. However, many companies find that over time the value of outsourcing really never materializes for various reasons. One reason is that a service may be contracted to support a current level of business, but after that business has atrophied somewhat, the contracted service level is never reduced. On the opposite end of that arrangement, perhaps a company's business really takes off, but the outsourcing provider starts demanding a much higher fee. Trying to negotiate those fees down takes a long time and may prevent a business from growing. Many businesses neglect to consider the cost that will be required to bring those processes back in-house when the service contract is up. All of these problems can be addressed by looking at the total cost of ownership, or TCO.

Other impacts to consider before hopping on the outsourcing bandwagon are the following seven:

- The company may lose essential skills
- There will be a lack of visibility into security processes
- New access risks are guaranteed to happen
- The long-term viability of the third-party vendor will now impact us
- The complexity of incident management goes way up
- There will be cultural and ethical differences to overcome
- There will be unanticipated costs and service short-comings

A vendor's security controls must be audited before, and during the life of, the service contract to make sure security is not compromised in the interest of cutting costs. This is most often performed by an external auditor who visits the vendor's facilities. If privacy laws apply to an organization's data, the vendor must obey the same laws. This is particularly important when the vendor is in a different jurisdiction than the organization, such as off-shore contracts. Ensuring that technical controls are in-place is a fairly straightforward activity. But, enforcing that the proper processes, procedures and activities are taking place will be more difficult and proper monitoring must be established. When outsourcing security services, special attention needs to be paid to the level at which a vendor meets the organization's security policies and standards.

All of the activities that we just covered can be summed up with two major aspects that must be examined when vetting a potential vendor:

1) The maturity of the vendor's security program must be high
2) The level of compliance assurance the vendor is willing to provide must be high

Outsourcing Contracts

There are two primary purposes for a contract:

1) To clearly spell out **rights and responsibilities**
2) To provide a way to handle **disagreements** after the contract is signed

The most common security provision in a contract is to address confidentiality or nondisclosure, usually in the sense that any information exchanged will not be shared beyond the relationship specified in the contract. Any referenced information should have a maximum retention time specified, and the manner in which information is destroyed should be spelled out as well. Additionally, the contract should state that appropriate security controls must be maintained, with the term 'appropriate' being well-defined in terms of a referenced standard such as ISO 27000, or COBIT 5. If the contract allows for a network connection between the two parties, it should assign responsibility for the security of that connection. Finally, specific security controls such as firewalls or monitoring should be included.

Even if a service provider has passed an initial audit proving that the vendor is an acceptable security risk, allowances for a right-to-audit and right-to-inspect without notice should be contained within the contract. A *right-to-audit* allows the customer to initiate an audit given sufficient notice to the vendor. A *right-to-inspect* requires little or no advanced notice and provides a greater assurance that the vendor will keep all security controls up to par at all times.

If a breach occurs, the contract should specify the roles each party will play with respect to investigation and remediation. Since emotions will be running high during a security event, ensuring these assignments are part of the contract will make it much easier to carry out the required tasks in a timely manner.

Special attention should be paid to indemnity clauses within the contract. *Indemnity* is the act of protecting one's self against loss or damage in the event of a security incident. Service providers will normally try to write a contract in a way that favors them by limiting the amount of compensation the provider must pay if it fails to meet contractual obligations. Another indemnity 'gotcha' to look out for is a 'choice of law' provision that may require any potential litigation to take place in a jurisdiction favorable to the provider.

Third-Party Access

Access to an organization's information, systems and facilities by third-parties must be strictly controlled and monitored. Any access should be granted using the principles of least-privilege and need-to-know. Any access must be authorized by the asset owner. All usage should be fully logged and routinely reviewed by the security team on a regular basis. The frequency is based on three factors:

1) Criticality of information
2) Criticality of privileges
3) Length of the contract

All access rights should never be granted until after the contract has been signed and should be removed immediately upon the termination of the contract.

Chapter 35: Information Risk Management – The Goal

Objectives of Information Security

One of the key reasons for using an architecture is to provide a framework which can handle complexity. It also acts as a road map that brings together multiple smaller projects into a single, cohesive whole, allowing multiple project teams to coordinate.

Getting a little deeper, information systems architecture considers three things:

- The **goals** that will be achieved through the systems
- The **environment** in which the systems will be built and used
- The **technical skills** of the people who will construct and operate the systems

However, information systems architecture goes beyond just technical factors. It looks at the entire enterprise as having a single mission and purpose, and how the systems will deliver at that level. If we fail to rise up and look around at this higher level, our technical implementations will ultimately fail to deliver what the business needs and expects.

When we consider security control goals, we are free to use a number of technologies to achieve it. This means that we can create 'control points' in which a single point is able to effect controls on behalf of the rest of the architecture. Because technology is not specified by the architecture, we have a good deal of latitude in how we implement controls. For example, a single firewall at the point where our network connects to the Internet will provide some protection for everything in our network. Or, installing a biometric scanner before granting access to a server room will provide some level of physical protection for all servers in that facility. These are both examples of control points.

Goal

There are seven elements that must be established before we can develop an effective risk management program. We will list each here but will then cover all of them in more detail.

- Context and purpose of the program
- Scope and charter
- Authority, structure and reporting relationship
- Asset identification, classification and ownership
- Risk management objectives
- The methodology to be used

- The implementation team

Let's quickly cover each.

Establish Context and Purpose

Unless we understand the need for risk management, the result will probably miss the mark by a wide margin. For example, if our goal is to meet regulatory compliance, but we somehow get distracted in protecting ourselves from Internet-based attacks, the result will not protect the organization. That is why we must clearly communicate the 'why' and continuously refer back to it along the way. A core part of this effort is establishing both risk appetite and tolerance as dictated by senior management. This activity will also highlight the security stance of the organization – risk averse or risk-aggressive – because the tone set at the top cascades all the way down to the bottom.

Define Scope and Charter

If the information security manager does not have the authority to carry out his or her function, all of the planning and meetings in the world will not result in an effective information security program. This must be firmly stated from the beginning, and a RACI chart can be of great help here.

Define Authority, Structure and Reporting

Authority below the information security manager must also be established, and the same RACI chart can help. Additionally, it is crucial that organizational structure and reporting hierarchies be established to prevent turf wars and missed communications. This often happens when people report up through different senior managers, resulting in conflicting directions being provided, as well as important information making its way up the chain never reaching the right people.

Ensure Asset Identification, Classification and Ownership

If we don't know what to protect, then gaps will form, and all of our efforts will be rendered useless. This is why an information asset register must be created and filled in. Following the identification of all information, we then need to classify each asset by sensitivity and criticality. Lastly, a single owner must be identified, preferably as a role and not an individual.

Determine Objectives

There is a saying, 'If everything is a priority, then nothing is.' What this means is that if we attempt to address everything, we will fail due to lack of resources and time. Therefore, we must prioritize our goals – in this case risks – and work from the top down.

Determine Methodologies

There are many choices for the methodology we select to assess, analyze and mitigate risks. But beware – just because one is already in-use and known should not prevent us from tossing it in favor of a distinctly better candidate.

Designate Program Development Team

An individual or team must be selected to develop and implement the information risk management program. Because security goals must align with business goals, it is important that non-security representatives from the business side be involved.

Chapter 36: Information Risk Management – The Strategy

A *risk management strategy* is the plan to achieve the risk management goals. What are those goals? In general, to get to a position where the entire organization experiences an acceptable level of risk, resulting in an acceptable level of disruption to business activities. The 'acceptable level of risk' is a management decision based on four things:

- The ability to **absorb** loss
- The risk **appetite**
- The **cost** to achieve acceptable risk levels
- Risk/benefit **ratios**

We have previously discussed the need for clear communication channels and training so that employees understand the importance of, and their role in, establishing a security-conscious culture. Every employee can help identify vulnerabilities, suspicious activity and possible attacks. We must foster a healthy attitude toward risk that focuses on several key elements. First, employees need to understand what risk is and how to recognize it. Then they must be able to identify information risks within our business and should understand that risk can affect each of us personally. And finally, the entire organization, as individuals and as a whole, must actively manage the risk.

However, an awareness program should not disclose vulnerabilities or ongoing investigations unless the problem has already been addressed. The use of examples can help understanding and underscore the need for diligence. To avoid employees from seeing security measures as just another inconvenience, training must clearly communicate the risk and its impact. Periodically changing up the message and how it is delivered will help maintain a higher awareness. To gauge awareness levels, the information security manager should use a standardized approach such as short computer or paper-based quizzes. Awareness training for management should emphasize the need for management to play a supervisory role in protecting systems from attack, and to ensure compliance by the people under their supervision. Awareness training for senior management should highlight the following six items:

- Liability
- The need for compliance
- Due care
- Due diligence

- Setting the tone and culture
- They are responsible for setting risk acceptance levels

Chapter 37: Information Risk Management – Who Does What

Information Security Liaison Responsibilities

Each information security program is unique, but we can expect to run across the same roles repeated across organizations that the security manager must successfully interact with. Let's walk through the most common.

Most large organizations have a **physical corporate security** department staffed with law enforcement individuals having limited information security experience. In smaller companies, physical security may fall to facilities management. The security manager must have a good understanding of the physical security policies to avoid the situation in which inadequate physical security undermines the information security program.

IT or internal audit is concerned with ensuring policy compliance and identifying risk. Unfortunately, if policies and standards are not complete, these auditors will fill in the blanks which may not agree with the security manager's view. This is one reason why complete governance documentation is so important.

Information Technology represent the hands-on implementers and operators of information processing systems. Unfortunately, IT often regards security as just something else getting in their way, so fostering a good working relationship with IT is essential. We have mentioned this before, but security is often at odds with performance and usability, and since IT can usually ignore security if they want to, gaps will appear unless a good rapport is present. On the flip side, IT must understand that if a serious compromise is encountered, their ability to deliver performance will be severely limited. Therefore, it is in the best interest of everyone involved to try and find controls that provide a good balance of security and performance.

Of course, we need to mention the neon-purple elephant in the room – IT is almost always the ones who implement and maintain security measures such as firewalls and encryption technologies on behalf of the security department. But, while security is usually at the mercy of IT's ability to implement proper security controls, in a healthy, security-conscious organization the C-levels will have included a mandate in IT's charter that expects an acceptable level of security – and this means that the IT manager will need the security manager every bit as the other way around!

The information security manager should engage **business unit managers** early and often. This not only assures that business has a voice in security decisions, but greatly increases the likelihood that security will be properly implemented in those units. This outcome is most effectively reached when business has a seat on the security steering committee.

On the opposite side of the relationship, security should make sure to be a part of all new product development efforts, whether the audience is internal or external. By doing so, security can be baked in from the beginning and security resources have a decent heads-up concerning work it will need to perform. No one likes to be surprised with last-minute requests!

The **HR department** has significant security responsibilities such as policy distribution, background checks, education and enforcement. The information security manager should work closely with HR so that the best methods of administering education is used, and agreements are reached in regard to proper computer resource usage. Improper use of computing resources – such as the viewing of pornography - should be of concern to both HR and the legal department. Therefore, both should be represented on the steering committee.

Information security issues such as compliance, liability and due diligence are also key matters for the **legal department**. Additionally, outsourcing contracts are primarily a legal concern, but with great security implications. That is why it is so important that the security and legal departments work closely with each other.

Employees are the first line of defense when it comes to security, but only if they are properly trained and aware of security concerns. Employees must be trained to report potential threats and offer suggestions for improvements to the security information program.

When it comes to purchasing equipment and other goods, most organizations have a **procurement** department. The security department should always be concerned with any physical items that come into a facility. Mature companies normally have an approved list of equipment that has been vetted for vulnerabilities. If such a process is not in-place, the information security manager should be afforded the opportunity to inspect proposed acquisitions to determine if there is risk.

More companies are starting to create a **compliance** department that may be a part of the legal department or might be completely separate. Compliance and security go hand-in-hand, so this relationship needs to be maintained.

In areas where privacy regulations are strenuously enforced, a company may have a dedicated **privacy** office. In this case, security and the privacy office must remain in lockstep to avoid sanctions or fines that are growing increasingly severe.

If a company has a **training** department, security should leverage its expertise in creating an effective awareness education program.

While we normally equate **quality assurance** with making sure that a product has minimal defects, it must also ensure an acceptable level of security controls around the design and production processes.

Most organizations have purchased **insurance** to mitigate certain types of risks, such as business interruption insurance. The security manager must remain aware of the types and coverage of such insurance policies, so they are included in risk analysis and recovery planning.

Any outsourced function is a possible source of severe risk, and the information security manager must remain informed of new and updated **third-party** relationships.

If a security department is not aware of new or ongoing projects, then it cannot ensure a proper level of security. The one department that usually is 'in the know' for these types of activities will be the **project management office**, or the PMO. The security manager must maintain a good working relationship with the PMO so that new or updated changes are pushed to the security department.

Cross-Organizational Responsibilities

It is important that an organization keeps too much responsibility from residing in a single role or individual. Separation of duties, or SoD, is a control designed to ensure just such a thing by dividing dependent responsibilities between two different parties. If SoD is not properly carried, unhealthy conflicts of interest can develop. For example, giving the same individual responsibility for security and performance will almost always result in performance being chosen over security, because a degradation in performance is always immediately noticeable, whereas security weaknesses may not be visible for some time. Another example is in the case of security, audit and quality control – these functions cannot be under the control of those responsible for monitoring them. It does no good for a fox to guard the henhouse – when that happens, hens start to mysteriously disappear!

As each phase of a security program is reached, the content should be actively spread among various parties in the organization so that areas of responsibility can be assigned. The information security manager will need to work with senior management to ensure that those responsible for specific activities understand, accept and have the resources necessary to carry out those activities. The security steering committee can be invaluable with this.

Management

Management can be loosely defined as...

> ...achieving defined goals by bringing together human, physical and financial resources to make the best decisions.

Managing a security program includes both short and long-term planning – from daily activities to governance responsibilities. Senior management must make sure that enough resources are made available for the security manager to do her job effectively. Management activities include the following six:

- **Directing** various projects and initiatives
- **Risk management** activities
- Incident management and **response**
- **Oversight** and monitoring
- **Development** of policies and standards
- **Creation** of procedures and general rules

Administration

While management is all about strategy and planning, and bringing the right resources together, administration describes the repetitive, often times daily tasks that need to be executed to keep the mechanisms moving so that we ultimately achieve our goals. Using our car example, management would identify the people to create the various parts, and setup the processes and how they work together. Administration ensures that each person shows up on-time and has the necessary raw materials.

However, administration of *developing* programs will not be the same as administrating the *operation* of a program after it has been developed. Some things administration must deal with are the following, which is *not* a comprehensive list:

- Personnel performance
- Time tracking
- Purchasing
- Inventory management
- Project monitoring and tracking

- Budgeting control
- Business case development
- Project management (this is a *not* security program management!)

Some technical and operational administrative duties are the following, also not a comprehensive list:

- Encryption key management
- Log monitoring
- Change request approval
- OS patching oversight
- Vulnerability scanning
- Penetration testing

An effective information security manager has a good working knowledge of all existing frameworks and major standards for IT and security management, as some will be a better fit for his organization than others. He must also act as a facilitator to resolve competing goals between security and performance, and to ensure that the organization's life cycle considers security concerns. The bottom line is that the security manager has to position himself right in the middle of everything without making himself a burden. People should *want* to seek out this person because of his value and expertise, instead of avoiding him because of the perception that he will just add more work.

There are many responsibilities that must be executed in an effective security organization, such as security engineers, QA, testing specialists, project managers, access administrators, security architects and auditors. Smaller companies must assign multiple responsibilities to a single individual, but they must be carried out regardless. The required skills needed to execute each responsibility must be acquired and purposefully maintained. Of course, those skills will probably vary between organizations.

The skills needed to spin up a given program will not necessarily be the same skills required to maintain that program. In these cases, it is often useful to temporarily outsource some responsibilities. One great example is to rely on an external provider to perform background checks as-needed on employee candidates. While most organizations have some type of an internal project management capability, larger organizations may have a *project management*

199

office, or *PMO*, which oversees all projects and which the security manager can take advantage of.

Every person in an organization should be able to articulate how their responsibilities and actions protect information assets.

Chapter 38: Information Risk Management – Resources That Help

Information Asset Classification

Business value of information assets can be represented by the sensitivity and criticality assigned to that asset. While defining both attributes can be a daunting task, if we do not undertake the effort we will not be able to create an effective risk management program.

In some cases, it is just too costly to perform comprehensive classification. In these cases, it may be acceptable to perform a business dependency assessment instead, where we simply look at critical business processes, and identify assets that are required for those processes.

The first step in classification is to make sure the asset inventory is complete, and the location of each asset has been identified. Assets housed by external service providers must be included. In addition to location, the data owners, users and custodians must also be identified.

The number of classification levels should be kept to a minimum, and all IT stakeholders should have the chance to review and approve them before being published. For organizations that have a blame culture, special care must be taken that assets are not overclassified so that people feel protected in case of a breach. Over classification can be a costly mistake, since low value assets will end up being unnecessarily protected.

Once a classification label has been applied to all assets, security measures need to be identified that apply to all assets for a given classification. Keep in mind that sensitivity and criticality each will more than likely require different security measures.

Methods to Determine Criticality and Impact of Adverse Effects

When determining criticality and sensitivity, it is common practice to focus on the impact that a loss of information assets will have, as opposed to looking at a specific adverse event. In other words, we don't focus on what would case a loss of information, we instead focus on the resulting impact that loss would have. The reasoning is simple – if we focus on specific events, we would have to look at _all_ that lead to a loss. To determine that impact, we usually perform a business impact analysis, or BIA.

The first step in determining asset importance is to break the entire organization down into business units, as illustrated in **Figure 28**. We also need to rate the relative importance of each business unit – that is the number in parenthesis.

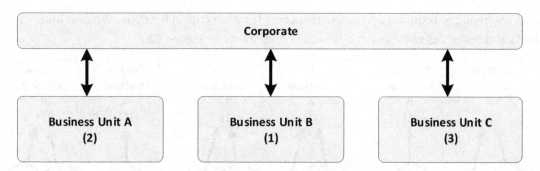

Figure 28: Top Layer of Business Risk Structure

In our example, Business Unit B is rated as the most important – this rating usually correlates to revenue generated by the unit, but it could be based on other attributes instead. This rating should be done by senior management.

The second step is to identify the critical functions across the organization and note each under the appropriate business unit, as shown in **Figure 29**. Of course, when we say, 'critical function' we're referring to whatever tasks are absolutely required for that business unit to function. Each critical function is assigned a priority within each business unit. For example, Business Unit A has two critical functions, and we assign one function a priority of '1' and the other '2'.

Likewise, Business Unit B has two critical functions, and the most important one is assigned a ranking value of '1', and the other '2'. We are not concerned how critical functions are ranked across all business units – just within the business unit that requires the function. When the second step has been completed, it will look very similar to the structure used in a BIA.

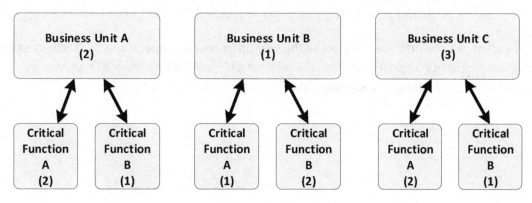

Figure 29: Critical Function Layer of Business Risk Structure

Next, we need the required assets and resources for each critical function. We also must rank all assets and resources within each business unit as shown in **Figure 30**.

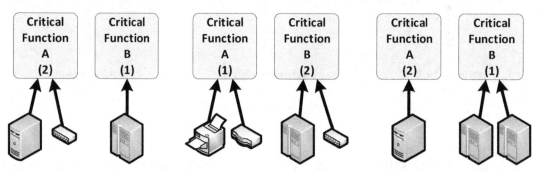

Figure 30: Aligning Assets to the Critical Layer Function

Assets and resources can contain vulnerabilities, and therefore they represent a source of risk as shown in **Figure 31**.

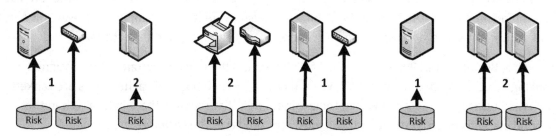

Figure 31: Asset Vulnerabilities

At this point, we can map specific risks all the way up to business operations. This allows us to easily see where risk originates, particularly when we view the entire organization map as shown in **Figure 32**. Using this approach, it is much easier to prioritize risk.

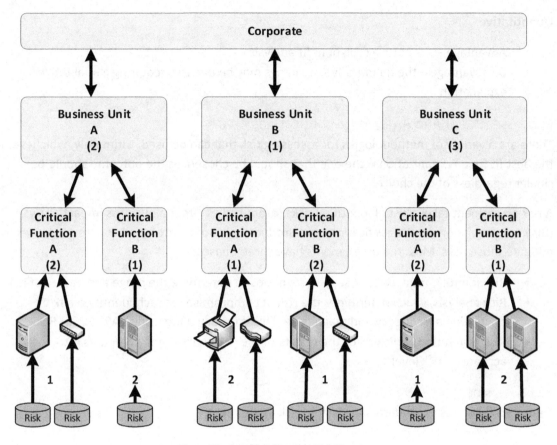

Figure 32: Combined Impact Risk Structure

Impact Assessment and Analysis

When assessing impact, we can use either a qualitative or quantitative approach, and there are pros and cons for each.

Qualitative

- Advantage – prioritizes risk and identifies areas for immediate improvement
- Disadvantage – does not provide a measurable magnitude, making a cost-benefit analysis difficult

Quantitative

- Advantage – supports a cost/benefit analysis
- Disadvantage – the quantitative meanings may be unclear, requiring a qualitative explanation

Risk Assessment and Analysis Methodologies

There are a variety of methodologies for assessing risk that can be used. Ultimately, whichever is the best fit for an organization is the one that should be chosen, as the outcome should be similar regardless of the choice.

A risk assessment takes a list of identified risks (produced as either a business impact analysis (BIA) or information asset classification) and produces a list of controls and countermeasures to mitigate those risks. Most risk assessments have three phases:

- **Risk identification**, which uses risk scenarios to determine the range and nature of risk.
- **Risk analysis**, which determines the risk of compromise for each identified risk by calculating a frequency and magnitude. This is usually done using VAR, ALE or ROSI.
- **Risk evaluation**, which takes the results of the risk analysis and compares it to acceptable risk levels.

Risk Assessment

Figure 33 illustrates a standard approach to risk assessment.

Figure 33: Risk Analysis Framework

The location and identification of information assets should be done based on criticality and sensitivity. It is essential that we have an accurate inventory of assets for this to be successful, or we will have unknown gaps that will eventually come back to haunt us when they are compromised – all because we didn't know they should be protected! Determining the value of each asset will be important later when assessing risk to this asset – after all, do we really want to spend $5,000 each year to protect something we can simply replace for $500? Value will also be used later to classify the asset.

For some assets, valuation into a common financial form (e.g. dollars) is easy, such as with hardware – how much does it cost to replace? Unfortunately, information assets can be much harder to valuate. Valuation can simply be the cost of recreating it or restoring it from a backup, or it might be based on how much it contributes to generating revenue. In other cases, the value is related to consequences or regulatory fines if confidential information or trade secrets are compromised.

Personally identifiable information (PII), such as social security numbers or full names, are particularly troublesome as the organization may incur regulatory fines as well as lawsuits resulting from identity theft. Slightly less tangible are reputation losses, which result in share losses. In these cases, the value is not in the data itself, but in the impact of leaking the data.

Marketing materials, while having little intrinsic value, can create unintended consequences and therefore represent risk. For example, inaccurate descriptions of products or services, or information leading to wrong investment decisions can bring on lawsuits, resulting in significant financial hardship.

Typical information asset categories that should be looked at are:

- Proprietary information and processes
- Current financial records and future projections
- Acquisition and merger plans
- Strategic marketing plans
- Trade secrets
- Patent-related information
- PII

Information Asset Valuation Strategies

Companies often find the task of inventorying and valuating information assets to be daunting, and therefore never carry it out. However, there are ways to simplify the seemingly overwhelming task. For example, a matrix of loss scenarios showing possible impacts can help tremendously. The accuracy of the valuation is really not as important – what really matters is having a way to prioritize the efforts. Simply grouping values within the same order of magnitude usually does the trick. If nothing else, media reports of high-profile breaches contain a great deal of information to aid in arriving at a rough approximation of loss potential.

Information Asset Valuation Methodologies

Quantitative valuation methodologies are the most precise but can be very complex once we factor in actual and downstream impacts. Instead, we might choose to use a qualitative approach in which a decision is made based on business knowledge and goals. In some cases, this is the only option as quantitative information is simply not available. Most information security managers use a combination of the two. In fact, in some cases simply assigning a subjective label of low, medium and high works quite well.

The most direct approach is to use a quantitative value based on purchase or replacement price. An alternative approach is to consider value-add or other more intangible values. For example, a hardware server and the software running on it may cost only $20,000, but if we lost the use of it, we would experience a monthly loss of millions of dollars. In this case value would be based on the lost revenue during the down-time, not simply the cost of replacement.

Intangible assets are usually intellectual property such as trade secrets, patents, copyrights, brand reputation, and customer loyalty. Auditors may represent intangibles under the heading of 'goodwill'.

In a publicly traded company, intangible assets represent the difference between tangibles recorded in financials and the company's market capitalization.

Risk Assessment and Management Approaches

There are several risk management models that we can choose from, including:

- COBIT
- OCTAVE
- NIST 800-39
- HB 158-2010

- ISO/IEC 31000
- ITIL
- CRAMM
- FAIR
- VAR

Aggregated and Cascading Risk

Aggregated risk occurs when a specific threat affects a large number of minor vulnerabilities. It can also refer to a large number of threats affecting a large number of minor vulnerabilities. In these cases, it is possible for a risk that individually is acceptable to become unacceptable if looked at collectively.

Cascading risk occurs when a single failure leads to a chain reaction of other failures. As an example, this happened recently when a small power utility in the Midwest failed, causing a cascade of failures across the power grid. When it was all done, most of the northeastern United States experienced a loss of power as well. Within IT systems, one system can cause one or more other systems to go down due to dependencies.

Other Risk Assessment Approaches

Some methods that originated outside of the information security arena are starting to see adoption by information security. Let's discuss the two most promising.

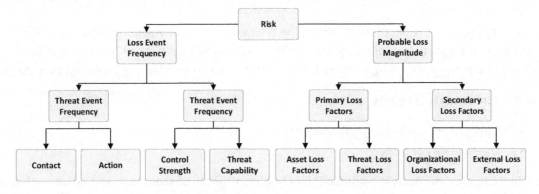

Figure 34: Factor analysis of information risk (FAIR)

Factor analysis of information risk, or *FAIR*, allows us to decompose risk and understand the underlying components. FAIR is designed to complement other approaches by increasing accuracy. The framework, which can is illustrated in **Figure 34**, consists of four elements:

- A **taxonomy** of the factors that make up information risk, by providing a set of standard definitions.
- A **method for measuring** the factors that drive information risk.
- A **computational engine** that derives risk mathematically and simulates the relationships between the measured factors.
- A **simulation model** that takes the three components above analyzes risk scenarios.

When dealing with risk taxonomy, there are four characteristics we need to look at:

- The **frequency** with which threat agents contact assets at-risk.
- The **probability of action** by threat agents.
- The **probability of success** by threat agents.
- The **type and severity** of the impact to assets.

A *probabilistic risk assessment (PRA)* is a methodology to look at complex life cycles from concept to retirement. PRA was created by NASA and is very time-consuming but works well in a high network security environment. It basically asks three questions:

- What can go wrong?
- How likely is it?
- What are the consequences?

Identification of Risk

Risk identification is the act of determining the type and nature of viable threats, and which vulnerabilities might be exploited by each threat – a vulnerability that can be exploited by a viable threat is a *risk*. *Exposure* is the potential loss when a vulnerability is exploited by a threat.

A viable threat has two factors:

- They exist or could reasonably appear
- They can be controlled

Risk identification normally is carried out by creating a variety of scenarios, and assumes that all assets, vulnerabilities and threats have been identified. This may not be possible due to a lack of knowledge, and in this case the lack of knowledge itself is a vulnerability. Vulnerabilities that cannot be tied to a specific threat should still be listed to be analyzed, since a threat may simply not have been identified yet. We should have the attitude of "if it can go wrong, it will". Even the process of risk identification itself is subject to error and could represent a vulnerability!

Some hints for a successful outcome when developing scenarios are the following:

- Make sure risk is kept **up-to-date**
- Start with **generic scenarios** and add detail when needed
- The **number of scenarios** should reflect the complexity of the business
- The **taxonomy** should reflect the complexity of the business
- When reporting risk, use a **generic structure** (avoid too much detail)
- Make sure to **include people** with the appropriate amount of skills and knowledge
- Use the process to **get buy-in** from all departments
- **Involve staff** who represent the first line of defense
- **Don't focus** only on rare or extreme scenarios
- **Combine simple scenarios** to make complex scenarios
- Consider **system and contagious risk:**
  - *Systemic risk* represents a negative event affecting a large part of the area or industry. For example, an unrelated air carrier's system goes down for 24 hours and cause the entire traffic control system to become backed up
  - *Contagious risk* occurs when multiple failures happen within a very short time frame of each other. For example, an earthquake (risk 1) causes online traffic to be diverted to a backup data center on the other side of the country, only to discover that misconfigured firewalls (risk 2) at that location prevent it from coming online.
- Use the exercise to **build awareness** around risk detection

Once the assets, threats, vulnerabilities, risk and exposures have been identified, a list of events representing those needs to be generated. A risk can be characterized by the following six attributes:

1) **The origin**, such as hostile employees, employees who have not been well trained, competitors of governments.
2) The **threat**, which can be an activity, a specific event or an incident.
3) The **impact** that results when the risk is exposed.
4) The **specific reason for its occurrence**, such as design error, human interaction or a failure to predict competitor activity.

5) The **exposure and controls**, or the extent of loss and how it can be mitigated.
6) The **time and place of occurrence**.

Historical information about the organization, or similar organizations, can be very helpful since it can lead to reasonable predictions about current and future issues that are not yet obvious.

When selecting a risk identification methodology, the following techniques should be employed:

- Team-based **brainstorming**
- **Flowcharting** and modeling
- What-if **scenarios**
- **Mapping threats** to both identified and suspected vulnerabilities

Risk scenarios are created by describing a potential risk event and then writing down the assets that might be affected. Some examples of risk events are:

- System failure
- Loss of key personnel
- Theft
- Network outages
- Power failures
- Natural disasters

Each risk scenario should be related to a business goal or impact. Only real and relevant scenarios should be considered. For example, while it is technically possible for Canada to invade the U.S., it is highly unlikely. However, it could be a very real threat that the Canadian government could pass a law that restricts import of our product – that's a risk that definitely should be "what-if'd". **Figure 35** represents inputs that should be considered when creating scenarios.

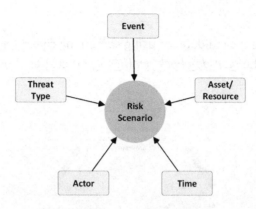

Figure 35: Risk Scenario Structure

Other Organizational Support

There are a number of security services that can be tied into an information security program. These services allow us to gain access to the expertise of external service providers without actually giving them responsibility. They are the following:

- **Good practices published by organizations**, including ISACA, the SANS Institute, and the International Information Systems Security Certification Consortium, or (ISC)^2.
- **Security networking roundtables**, which are organizations that gather information security professionals from similar industries to discuss topics of common interest. Some are free while others require a fee. Still others are sponsored by a technology vendor, and the information security manager may consider restricting attendance to these to avoid pressure to purchase that vendor's products.
- **Security news organizations**, such as Computer World, SANS, Tech Target and CIO Magazine. These publish daily or weekly news relevant to information security.
- **Security-related studies**, which are annual studies regarding a number of security-related matters published by PricewaterhouseCoopers (PwC), Ernst and Young (EY), Verizon, Symantec and Ponemon.
- **Security training organizations**, which provide classes on information security topics.
- **Vulnerability alerting services**, who notifies information security managers about vulnerabilities specific to the technology their organization uses.

Plan-Do-Check-Act

Information security is a great candidate for using something called *total quality management*, or *TQM*. TQM is based on the *plan-do-check-act* (*PDCA*) process as shown in **Figure 36**.

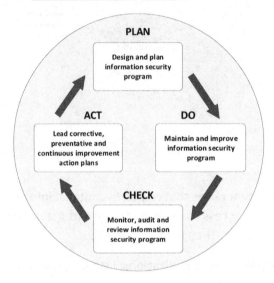

Figure 36: PDCA Methodology

The components of TQM as carried out with information security are shown in **Figure 37**.

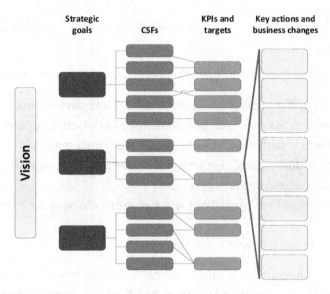

Figure 37: Strategic Goals, CSFs, KPIs and Key Actions

Vision is a clear statement describing the organization's purpose and should include goals for the information security program.

Strategic goals are the objectives necessary to reach the organization's vision. The goals should be reflected in the selected KPIs.

We have already discussed KGIs and CSFs in Section. *Key actions and business changes* are the initiatives needed to achieve the strategic goals and KGIs.

Chapter 39: Information Risk Management – Constraints That Hurt

Third-Party Services

When dealing with third-parties, the information security manager must ensure:

- Proper controls and processes are in place to facilitate outsourcing
- Proper information risk management clauses are in outsourcing contracts
- A risk assessment is performed for any outsourced processes
- A proper level of due diligence is carried out prior to signing contracts
- Manage risk for outsourced processes daily
- New risk assessments are carried out when material changes are made to an outsourced process
- Proper processes are followed when relationships end

We must recognize that outsourcing business-critical functions generally increases risk instead of decreasing it, because specification of controls, and the implementation of those controls, are now carried out by two different organizations, and we depend on the contract specifics to make sure it happens. **Figure 38** illustrates this relationship.

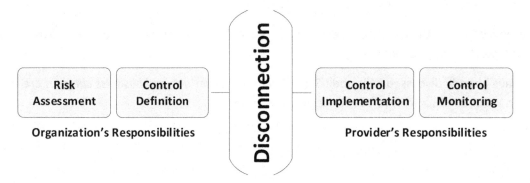

Figure 38: Disconnect of Responsibilities with Outsourced Providers

Additionally, when involving third-parties the number of information risk areas to assess grows from two to three: our business, the outsourced process, and the third-party themselves. If the business operates in a regulated industry, the contract should explicitly state those regulatory requirements. Of course, the more we rely on innovation from the third-party – as opposed to heavily dictating performance in the contract - the greater the risk we create. All of these points underline why we should restrict outsourcing to those functions that are outside of the organization's core expertise. Do what we do best internally, and potentially outsource other processes only.

The exit strategy needs to be considered before an agreement is finalized and must be specified in the contract to ensure that the outsourced process continues to be available while transitioning away from the third-party. Because few businesses remain static, the information security manager needs to stay on top of the contract and make sure that it reflects the current relationship.

Keep in mind one very important detail – while we can outsource information risk management to a third-party, we can never outsource ultimate responsibility. Even if we do a great job of dictating controls and making sure the third-party implements them properly, if a security event occurs, we are still responsible for any fallout from that event, particularly in the eyes of the law.

Outsourcing providers may be reluctant to share details on the nature and extent of their internal protection mechanisms. This makes it even more important to include service-level agreements (SLAs) and other performance requirements in the contract. Since we will not be able to peer inside of their day-to-day operations, we must rely on the contract to force the provider to behave properly. One common approach for this is to require specific audits such as SOC 2, or perhaps require the outsourced business to acquire an ISO 27001 certification. Care must be taken with SOC 2 audits, as the outsourced provider is the one who defines the criteria. Even with ISO 27001, it is important to review the external audit report performed on the provider for comments.

If the organization operates in a regulated industry such as finances, there will probably be requirements on reporting security events such as the time allowed before the report is submitted to the governing agency. In these cases, the contract must reference such notifications.

The financial viability of providers must also be addressed to ensure they will be able to operate and meet the requirements of the contract. Since outsourcing often is awarded to the lowest bidder, this is a very important aspect to consider. The BC and DR plans should reference all outsourced relationships, and should cover the loss of critical outsourcing providers, including insolvency or bankruptcy scenarios.

Some sources of outsourcing risk can be transferred by including indemnity clauses in the contract. Some examples are:

- The right to software source code in the event of a default, usually carried out by employing source code escrow with a neutral party
- Requirements that the provider remain timely with compliance
- The right to audit the provider's books, premises and processes
- The right to assess the skill sets of the provider's resources (employees)
- Advance information if the provider's resources are to be changed

Legal and Regulatory Compliance

Organizations must evaluate their level of compliance relative to other organizations in the same industry, as enforcement actions are taken against those that are least compliant first. Management may decide that non-compliance is the correct decision due to the lower costs of fines or the fact that enforcement may not be likely.

While corporate legal departments should be concerned with regulatory requirements, most are not aware of any such constraints, and the information security manager should therefore help identify them. The security manager will probably be required to support the legal standards related to the following areas:

- Privacy of information and transactions
- Collection and handling of audit records
- Email retention policies
- Incident investigation procedures
- Cooperation with legal authorities

Since legal and regulatory requirements can vary quite a bit between different jurisdictions, the HR and legal departments should be consulted before action is taken.

Physical and Environmental Factors

The level of security applied to various hardware, software and information assets should be based on the following aspects:

- **Criticality** of systems
- **Sensitivity** of information
- **Significance** of applications

- **Cost** of replacement hardware
- **Availability** of backup equipment

Control of physical security may reside with the information security group or not, but regardless it is the responsibility of the information security manager to ensure security policies, standards and activities sufficiently protect those assets. Physical control of access to computing resources should be determined by the sensitivity of the information being accessed and should always be on an as-needed basis.

The physical location within a facility is important as well. For example, putting servers in a room prone to flooding is not such a great idea. The ability to control temperature, humidity and electrical power needs to be looked at as well. Personal computers with special access should not be placed in heavily-trafficked areas. Physically locking a device down or disabling methods for copying data off (such as USB ports and removable media drives) should be considered. Laptops and other mobile devices are particularly problematic as they are designed to be taken out of a secure facility. Encryption of the entire storage disk in such devices is one option to mitigate the risk of a device being stolen.

Physical media such as optical disks, magnetic disks, USB drives and even printed hardcopies are as great a risk as online compromises, so they should be stored in a secure location. The transport and storage of backup media must be encrypted, particularly if stored at an off-site location. A clean desk policy in which no cluttered desks are allowed should be enforced in less secure office spaces. This prevents sticky fingers or wandering eyes from accessing sensitive information.

Locations that reside in a geographical area prone to earthquakes, flooding, hurricanes or other natural disasters should be avoided when selecting sites for facilities. Even if an area is safe geographically but located next to special risk infrastructure, such as nuclear power plants, airports or chemical production facilities, then additional consideration must be applied before selecting it as a site for a facility. Finally, primary and backup facilities should be located far enough from each other that a single disaster event does not take out both locations.

Cultural and Regional Variances

It is the job of the information security manager to be aware of local culture and customs, and how certain actions that may be appropriate in one area may be deemed offensive or unacceptable to that locale. Any risk from such an incident must be considered and mitigated if it falls above the acceptable risk and risk tolerance levels for an organization. Different countries have varying laws regarding the sharing of personal information, and the information security manager needs to be aware of those complications. If the information security manager has any doubts about possible risks, he should work with the legal and HR departments to identify problems and to come up with solutions.

Logistics

Because of the need to interact with other business units and people, the information security manager must consider logistical issues such as coordinating meetings, development of schedules for recurring procedures, and managing workload across resources. Fortunately, there are a lot of online systems to help with this task. However, undergoing logistics training will go a long way to help the security manager deal with these types of duties efficiently.

Chapter 40: Information Risk Management – The Action Plan

Often an organization will have such a level of expertise or experience with a specific technology that it will reference that technology at the policy level. For example, transport layer security, or TLS, is so ubiquitous in today's world that it is often named in security policies, even though it is only one way to encrypt data and provide confidentiality.

Another reality that exists is that many organizations have multiple, unrelated architectures such as a database architecture, server architecture, identity management, etc. Apart from each other they function well, but if you were to try and combine them into a single enterprise architecture you would find the result less than usable. As an analogy, consider different people creating parts of a car without working with each other – wheels, the engine, seats and the transmission – all created without each person comparing their blueprint with others. When it comes time to assemble the vehicle, nothing is really going to fit together and work. This is why we have architectural frameworks – to ensure each group carries out their respective tasks underneath a watchful umbrella of architectural goodness. Examples of these are COBIT, ITIL and ISO 27001.

Information Security Framework

An information security management framework describes information security management components and their interactions at a high-level. 'Components' would be things like roles, policies, standard operating procedures (SOPs), security architectures, etc. However, a framework also facilitates deliverables that are more short-term, such as possible risk mitigation options, facilitation of conversations with subject matter experts (SMEs), or ensuring policies are followed. Some other goals a framework helps with are ensuring that:

- The program **adds value**
- The program is **efficient and low-cost**
- Management clearly understands information **security drivers and benefits**
- Information security knowledge and **capabilities grow**
- The program fosters **cooperation and goodwill** among business units
- Stakeholder **understand their roles**
- **Continuity of business** is addressed

Components

The various components of a security management framework can be broken down into five areas:

- Technical
- Operational
- Management
- Administrative
- Educational and Informational

Let's dive into each area one at a time.

Technical Components

For our purposes, 'technical' refers to IT systems, which have an owner and a custodian. The owner is responsible for costs and behavior of the system, while the custodian is responsible for the day-to-day management of the system. IT is always the custodian of an IT system, but often the business unit that requires a system is the owner. Regardless of who it may be, it is crucial that all systems have an identified owner. Otherwise, there is no one accountable for ensuring that a system remains compliant with security policies and that risk is properly addressed. Given that the vast majority of information resides in systems maintained by IT, that department is a major focus of an information security framework.

Operational Components

Operational components of a security program are the management and administrative activities conducted either daily or weekly such as maintenance of security technologies, security practices and keeping procedures updated. The information security manager manages these areas, but since the actual execution usually requires a different department (such as applying security patches) he will need to work with and provide oversight of those departments.

Some examples of operational components are:

- Credential administration
- Security event monitoring
- System patching procedures
- Change control procedures

- Collection of security metrics and reporting
- Maintenance of control technologies
- Security incident response, investigation and resolution
- Retirement and sanitization of hardware

For each operational component, the information security manager will need to identify the owner and ensure documentation is kept up to date. Additionally, the security manager must ensure that procedures for appropriate security-related areas are created and maintained, and that roles and responsibilities documentation is kept current.

Management Components

While operational components are addressed on a daily or weekly basis, management components are visited periodically every few months, quarters or even years. Examples are the development of standards, reviewing policies, and executing oversight of initiatives or programs.

Management goals shape the security program, which in turn defines what must be managed. Often, early versions of a security program are too lenient or strict and the management components must allow for timely modification. When developing the management components, it is important that proper oversight from senior management takes place.

Administrative Components

We have discussed to a great extent how the information security management role needs to provide oversight for other departments, but we need to keep in mind that information security is itself a department, and so we can't ignore all of the normal functions that come along with a group of people trying to accomplish a mission. This means we need to manage resources, personnel and the financial aspect of running a business unit. Rarely does an information security program have a sufficient number of resources, and so security efforts must be prioritized.

It is not uncommon for the information security manager to experience pressure to take shortcuts, and if this cannot be handled between the two departments, the manager needs to escalate it to senior management so that a decision can be made. Executive management must understand the risks of moving an initiative ahead without a full security diligence, but they may ultimately decide to do so. If this happens, the information security manager should take the first available opportunity to certify the compromised system or initiatives.

To ensure sufficient resources are available to address incidents as they arise, the manager must make sure that business units understand that some ad-hoc conditions may cause a temporary shortage of security resources.

Educational and Informational Components

It is crucial to educate employees and provide training on security awareness across the organization. The type of material and the target audience can change how and when this training is carried out. **Table 4** provides a brief list.

Content	Application
Security risk and awareness	Orientation and initial training
General policies and procedures	HR Level
Role-specific training	Business unit level

Table 4: Security Content and Application

Interactive techniques such as online testing and role-playing will usually be more effective than an informational session. Collaboration with both HR and business units is required to identify what information needs to be covered. To ensure progress is being made, metrics such as average quiz scores or the average time elapsed since the last training period, should be communicated to the steering committee and senior management.

Defining an Information Security Program Road Map

We previously covered the six outcomes of a successful security program – strategic alignment, risk management, value delivery, resource management, assurance process integration and performance measurement. All outcomes should appear on a road map, showing how we will achieve each. However, the targeted outcomes will probably now be well-understood by management and stakeholders, leading to unrealistic expectations and poorly-defined goals. To avoid this pitfall, the information security manager can develop a road map in stages, with each stage focusing on just a portion of the overall success.

To illustrate this approach further, let's explore an example in which we implement the road map in four stages.

Stage 1 will highlight how security will align with business goals, and how we will start improvements over what is in place today. This will require the security manager to interview various stakeholders and will provide a great deal of insight to possible members of the steering committee.

Stage 2 leverages the steering committee to draft policies for a security program for senior management to approve. Since business unit owners are part of that committee, we will also have identified business goals.

Stage 3 sees the committee members conducting internal reviews to see how far away they are from the goals that they themselves have identified. A nice side-effect is that they are now promoting awareness of the security program.

Stage 4 implements change to address the gaps revealed in the previous stage, while a monitoring approach is developed at the same time. The security manager can then get consensus on roles and responsibilities, processes and procedures.

Job done!

Elements of a Road Map

If some type of a security strategy is already in place, then a road map should also exist. In this case, the manager simply needs to turn the conceptual architecture into reality. Basically, we have been given a blueprint, and we need to simply build it.

On the other hand, if a security strategy does not exist, we need to recognize that there is a risk that the elements and work needed for a successful security program may not be prioritized. Add to that a lack of metrics, and we are setting ourselves up for failure. So, a security strategy is essential to success.

A lot of the effort required for developing a security program is in designing controls that meet our control goals, and then creating, deploying and testing those controls. All of this means that the organization is going to need to be receptive to the addition of new security activities, including the inevitable disruptions.

Developing an Information Security Program Road Map

If we want to be successful in developing a security program, an essential skill to have is the ability to review existing data, applications, systems, facilities and processes. This will give us an excellent insight into the new projects we will have to undertake.

An implementation road map can serve the same purpose by defining each step necessary to get to a particular goal of the program. Not only does it provide an overview of the entire scope, but it also shows the sequence in which the steps need to be executed. Milestones should be present that represent when we will have access to KGIs, KPIs and critical success factors (CSFs).

It is more important that we establish a process for monitoring KGIs and KPIs than demonstrating the values are correct during the first few times that we collect them.

The Risk Management Process

Risk management consists of a series of processes in which we identify, analyze, evaluate and maintain risk at acceptable levels. Let's go through each process in the order each should be carried out.

First, we **establish scope and boundaries**, resulting in a set of global parameters used by risk management, both inside and outside of the organization.

Second, we **identify information assets and valuation** in which at-risk assets are identified and the potential impact is estimated.

The third step is to **perform the risk assessment**, which itself consist of 3 steps – identify, analyze and decide what to do. More specifically, we must:

- Identify threats, vulnerabilities and exposures
- Analyze the level of risk and potential impact
- Determine if the risk meets the criteria for acceptance

Then, for each risk that is unacceptable, we **determine risk treatment or response** by selecting a strategy to deal with it. If you recall, the possible strategies will be to avoid, mitigate, transfer or accept risk.

Risk is usually accepted if it is minor, too expensive to mitigate, or simply cannot be mitigated.

The fifth step is to **accept residual risk**, which is the risk remaining after mitigation steps.

The sixth, and last, step is to **communicate about and monitor risk**. Communication happens between decision makers and other internal and external stakeholders.

For any security program to be successful, we must be sure that it is a continuous process as shown in **Figure 39**.

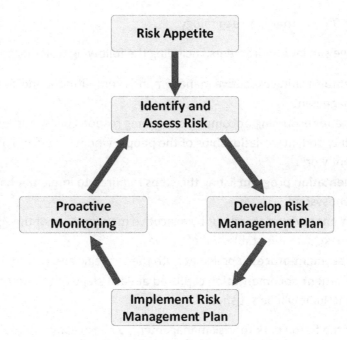

Figure 39: Continuous Risk Management Steps

The information security manager should setup a formal, repeating process to perform risk assessments at the organizational, system and application levels, including both logical and physical processes. Naturally, useful metrics are part of this process to ensure we can measure success, and it is the information security manager's duty to recommend to asset owners manual and automated techniques to continuously monitor risk. Resist the temptation to apply general risk profiles across regions or industries – each location will probably be unique. Remember that controls degrade over time, so periodic testing is crucial.

Defining a Risk Management Framework

The best approach to implementing a risk management program is to use a reference model from the following choices:

- COBIT 5
- ISO 31000 Risk Management
- IEC 21010: Risk Management
- NIST SP 800-39: Managing Information Security Risk
- HB 158-2010: Delivering Assurance based on ISO 31000

- ISO/IEC 27005: Information Technology

All of the above have similar requirements, including the following 6 elements.

- A **policy** demonstrating executive management's commitment and containing the goals of risk management.
- A **planning and resourcing** document, containing responsibility, authority, accountability and interrelationships of the people who will perform and verify risk management work.
- An **implementation program** listing the steps required to implement an effective risk management system.
- A **management review** carried out by executive management of the risk management system to make sure it is stable and effective.
- A **risk management process** applied at both the strategic and tactical levels.
- **Risk management documentation** captured at each stage of the process so that an independent audit will be satisfied.

When we establish the framework for risk management, we also establish the criteria for acceptable risk, control goals, and scope. But, before we can define a great framework, we have to do the following:

- Understand the background of the organization and its risk
- Look at existing risk management activities and acceptable risk criteria
- Develop a process to create risk management initiatives and controls that will get us to acceptable risk levels

Defining the External Environment

Several times to this point we have referenced things that are 'external' to the organization. External in this case refers to:

- The local market
- Our industry
- The competitive, financial and political; environments
- The law and regulatory environment
- Social and cultural conditions
- External stakeholders

Additionally, we must also consider the perceptions and values of external stakeholders, and any externally generated threats or opportunities.

Defining the Internal Environment

Let' define the internal environment while we're at it:

- Key business **drivers**
- The organization's **SWOT** (strengths, weaknesses, opportunities, and threats)
- Internal **stakeholders**
- Organization structure and **culture**
- **Assets**, such as people, processes, systems and capital
- **Goals**, objectives and strategies

Determining the Risk Management Context

When we use the term 'context' when discussing risk management, we're talking about the environment or activities where the risk occurs. There are four things we need to define before being able to nail down the risk management context:

- How much of the organization and activities we need to **assess**
- The full **scope** of risk management activities
- The **roles and responsibilities** of the people and groups participating in risk management
- How **risk-averse or risk-aggressive** the organization is

Once that is done, we can establish the criteria by which risk will be evaluated. There are three considerations we must consider when selecting criteria:

- The **impact**, or the kinds of consequences we need to consider
- The **likelihood**, or the probability of being compromised
- The **rules** that establish what is acceptable risk

Note that these criteria may need to change in the later phases of the risk management process due to changing circumstances, or as consequences of the risk assessment itself.

Gap Analysis

A 'gap analysis' means measuring the difference between two states. When it comes to risk management, we are measuring the difference between existing controls and our control goals

– the current state and the desired state. Control objectives should result in acceptable risk, which in turn establishes the information security baseline.

Control objectives can change during the risk management process, so we must be sure to periodically review previous gap analysis to ensure they remain accurate. This should be automatically covered when testing for control effectiveness.

Costs and Benefits
Three common measurements of potential losses are:

- Employee productivity impacts (virus and worm attacks, PII compromise are the most often reported)
- Revenue losses
- Direct cost loss events

Events Affecting Security Baselines
Baseline security is defined as the minimum security level across the entire organization. The baseline for higher classifications of information assets should be higher as well. For example, access to higher-classified assets might require two-factor authentication, while lower levels may only require a username and password.

Any security incident can be traced back to a control failure or lack of a control. When a significant incident occurs, a root cause must be found, and a reassessment executed. Baselines may need to be temporarily changed based on external threat changes. Other events that might cause changes to a baseline are:

- New or changing laws and regulations
- New or changing threats result in unacceptable risk levels
- Degradation of controls over time
- System changes creating new vulnerabilities

Integration with IT Processes
The security manager must ensure that security programs properly integrate with other assurance functions within the organization. These interfaces are bidirectional, in that while security-related information is provided to other departments, those departments also provide information back to the security department. For example, a business unit may provide

requirements to the security department, while the security manager may provide meaningful metrics back to the business unit.

Security added after the fact is usually not effective security at all. That is why it is important to bake security into projects from the beginning of the system development life cycle, or SDLC. However, the SDLC is seldom controlled by the security manager, and therefore he must foster collaborative relationships with his colleagues in other departments.

The traditional SDLC goes through five stages:

- Initiation
- Development or acquisition
- Implementation
- Operation or maintenance
- End of life or disposition

Change management needs to be an area in which the security manager takes special interest, since it is through change management processes that she will be able to inject risk assessments and apply the appropriate treatments. Another approach is to make sure that security implications are part of the standard practice when making changes. This can be done by requiring all changes to be accompanied by the results of a risk analysis. In addition, it is a wise precaution for the security manager to identify where changes are initiated, funded and deployed. By hooking into these locations, the manager has a much greater chance at detecting changes as they occur.

Security controls lose their effectiveness over time due to changes in the systems and processes they are designed to protect, and therefore a periodic review of all existing controls is absolutely essential to keep a proper security posture.

Closely related to change management is configuration management, which is the primary culprit that contribute to security breaches. The main two reason systems are improperly configured are:

- A lack of clear standards or procedures
- Shorthanded staff who take shortcuts

If proper documentation exists and the staff is properly trained, but we are still experiencing poorly configured systems, then we need to take a look at the time constraints placed on the existing staff. It may be they are so overworked that they do not have the time to perform the configuration operations properly.

Release management is the process of rolling out new capabilities or updates to existing capabilities. The key component for success is proper testing *before* deployment. The security manager should ensure that proper procedures and standards exist to prevent products from being deployed to the production environment prematurely. Proper monitoring to ensure staff are following the procedures must also be carried out.

Security Awareness Training and Education

Security can never be addressed solely through technical mechanisms. The behavioral aspect – meaning the behavior of people – must be addressed as well through engaging and repeated training. Security awareness programs should focus on topics such as:

- Password selection
- Appropriate use of computers
- Email safety
- Web browsing safety
- Social engineering

Since employees are the ones who will be in the best position to recognize threats that automated mechanisms may miss, they should be taught how to recognize and escalate security events.

Special attention needs to be paid to the positions that have unlimited data access. Examples of duties that often require this are:

- Transferring data between systems
- Performance tuning
- Scheduling batch jobs
- Programmers changing application code

Since security management seldom has oversight into these areas, management in those areas must take on the responsibility of understanding security requirements and assisting in providing oversight.

Employee awareness training should begin on the day the employee starts and continue regularly. The training techniques used should vary to prevent the material from becoming stale or boring. Programs should incorporate the following:

- Quizzes to gauge retention
- Reminders such as posters, newsletter or screen savers
- A regular schedule of refreshers

Awareness program should consider the following aspects:

- Who is the intended **audience**? Is it senior management, business managers, IT staff, or end users?
- What is the intended **message**? Is it policies, procedures or perhaps recent events?
- What is the intended **result**? For example, improved policy compliance, changing a behavior, or executing better practices?
- What **communication method** will be used? Possibilities include computer-based training, or CBT, an all-hands meeting, using the intranet, or newsletters.
- What is the organizational **structure and culture**?

There are a number of effective mechanisms we can use to raise awareness for information security, including:

- Computer-based training
- Email reminders
- Written security policies
- Non-disclosure agreements signed by employees
- Newsletters, web pages, videos, posters, login reminders
- Visible enforcement of security policies
- Simulated security incidents
- Rewarding employees for reporting suspicious behavior
- Job descriptions
- Performance reviews

General Rules of Use/Acceptable Use Policy

Some employees are very interested in adhering to good security practices but would simply rather read a comprehensive summary of everything the organization expects and requires. By creating a user-friendly summary of what they should do and should not do to comply with policy, we have an effective way of reaching these individuals. The policy can detail in everyday language and in a straight-forward manner all obligations and responsibilities of everyone. However, we must also make sure that the policy is read and understood. The policy should be given to all new employees, regardless of employment status.

The policy normally includes the following elements:

- **Policy and standards** for access controls
- **Classification** of information
- **Marking and handling** of documents and information
- **Reporting** requirements
- **Disclosure** constraints
- Email and Internet **usage policy**

Ethics

Ethics training is usually provided for employees who engage in activities of a particularly sensitive nature, such as monitoring user activities, performing penetration testing, or having access to sensitive personal data, such as those in HR. Additionally, information security personnel must be aware of potential conflicts of interest or activities. A signed acceptance of the code of ethics should remain a permanent part of the employee's records.

Documentation

An important part of a good information security program is ensuring effective oversight of the creation and maintenance of security-related documentation. Some document examples are:

- Our good friends policies, standards, procedures and guidelines
- Technical diagrams of infrastructure, architectures and data flows
- Training and awareness documentation
- Risk analysis
- Security system designs
- Incident tracking reports
- Operational procedures

Every document should be assigned an owner who is responsible for keeping it updated and controlling changes to it. The information security manager should also make sure that enablers we discussed earlier are available that address each step in the life cycle of documents, such as creation, approval, change control and retirement. Version control is an absolute must – this ensures that previous versions are kept in an original state, and that everyone is working from the same version. Other attributes that need to be managed include markings, classification, release date, version and owner.

All changes to documentation must be managed through a formal change request process. The information security manager should track all proposed changes to policies and ensure each is properly reviewed.

However, changes to standards will happen more frequently than to policies due to evolving technologies, changes in risk or new business initiatives. Proposed standard changes should be reviewed by those impacted by the changes, with the opportunity to provide input before approval – this will maximize cooperation and compliance.

Modifications to either a policy or standard should trigger procedures to update compliance monitoring tools and processes. If auditors or compliance people are not directly involved with that process, they should be periodically kept up-to-date.

Program Development and Project Management

Ideally, most security projects will result in making existing technology more secure. Each project should have time, budget and a measurable risk, and should make the overall environment more secure without causing weaknesses in other areas. Projects should also be prioritized so that those that overlay others do not cause delays.

Program Budgeting

The success of an information security program depends on having the necessary resources, and having the necessary resources depends on how well the budget is managed. We're not talking just spreadsheets here – effective budget management includes presenting to and convincing senior management to approve a budget. This is why self-education and advanced planning are so important. Well-before the fiscal cycle starts the information security manager must be sure he or she is familiar with the processes and methods the organization uses. Another crucial aspect is to ensure the security strategy is laid out in a well thought-through road map. If the strategy has been reviewed and approved before the budgeting cycle begins, we have a much better chance of getting a budget that aligns with that strategy approved.

Most budgetary expenses for an information security program are pretty easy to understand - we have personnel, hardware, software and subscription costs. Slightly more difficult to get a grasp on are expenses related to projects with timed deliverables. The security manager must work with the PMO and SMEs to estimate reasonably accurate costs for each fiscal year. Some elements that need to be considered are the following:

- Employee time
- Contractor and consultant fees
- Hardware and software costs
- Hardware space requirements
- Testing resources
- Training costs
- Travel
- Creation of supporting documentation
- Ongoing maintenance
- Contingencies for unexpected costs

One area that is the most problematic to estimate are the costs involved with responding to incidents, because often the need arises to engage with external resources. The best way to estimate this type of costs is to use historical data and extrapolate for the coming year. If historical data within the organization is not available, estimates can be based on information from peer organizations.

Information Security Problem Management Practices

Problem management is focused on finding the root cause of an emerging issue. As information systems get updated and are enhanced, it is likely that security controls will start having problems or stop working altogether. The security manager will then need to identify the problem and assign a priority to it. The steps involved are:

- **Understanding** the issue
- **Defining** the problem
- **Designing** an action program
- **Assigning responsibility**
- **Assigning due dates** for resolution

Some type of reporting process needs to track the issue until it is resolved.

At times, the security manager will need to take immediate steps to implement a secondary control if the primary fails. For example, if a firewall stops filtering traffic, the security manager might disconnect certain systems from the network until the firewall has been replaced. Of course, this will almost certainly result in a business interruption, so the authority to take such an action would need to be assigned to the security manager before the event took place.

Vendor Management

External vendors often provide a valuable benefit in either capabilities an organization does not yet possess, or by providing capabilities at a lower cost than the organization could provide for itself. Security service providers can provide a range of functions such as:

- Assessment and Audit
- Engineering
- Operational support
- Security architecture and design
- Advisory services
- Forensics support

However, it is up to the security manager to oversee and monitor external providers of hardware, software, general supplies and other services. Services needing monitoring specific to security are:

- Financial viability
- Quality of service
- Adequate staffing
- Adherence to security policies
- Right to audit

By monitoring these services, the security manager ensures that risk introduced by those providers is managed properly.

Program Management Evaluation

The information security manager must periodically reevaluate the effectiveness of a security program based on changes in organizational demands, environments and other needs. Or, perhaps the program needs be reviewed when a new information security manager or CSO is hired. In either case, the results should be shared with the information security steering committee or other stakeholders. There are six areas that are critical for evaluation, which are:

- Program objectives
- Compliance requirements
- Program management
- Security operations management
- Technical security management
- Resource levels

Program Objectives

The first evaluation area, program objectives, deals with ensuring that the program's security goals are sound. Here, we need to ensure that there is a solid security strategy and road map, and that there is well-defined criterion for acceptable risk. Once we have that established we then need to make sure that the program's goals align with governance goals, and that those goals are SMART. When defining those goals, we need to be sure that they are developed collaboratively among all stakeholders so that we can reach consensus. If policies, standards and procedures do not exist, then this is the time to create them. This is also the time to define whatever metrics we will be using to measure success.

Compliance Requirements

The second evaluation area, compliance requirements, comes into play if the purpose of a program is to ensure compliance with a regulatory standard. If compliance is not a concern, then we can skip this step.

Assuming compliance is needed, then we will first need to determine the level of compliance we will need to meet. As part of that effort, the program will need to be examined to see if its components align with the components required by regulatory standards. Looking at the results from recent audit and compliance reviews will help with this activity, as will ensuring that there is a close level of communication between compliance and security groups. Since policies, standards, procedures and metrics were already covered in the previous area, program objectives, we simply need to make sure that compliance requirements are integrated into each of those. Finally, we just need to examine compliance management technologies in-use, and ensure that deficiencies are tracked, reported and addressed in a timely manner.

237

Program Management

The third evaluation area, program management, will reveal the extent of management support and how comprehensive the existing program is. The level of management each program contains will vary, but generally speaking, technical security programs will be light on management, while programs driven by standards, compliance or governance will have a greater level of management oversight.

In this area, we need to ensure everyone understands their assigned roles and responsibilities, including senior management. Information security responsibilities should be a part of each business manager's goals, and it should be reflected in his/her individual performance rating. It should be clear who is accountable for the program, and that person or group must have sufficient authority and visibility for the program to succeed.

This evaluation area also covers ensuring that sufficient documentation of the program exists, and that policies and standards are complete, formally approved and distributed to the appropriate audiences. Formalizing a steering committee is covered, as well as ensuring that management regularly reassesses the program's effectiveness. Finally, this step ensures that the metrics defined earlier are regularly collected and reported.

Security Operations Management

The fourth evaluation area, security operations management, looks at how well a program implements security operational activities. A large part of this area focuses on standard operating procedures, or SOPs. SOPs are examined to ensure that they include security requirements and processes, and that SOPs exist for configuration and access management, systems maintenance, event analysis and incident response.

Other topics addressed in the security operations area are ensuring proper segregation of duties, validating that a schedule for regularly performed activities exists, checking to see if metrics produce meaningful results, and that there is a path for escalating issues to management so that they will be resolved.

Technical Security Management

The fifth area, technical security management, covers the technical security environment and makes sure that systems and security mechanisms have been implemented properly. A major focus is placed on the implementation and success of standards. For example, security configuration standards for network, system and application components are checked, as are standards for topology, communication protocols and compartmentalization of critical systems. In addition to validating that they even exist, standards must also follow high-level policy and requirements, and should be a result of collaborative efforts. If implemented correctly, standards will be uniformly implemented, and there will be a process to report exceptions.

Other topics of interest in the technical security management area are ensuring that key controls are continuously monitored, and that they notify on failure. Development, test and production environments should be kept separate, and SoD is properly enforced on systems. Logging must be reliable and visible, and there should be proper decommissioning processes to prevent data leakage.

SoD — segregation of duties

Resource Levels

The final evaluation area is that of resource levels, including financial, human and technical resources. This area examines current funding levels and makes sure that the budget and available money line up. This is carried out by ensuring that resources align with business goals, and that program functions are prioritized by the amount of money available.

Specific to human resources, the resource level evaluation area will inquire about the current staffing level to see if existing resources are being fully utilized. Part of this activity is to ensure that existing resources are adequately skilled for the roles they are assigned, and to search for low-value tasks that other resources could carry out. A special consideration is finding out if there are other HR resources the program is dependent on to succeed.

When it comes to technical resources, this area will ask about any technologies needed to support information security program goals, and if the current capacity of those technologies is sufficient for our current and future needs. The maintenance and replacement of the technology is considered, and other technologies that could make the program more efficient are examined.

Current State of Incident Response Capability

Most organizations have some sort of capability for reporting incidents, and the information security manager must identify what this capability is. The three most common ways to collect this information are by:

- Surveying senior management, business managers and IT representatives.

- Using a self-assessment, which is the easiest method as it does not require participation from stakeholders, but it also may produce the most limited view.
- Using an external assessment or audit, which is the most comprehensive approach.

Past incidents can provide a wealth of knowledge on trends, types of events encountered in the past and the subsequent impact on the business. This information can then be used as an input to decide on the types of events we need to plan for.

Developing an Incident Response Plan

The *incident response plan*, or *IRP*, is the operational component of incident management.

Elements of an Incident Response Plan

A common approach to develop an incident response plan is based on a six-phase model or preparation, identification, containment, eradication, recovery and lessons learned. Let's walk through each of the six phases.

The first phase, **preparation**, prepares an organization to develop the incident response plan prior to an incident. Activities include:

- Establish how we will handle incidents
- Establish policy and warning banners in information systems
- Establish a communication plan to stakeholders
- Develop the criteria used to decide when to report an incident to authorities
- Develop the process to activate the incident management team
- Establish a secure location to execute the IRP
- Ensure equipment is available when needed

The second phase, **identification**, verifies that an incident has happened and tries to find out more details about it – not all reports are real incidents. Activities include:

- Assign ownership of a reported incident to a handler
- Verify the report is an incident
- Establish a chain of custody for handling evidence
- Determine the severity and escalate if needed

The third phase, **containment**, is designed to limit exposure. The incident management team is activated and conducts a detailed assessment. Activities include:

- Activating the incident management team and/or incident response team to contain the incident
- Notify appropriate stakeholders
- Get agreement on actions
- Get the IT representative and team members involved
- Obtain and preserve evidence
- Document and take backups
- Manage communication to the public by the PR team

The fourth phase, **eradication**, is where we determine root cause and eradicate the threat. Activities include:

- Determine the root cause
- Locate the most recent backup
- Remove the root cause
- Improve defenses by implementing protection techniques
- Perform a vulnerability analysis to find new vulnerabilities introduced by the root cause

The fifth phase, **recovery**, restores affected systems and services to a condition as specified in the service delivery objectives (SDO) or BCP. The amount of time we have to perform this step is defined by the RTO. Activities include:

- Restore operations as defined in the SDO
- Validate the restoration was successful
- Get system owners to test affected systems
- Facilitate system owners to declare normal operation

The last phase, **lessons learned**, is where we create a report that contains the following items:

- What happened
- What measures were taken
- Results after the plan was executed

The report also contains a list of lessons learned that should be developed into a plan to change the incident management responses. Activities include:

- Analyzing issues encountered during the response efforts

- Proposing improvement based on issues encountered
- Writing the report
- Presenting the report to stakeholders

Business Impact Analysis

The BIA was introduced in Section 1, but we're going to dive in a little deeper at this point.

A BIA will tell us about potential incidents and any related business impacts – and it will prioritize them for us. Whereas risk calculates the probability of compromise, the BIA determines the consequences of compromise.

A BIA must do the following four things at a minimum:

1) Determine the loss resulting from some function no longer being available
2) Figure out how that loss will escalate over time
3) Identify the minimum resources needed to recover from that loss
4) Prioritize the recovery of processes and systems for all losses

The BIA ultimately creates a report that stakeholders use to understand the business impact that various incidents will cause. Each impact will be expressed in either quantitative terms, such as money, or qualitative values, such as a relative rating. To be successful, the BIA will need to include participation from business process owners, senior management, IT, physical security and end users.

The assessment includes three steps. The first step is to **gather assessment material** where we identify the business units that are crucial to an organization's survival. We then drill down and identify the critical tasks within each unit.

The second step is to **analyze the information** gathered in the first step. Activities carried include:

- For critical and high-impact areas, figure out if there are interdependencies
- Discover all possible disruptions that might cause the interdependencies to fail
- Identify potential threats that could interrupt interdepartmental communication
- Gather quantitative and qualitative data for those threats
- Come up with alternative means for restoring functionality and communication
- Write a brief description of each threat

The third step is to **document the result and present recommendations**.

Despite the importance of carrying out a BIA, many organizations fail to do so. And even if they do, some businesses fail to keep the BIA up to date when systems and business functions change.

A typical BIA will include the following information about each business unit:

- **Function description** – what is the function of the business unit?
- **Dependencies** – what is dependent on this function?
- **Impact profile** – is there a specific time window where the function would be more vulnerable to risk?
- **Operational impacts** – when would the operational impact be felt if this function were no longer available?
- **Financial impacts** – when would the financial impact be felt if this function were no longer available?
- **Work backlog** – when would the backlog of work start being felt?
- **Recovery resources** – what kind of resources are needed now, and how many and when would they be needed after a disruption?
- **Technology resources** – what software is needed for this function to operate?
- **Stand-alone PCs or workstations** – does the function require PCs?
- **Local area networks** – does the function require access to a LAN?
- **Workaround procedures** – are there any manual workaround procedures in place?
- **Work-at-home** – can the function be performed from home?
- **Workload shifting** – can we shift the work to another part of the business?
- **Business records** – are business records required for this function?
- **Regulatory reporting** – are regulatory documents created by this function?
- **Work inflows** – what input is received necessary for the function to perform properly?
- **Business disruption experience** – has there ever been a disruption?
- **Competitive analysis** – would there be a competitive impact if the function were no longer available?
- **Other issues and concerns** - what other relevant issues or concerns are there?

Conducting a BIA has several benefits, including:

- Increases the understand around loss of a particular function

- Prioritizes restoration activities
- Increases visibility of various functions and their dependencies
- Raises the level of awareness for response management

Escalation Process for Effective Incident Management

It is up to the information security manager to establish a clear escalation process well in advance of an incident so there are no questions on when to escalate an issue and to whom. For every type of event, the process should contain a list of actions and the order in which they should be carried out. For each action, the following should be listed:

- Who is responsible for carrying out the action
- At least one backup person
- How long it should take for the action to be completed

If any action cannot be executed, or the allowed time has elapsed according to the RTO, the next action should be started. If the overall elapsed time reaches a predefined limit, then the issue should be escalated even further to an alert – low, medium or high. When an alert level is reached, notifications should be sent to people with executive responsibilities, including the following groups:

- Senior management
- Response and recovery teams
- HR
- Insurance companies
- Backup facilities
- Vendors
- Customers

The process continues until either the emergency is resolved, or the last alert notification has been sent.

The exact escalation process will vary based on the level of the emergency event, which in turn depends on the severity, the number of organizations affected, and their need to be notified. If email is used for notifications, the security manager may wish to encrypt such messages as email is sent in clear text by default.

Help or Service Desk Processes for Identifying Security Incidents

Since help or service desk employees are likely to be the first to receive an incident report, they should have guidelines on what looks like a typical request and what is a possible security incident. This also serves to reduce the risk that the service or help desk will be targeted in a social engineering attack.

Incident Management and Response Teams

The incident response plan should identify all teams needed to handle the various activities. It is helpful to create a matrix matching teams to the activities they are capable of carrying out, as this will assist the response process in quickly activating the correct teams. There are five common teams in this matrix:

- The **emergency action team** deals with fires and other emergency scenarios
- The **damage assessment team** assesses the physical damage and decides what is a total loss or can be salvaged
- The **relocation team** moves operations from the affected site to an alternate site, and then back once the original site has been restored
- The **security team**, often called a CSIRT which is short for computer security incident response team, takes care of all security concerns, including monitoring the security of systems and communications.
- The **emergency management team** coordinates the activities of all other teams and makes the key decisions

Organizing, Training and Equipping the Response Staff

Running the teams through test scenarios is key to being prepared. This process will identify points of confusion, ambiguous procedures and help to highlight any missing equipment or training needed. At a minimum, team members should undergo the following training:

- **Induction**, which provides the essential information needed to be an effective member.
- **Mentoring on roles, responsibilities and procedures** by pairing experienced members with junior members.
- **On-the-job training** provides an understanding of the policies, procedures, standards and tools unique to the organization.
- **Formal training** may also be needed to bring members to the level of competency required to do their job well.

Chapter 41: Information Risk Management – Metrics, Monitoring and Reporting

Reporting Formats

Red-amber-green reports are sometimes referred to as security dashboards, heat charts or stoplights. We Americans always want to know why it is not called a red-yellow-green report, and the answer is two-fold:

- The Brits call a yellow stop light an 'amber light'.
- The acronym RAG is way easier to pronounce than RYG. Just sayin'.

A RAG report uses color to quickly convey status – green is good, amber/yellow is iffy, and red needs attention.

Other reports are more useful when conveying trends, such as bar graphs and spider charts. Regardless of the format, the information security manager needs to ensure these types of reports are periodically generated and reviewed by senior management.

Key Risk Indicators

When selecting individual KRIs, we should look at four criteria:

- The KRI should be an indicator for risks with high **impacts**.
- If two or more KRIs are equivalent, choose the one that is **easier to measure**.
- The KRI must be **reliable** in both predicting outcomes and having a high correlation with risk.
- The KRI must be able to accurately model variances in the risk level with a high degree of **sensitivity**.

We should also be looking at the selected KRIs as a group in the following manners:

- **Include** the different types of **stakeholders** in the selection decisions so that risk across the organization is represented.
- **Balance selected KRIs** so that they indicate how well we can prevent security events, the risk left after an incident, and reflect trends based on KRIs over time.
- Make sure the selected **KRIs can drill down to root cause** instead of just focusing on symptoms.

Reporting Significant Changes in Risk

In addition to periodic reporting to senior management, the security program should contain a process by which significant breach or security event triggers a report to senior management, followed by a risk reassessment. All security events result from a lack of a control, or the failure of an existing control.

Documentation

Documentation for a security program is a must if we hope for it to be effective. At any stage of the risk management process, we should have the following elements documented:

- Objectives
- Audience
- Information resources
- Assumptions
- Decisions

Typical documentation for risk management should include the following sections:

- A risk register
- Consequences and likelihood of compromise
- Initial risk rating
- Vulnerability to internal/external factors
- An inventory of information assets
- A risk mitigation and action plan
- Monitoring and audit documents

All documentation must be properly versioned so that we can determine what policies were in effect at any given time.

Training and Awareness

People will probably always be the number one security risk due to either accidents or malicious intent. Training and awareness programs are the most effective methods to combat this top risk but must be targeted to different audiences. End-user information security training should include the following:

- The importance of following policies

- How to respond to emergency situations
- The importance of restricting access in an IT environment
- Privacy and confidentiality requirements
- Recognizing and reporting security events
- Recognizing and dealing with social engineering

Technical Control Components and Architecture

A recurring pitfall that organizations fall into is one of overreliance on technology to provide security. Instead, the security manager must align technology goals with the organization's goals and let administrative and physical controls take their proper place. This allows us to design an effective technical architecture that uses technology only when appropriate.

The best way to approach designing this technical architecture is to ask a series of questions and let the answers do the work for us. There are five groups of questions we need to ask.

The first has to do with the **placement** of controls, relative to both systems and other controls. Questions to ask are:

- Where are the controls located in the enterprise?
- Are controls layered?
- Do we need control redundancy?
- Do perimeter controls really protect us?
- Are there any uncontrolled access channels, such as physical, network, system-level, application-level?

The next group of questions are designed to figure out how **effective** existing controls are and need to be. Questions to ask are:

- Are the controls reliable?
- Are the controls the minimum required?
- Do the controls inhibit productivity?
- Are the controls manual or automated?
- Are the key controls monitored?
- Are they monitored in real-time or after-the-fact?
- Are the controls easily circumvented?

Now, we need to figure out how **efficient** the controls are by asking the following questions:

- How broadly do the controls protect our environment?
- Are the controls specific to one resource or asset?
- Are the controls fully utilized?
- Is a control a single point of application failure?
- Is a control a single point of security failure?
- Is there unnecessary redundancy?

Next, let's take a look at how well the **policies** around existing controls function. Questions to ask are:

- Do controls fail secure or fail open?
- Do controls implement a restrictive policy (deny access unless explicitly allowed) or a permissive policy (permission unless explicitly denied)?
- Is the principle of least-needed functionality and access enforced?
- Does the control configuration align with organizational policy?

Finally, we want to look at how existing controls are **implemented** by asking the following questions:

- Does the implementation of each control follow policies and standards?
- Are the controls self-protecting?
- Will the controls alert security personnel if they fail or detect an error condition?
- Have the controls been tested to verify they implement the right policy?
- Are control activities logged, monitored and reviewed?
- Do controls meet defined goals?
- Are the control goals mapped to an organizational goal?

Control Testing and Modification

As changes are made to systems and processes, security controls become less effective. Therefore, it is very important that controls are periodically tested for effectiveness, something that is actually required in most publicly traded organizations and should be followed for all businesses. Any change to a technical or operational control must undergo change management and approval processes. If additional staff training is required for a given change, then that change should not be rolled out until the training is complete.

249

Baseline Controls

Any new system should be subject to a minimum level of security controls, called the baseline. Examples are:

- Authentication
- Logging
- Role-based access
- Data transmission confidentiality, such as encryption

The information security manager should use both internal and external resources to ensure secure coding practices and logic during software development.

Just before deploying a new system, there are a series of steps that should be followed:

- Test the system against the original security requirements
- Test the system's interfaces for vulnerabilities
- Ensure the system provides sufficient security administration capabilities and feedback
- If flaws are detected, work with the project team to prioritize and resolve
- If an issue cannot be addressed before rollout, estimate risk to determine if the rollout should be postponed
- If the system is deployed with unresolved issues, make sure each is documented, and a time-to-fix is agreed on
- If no viable resolution is available at deployment, track and reassess the issue periodically to see if a solution becomes available

Code reviews from a security perspective must be carried out, often with the aid of an external party.

Chapter 42: Information Risk Management – What Success Looks Like

When we have achieved effective risk management, the following will be true:

- We can handle complexity
- Risk appetite and tolerance have been dictated by senior management
- The information security manager has the authority to carry out his or her function
- All Important assets have been identified, classified and have an owner
- Assets have been prioritized

Chapter 43: Information Security Program Development and Management – Overview

An *information security program* is comprised of all activities and resources that provide information security services to an organization. At times, an information security manager is required to create an information security program from the beginning, but more often than not he simply manages an existing one. Many information security managers have a technical background and have simply migrated to a management position.

To add some color, a security program is the process through which the organization's security systems are designed, implemented, maintained and retired. There are three elements absolutely required for a successful program:

1) The program must be the result of a well-developed security strategy that is closely aligned with business goals.
2) The program must be designed with the full cooperation of both management and stakeholders.
3) Effective metrics must be defined and properly collected to provide sufficient feedback.

Many frameworks suggest that the first step is to carry out a risk assessment. However, that approach ignores the need for a security program to address more than just risk. For example, we first need to ensure the goals for information security align with business goals.

An organization may not be ready to undertake the costs and efforts associated with information security governance. In this case, the information security manager may need to take a shortcut in developing objectives by using COBIT or ISO 27001, in combination with CMMI or PAM.

This domain is light in some areas – such as 'Who Does What' and 'Resources That Help', but more than makes up for it in the 'Metrics and Monitoring' section. This makes sense if you think about it. The security program is where we measure how well we are managing risk and how well we handle incidents, so it will be heavy on measuring success by design.

Chapter 44: Information Security Program Development and Management – The Goal

The primary goal of the information security program is to help achieve the business' goals while keeping downtime and costs low. We have already covered how governance and risk management helps us with this, and now we turn to information security program goals.

It is rare that an organization has no security activities – the new information security manager will almost always take over existing management. Therefore, a gap analysis between the current state and the desired state will need to be done before we can define our objectives.

Part of this is to define the forces that drive a need for a security program. Some of these might be:

- Regulatory compliance
- Security incidents increasing in frequency and cost
- Concern over damage to reputation
- Compliance with Payment Card Industry Data Security Standard (PCI DSS), which is not a governmental agency by the way – it is purely commercial
- Goals that may increase risk

Chapter 45: Information Security Program Development and Management – The Strategy

Scope and Charter of an Information Security Program

It is up to the information security manager to define scope, responsibilities and the charter for the information security department. Unlike general technical responsibilities, don't expect to find an abundance of documentation on this matter.

Coming into a new environment, the best approach is to first understand what those above expect, followed with an abundance of documentation of those expectations and agreement with management that the documentation is indeed accurate. We also need to understand where in the chain of command the information security function fits – who the position reports directly to all the way to the executives or board, and what positions report to the information security manager. This will serve to highlight potential conflicts and set the stage for future relationships that will need to be well-managed. The conflicts should be discussed with management to identify how they will be dealt with going forward.

The information security department largely exists to regulate internal behavior, and therefore it should not report up through those it is supposed to regulate. Information security managers who report up through technology or operational management tend to be much less effective.

If new to an existing position, it is likely that the former manager took on responsibilities that were not fully documented or known. This is a clear sign that the previous manager was effective due to being persuasive and influential rather than relying on a defined and documented process. If possible, the former manager should remain available for a short while to allow his or her successor to discover these little 'nuggets of opportunity'.

The subject of security is often politically charged, so the information security manager must be aware of the organization's culture. Success may hang more on the information security manager's ability to develop the right relationships than on any given area of expertise. The current state of security must be determined at the same time, usually by executing a BIA.

Figure 40 shows the steps in developing an information security program – the flow is pretty much self-explanatory. Note that most of the listed steps must be executed by the information security manager.

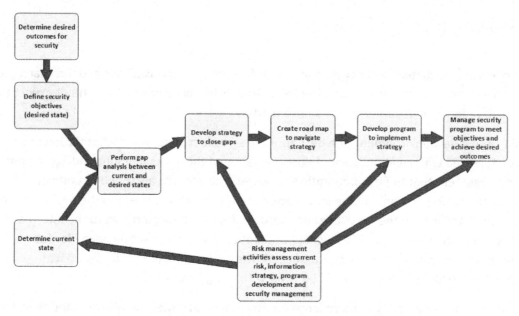

Figure 40: Steps to Information Security Program Development

If our security strategy has been well-developed, all we have to do at this point is to turn that strategy into logical and physical reality. Well, in theory anyway. The truth is that there will always be changes to our strategy because the world is always changing. Businesses requirements change. Infrastructure evolves. We encounter risks we didn't know existed a month ago. A new invention comes along that we need to adopt to reduce costs. We encounter unexpected resistance within our own organization. Change simply happens. Regardless, the adoption of a standard development life cycle (SDLC) approach will help.

Chapter 46: Information Security Program Development and Management – Who Does What

It is now more common to find that the information security manager is a member of senior leadership, such as V.P. of Security, chief information security officer (CISO) or chief security officer (CSO). In some large multi-national organizations, these functions may role up to the chief risk officer (CRO).

Chapter 47: Information Security Program Development and Management – Resources That Help

We're going to skip this chapter for the security program domain, because all 'helpful' resources will be covered in the 'Metrics and Monitoring' section.

Chapter 48: Information Security Program Development and Management – Constraints That Hurt

Anytime a security program is either initiated or extended, expect to encounter impediments. The most common are:

- Resistance due to changes in areas of responsibility, most commonly called turf wars
- A perception that increased security will reduce access required for someone to do their job
- An overreliance on the wrong metrics
- Failure of a strategy
- Assumptions that procedures will be followed without confirmation
- Bad project management, resulting in delays
- Previously undetected broken or buggy software

The capabilities an information security program will ultimately have depends on multiple constraints. Here are three scenarios:

- Limited funding and a lack of business owner buy-in will most likely result in documentation only with no process or control implementation.
- Turf wars, a strict focus on costs and inconsistent policy and procedure enforcement will result in processes being coordinated, but there will be no controls implemented.
- Good senior management examples, an adequate budget and business owner buy-in will result in control implementations.

The two most prevalent challenges facing a security manager are:

- A view that security can be fixed with technology
- Increased security simply makes my job harder

But, the situation is getting better due to the following influences:

- Legal and regulatory mandates requiring improved security
- Customer and business partner expectations
- PCI DSS requirements for credit card processing
- Increased litigation resulting in financial damage awards

- The rise of cyber insurance which requires an adequate level of risk management

There are three areas in which a security manager should focus to provide the best chance at success.

Senior management support is crucial, but in most smaller organizations or even larger companies not operating in a security-conscious industry, this will be a struggle to reach. In these cases, the security manager will have to resort to industry statistics, impact analyses and reviews of common threats. An overview of approaches that peer organizations in that industry are taking will help as well.

Inadequate **funding** is often a symptom of the lack of senior management support, but their view can be influenced if the following views are addressed:

- There is no value in security investments
- Security is a low-cost center
- We don't understand where the money is going
- There is no need for a security investment
- Our industry is not investing in security

Sometimes the security manager may have senior management's full support, but the money is just simply not there. In this case we can try three different approaches:

- Leverage the budgets of other business units to implement security program components
- Improve the efficiency of existing components
- Work with the steering committee to kick security resource allocations up in the list of priorities, and make sure they understand the risk if those items are not funded

Obtaining funding is a never-ending task for the security manager, and there is a no-win aspect of this thankless job. If the security department performs too well, then management may start wondering why they have to keep spending money on something that is not a problem. Perform too poorly and management may start wondering why they keep spending money on something that doesn't work. The only alternative is to perform well and to continuously show management why security has a direct impact on business goals.

Keeping an effective **staffing** level is also an unending challenge. Some obstacles to this are:

- A poor understanding of what new resources will be doing
- A poor understanding of the need for new activities
- A lack of awareness of existing staffing levels or utilization
- A belief that existing staff are underutilized
- A constant desire to examine outsourcing alternatives

To combat these pesky hurdles, the security manager should generate reports and metrics that demonstrate the current expenditure of effort by the security staff. Highlighting how the various security roles and responsibilities provide protection to enterprise assets will also help. It definitely helps if we can demonstrate that security staff are continuously becoming more efficient over time.

If the organization is still unwilling to increase staffing in spite of the above efforts, the following strategies can help:

- See if other business units can take on some security responsibilities
- Look into outsourcing high-volume operations, but be prepared to show how existing resources will be immediately assigned to higher-value activities
- Work with the steering committee to kick security resource allocations up in the list of priorities, and make sure they understand the risk if those items are not funded

There are five challenges commonly encountered when developing an incident management plan.

First, a **lack of management buy-in and organizational consensus** will often prevent effective incident responses. This happens primarily when senior management and other stakeholders are not involved in the planning process. A contributing factor may also be a lack of regular meetings.

Secondly, if the incident management process **does not align with the business goals or how it is organizationally structured**, it will be unable to detect incidents and protect the business.

Third, the **loss of a champion of incident management**, such as a senior management member or stakeholder, will cause the focus to be lost almost immediately.

Fourth, the **lack of a good communication process** will cause either under-communication or over-communication. Under-communication results in misunderstandings about the need for incident management. Over-communication will result in people becoming concerned that the plan is too much to handle or that it competes with their other priorities.

And finally, an **overly complex and broad plan** will overwhelm people, causing them to resist supporting it.

Chapter 49: Information Security Program Development and Management – The Action Plan

There are a number of approaches to developing an incident management action plan, also known as the _incident response plan_, or _IRP_.

CMU/SEI's _Defining Incident Management Processes_ describes 5 steps, as shown in **Figure 41**.

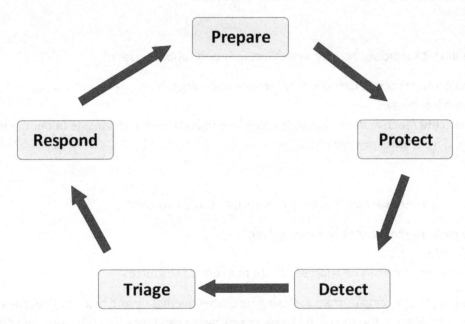

Figure 41: Incident Response Plan Process Flow

Let's walk through the steps and describe each.

Prepare

First, in the **prepare** step we do all of the footwork required before we can actually carry out protection. There are two subprocesses here:

1) Plan and design
2) Implement

Protect

Then, we **protect** the infrastructure by responding to incidents and carrying out improvements over time. There are four subprocesses:

1) **Measure** our current protection levels by performing security assessments
2) **Implement changes** to infrastructure to mitigate potential incidents
3) **Improve protection** based on postmortems after incidents
4) **Provide input** on how to detect future incidents

Detect

We then **detect** suspicious activity, which includes two subprocesses:

1) **Execute proactive detection** by carrying out vulnerability scans, network device alerts and log reviews
2) **Execute reactive detection** by tapping into reports from users inside of our organization and from other organizations

Triage

Triage is next, where we sort incoming reports into three categories:

1) Problems that cannot be easily solved
2) Problems that can wait
3) Problems that can be addressed with our current resources

Effective triaging prevents us from assigning resources needlessly and helps to float the most important problems to the top of the heap. Prioritization can be carried out using two different sets of criteria:

1) Based on a **tactical** set of criteria
2) Based on the **strategic** impact to the business

There are four subprocess for the triage step:

1) **Categorization**, where we assign the problem to one of the three categories defined earlier (cannot be solved, can wait, and can be solved now)
2) **Correlation**, where we associate other data points or information with the problem; this allows us to see the problem clearly and may change how we approach it

3) **Prioritization**, where we prioritize according to the two methods described earlier (tactical or strategic)
4) **Assignment**, where we assign the problem to be worked by team members based on current workload, experience with this problem, the category or priority of the problem, or to the relevant business unit

Respond

And finally, we **respond** to the incident in which we resolve or mitigate the problem. There are three types of response activities:

- A **technical response**, where we analyze and resolve the incident.
- A **management response**, which covers any type of supervisory intervention, notification, escalation or approval.
- A **legal response**, which is any activity related to investigation, prosecution, liability or other legal issues. This is usually referred to the corporate legal team.

Chapter 50: Information Security Program Development and Management – Metrics and Monitoring

We have previously stressed that if you can't measure something, then you will never know if it is successful or not. The same applies to a security program, but not all metrics are equal. While technical metrics are great for measuring how well specific controls are working, they do little to tell us how well our security program is aligned with organizational goals. To illustrate this, consider the following questions and see how we would determine the answer based on technical measurements alone:

- How secure is the organization?
- How much security is enough?
- What are the most effective solutions?
- How do we determine the degree of risk?
- Are we moving in the right direction?
- What impact would a catastrophic security breach have?

Obviously, we can't answer those questions by looking at logs or reports from some appliance. We need to collect some other type of metrics. But, we must first ensure we have properly defined goals. After all, if you don't what to measure, then how are you going to measure it? Ultimately, the point of collecting metrics is so we can make an informed decision. Is it working, or do we need to course correct? Are there gaps we have not closed yet?

Qualitative metrics that are properly monitored can be used to discover trends, and are represented by the following possibilities:

- CMMI levels
- KGIs
- KPIs
- KRIs
- Business balanced scorecard (BSC)
- Six Sigma quality indicators
- ISO 9001 quality indicators
- COBIT 5 PAM

While there are different ways to determine how effective a security program is over time, the most important thing is to be consistent. One approach is to regularly conduct risk assessments and track how they change over time. Or, we can use scanning and penetration testing to evaluate our progress, although this really only covers a single dimension of overall security. Another approach is to hook into change management activities, so changes can be evaluated and addressed.

Most monitoring will be implemented using technical controls, but training help desk personnel can be a great asset as many attacks will start with a social engineering aspect, and this can provide advanced warning of a pending event.

While it may not be apparent, effective monitoring is a crucial part of the budgeting process. Senior management is always on the lookout for cost-cutting measures or to shift money to the best ROI they can find. By agreeing on the correct KPIs from the beginning, it will be obvious if a given security program should continue to be funded.

Measuring Information Security Management Performance

Measuring success is not just about metrics, though – while metrics are the end result, a security manager must know how to implement processes and mechanisms that produce useful metrics. Measuring success consists of the following three steps:

1) Defining measurable goals
2) Tracking the most appropriate metrics
3) Periodically analyzing those results so we know where to make adjustments

Measuring Information Security Risk and Loss

It is impossible to address all risk in a system while not impacting some level of usability. Likewise, it is not possible to deliver the optimum user experience without impacting security. There must be a compromise in the middle where both aspects are considered to be acceptable. Achieving this balance can be reached in a number of ways. There are three approaches we can use to measure our success against loss prevention and risk management.

The **technical vulnerability management** approach examines the number of technical or operational vulnerabilities in a given system during a reporting period, and then looks to see how effective we have been in resolving them.

The **risk management** approach looks at the number of risks identified within a given reporting period, and then looks at how each was avoided, accepted, transferred or mitigated.

The **loss prevention** approach looks at the amount of losses incurred during a reporting period, and how many were preventable.

All three of these approaches result in a quantitative measurement. We can also take a qualitative approach by asking the following questions:

- Do risk management activities occur as scheduled?
- Do executive management oversight and review activities occur as scheduled?
- Have IRPs and BCPs been tested?
- Are asset inventories and risk analyses up-to-date?
- Is there a consensus among stakeholders on the amount of acceptable risk?

Measuring Support of Organizational Objectives

To measure how well aligned security goals are with business goals, we need to determine if there is a documented correlation between business milestones and the security program goals, and the number of security program goals that were successfully completed in support of those business goals. An interesting aspect of this measurement activity is to figure out if there were any business goals that were not met because information security goals were not met. A final consideration is to measure the strength of consensus among stakeholders that security program goals are complete and appropriate.

Measuring Compliance

Most security failures are the result of people not following the procedures that keep us in compliance with standards. When building jets or nuclear power plants any level of compliance with standards and regulations less than 100% is unacceptable. For the rest of the world, a 100% compliance level is not nearly as important. Instead, we need to weigh the acceptable level of compliance against benefits and potential impacts to figure out where we should land.

Of course, measuring compliance with a technical standard can often be automated and is relatively easy. Measuring compliance against procedures or standards is quite a bit more challenging. Sometimes constant monitoring is warranted, as in the case of protecting entrances controlled by guards. At other times a simple case of logging and checklists may be enough.

Compliance requirements will fall into one of three categories:

- *Statutory compliance*, in which external regulations and legislation demand compliance.
- *Contractual compliance*, where we are obligated by a contract to remain in compliance.
- *Internal compliance*, in which we impose self-constraints for our own benefit.

Measuring Operational Productivity

To measure productivity, we simply calculate the work produced per resource within a period of time. For example, if we want to measure productivity of analyzing a log, we could measure the number of entries analyzed per resource each hour. To see if a change has increased our productivity, we measure a baseline before the change, and take the same measurement after the change, and compare the results. In this manner we can easily see if automating certain tasks has achieved a productivity level that was worth the investment.

Measuring Security Cost-Effectiveness

Financial constraints are a common reason for security failures. We therefore have to be purposeful in ensuring we can get value out of every dollar spent. We do this by making sure we can properly forecast budgets when comparing initial and final expenditures for past projects. If we are consistently under-estimating costs, then we need to adjust how we arrive at those estimates.

We also need to track cost/result ratios to measure how cost-effective specific components are. Cost is not just the amount of money we spend on buying or building a control. It also includes maintenance, operations and administrative costs for the period being analyzed. This, along with other hidden costs, should give us a total cost of ownership, or TCO, for each component. Turning that cost value into a measurable metric allows us to track cost efficiency. For example, suppose we implement an IDS appliance, and set the annual cost to $150K, which is able to handle 24 billion network packets over the same period. We can then express the efficiency as work/cost, or 24 billion packets/$150K, or 160K packets per dollar spent.

Measuring Organizational Awareness

On the opposite end of the spectrum from technical metrics, we need to be able to measure how effective our security awareness training program is. Having vigilant employees is just as important, if not more so, than any technical control. Since success must be measured at the employee level, HR is a crucial partner for this activity. Records of initial training, and acceptance and acknowledgement of policies and usage agreements are valuable metrics by which we can measure how effective our awareness training is being. Additionally, HR can help us identify employees and units that are not fully engaged in the awareness program.

Another method for measuring awareness is by testing employees immediately after training sessions using online or paper quizzes. The same quizzes can be targeted to a random sampling of employees at any time to get additional measurements.

Measuring Effectiveness of Technical Security Architecture

Measuring the effectiveness of a technical security architecture is one of the best uses for a quantitative approach. Possible metrics include:

- The number of probe and attack attempts repelled by network access control devices
- The number of probe and attack attempts detected by IDSs on the internal network
- The number and type of actual compromises
- Statistics on viruses, worms and other malware identified and neutralized
- The amount of downtime attributed to security flaws and unpatched systems
- The number of messages, sessions or KB of data examined by an IDS

We can also collect qualitative metrics such as:

- If technical mechanisms have been tested
- If security controls are applied in a layered fashion
- If mechanisms are properly configured and monitored in real-time
- All critical systems stream events to security personnel in real-time

Keep in mind that the metrics we have just covered will have little meaning to senior management, and they will need to be summarized at a higher level before presentation to those stakeholders.

Measuring Effectiveness of Management Framework and Resources

Some methods for tracking the overall success of the security program include:

- How often issues reoccur
- How well operational knowledge is documented and spread
- How many processes refer to standards

- How well security roles and responsibilities are documented
- If every project plan incorporates security requirements
- How well security goals align with organizational goals

Measuring Operational Performance

It is important that the security controls put into place are supported by the operational components of the security program. Some ways to measure this include:

- The time required to detect, escalate, isolate and contain incidents
- The time between vulnerability detection and resolution
- The quantity, frequency and severity of incidents discovered after their occurrence
- The average time between a vendor's release of a patch and its rollout
- The percentage of systems that have been audited within a certain time period
- The number of changes that are released without full change control approval

Monitoring and Communication

All of the best controls in the world will be rendered completely useless unless they are monitored, and a communication path exists for them to get attention when needed. The security manager should consider implementing a centralized monitoring environment that provides visibility into all information resources. There will always be a large number of events that *could* be monitored, but a subset should be selected to keep scope within an acceptable size. Some commonly monitored events are:

- Failed access attempts
- Processing faults that might indicate someone is tampering with a system
- Outages, race conditions and faults related to design issues
- Changes to system configurations
- Privileged system access and activities
- Technical security component faults

A well-thought-out process for responding to events should be established, and all analysts should be properly trained. The escalation path for security events should be tested regularly.

The focus should not always be on real-time events, however. Figure out which are the most frequently targeted resources, or the types of attacks seen the most frequently. Keep in mind that log reviews, even if happening in real-time, will only reflect what has already happened – their main value is in figuring out *how* it happened. Even an IDS may not trigger a warning soon enough.

Chapter 51: Information Security Program Development and Management – What Success Looks Like

Outcomes of Information Security Program Management

The primary difficulty with implementing a security program is in translating design concepts into technologies and processes. If developing the security program is a major effort, a full security architecture should be used. If an enterprise architecture already exists, then the security architecture should be incorporated into that.

Any successful security program will result in the following six outcomes:

- Strategic alignment
- Risk management
- Value delivery
- Resource management
- Performance measurement
- Assurance process integration

Let's go through each outcome individually.

Strategic Alignment

Strategic alignment refers to the degree that security goals align with business goals. This requires frequent interaction with business owners so that we can understand their plans and goals. Topics to discuss include:

- Organizational information risk
- Selection of control goals and standards
- Gaining agreement on acceptable risk and risk tolerance
- Definitions of financial, operational and other constraints

This can occur through a security steering committee if business owners are members and actively participate. Daily interactions can serve to greatly enhance cooperation.

Risk Management

We have already covered risk management in great detail, as it is a core function for a security program. Enough said.

Value Delivery

Value delivery simply means that the security program delivers what it promises – to create the desired level of security effectively and efficiently. While even mentioning this might seem slightly obtuse, if it is not defined as an objective a program could easily focus on side-goals and not deliver the obvious. Continued delivery of value means that a security program is seen as 'normal' by everyone in the organization and is in fact expected because standards are in place. Security management cannot remain static and must purposefully strive to be in a state of constant improvement, because the nature of threats is always changing as well.

Resource Management

Recall that resources encompass people, technology and processes – all required to develop and manage a security program. Those resources can be further categorized as human, financial, technical and knowledge. That last one – knowledge – is particularly important, as good resource management captures knowledge and makes it available to those who need it. Applying that to security programs, we need to make sure that practices and processes are well-documented and consistently applied using standards and policies.

Performance Measurement

Any good information security strategy must identify how it will be monitored, and the metrics to be collected should be spelled out. Along the way, more metrics will become available or identified, and we will need processes for adding those to our strategy.

Not only do we need to measure how effective our security program is, we need to measure how we are doing in implementing that program itself. Sort of like making sure the building we are constructing will meet our needs when it is done, while simultaneously measuring progress with the construction process. We are measuring what we are building as well as how we are building. Independent auditors will need to be called in once we 'think' we are done building the program to tell us if we really are.

Assurance Process Integration

273

An _assurance provider_ is an individual or group that has an expertise level of knowledge and skills in a given area, and as a result helps us to identify and manage risk as well as monitor the effectiveness of mitigation controls in that area. Basically, they are the subject matter experts that the information security manager relies on to create an effective security program. Some examples might be a business manager, IT manager, or finance director – even the information security manager herself. Anyone who can contribute to security effectiveness.

The information security manager should actively cultivate good relationships with other assurance providers and strive to integrate their activities with information security activities.

Chapter 52: Information Security Incident Management – Overview

In a typical organization, there are many departments involved in the development of an incident management and response plan, including:

- IT department
- Internal audit
- HR department
- Legal department
- Physical security
- Risk management
- Insurance department
- PR department
- Sales and marketing
- Senior management
- Compliance officer
- Privacy officer

When an incident occurs, it is due to the failure or absence of a control, and security staff must act quickly. We usually think of incident management as the actions that take place during this time. However, the full scope of incident management are all actions taken before, during and after an incident. Those actions should all be designed with five goals in mind:

1) Provide a way to minimize the impact
2) Provide enough information so we can make the right decisions
3) Maintain or restore continuity of enterprise services
4) Provide a defense against subsequent attacks
5) Provide additional deterrence through technology, investigation and prosecution

Events deserving of an incident management response can be technical attacks, accidents, mistakes or the failure of a system or process. Any type of incident that can disrupt the normal operation of the business must be considered by the information security manager. Just like risk management, risk assessments and BIAs form the basis for how we prioritize the protection of resources and how we carry out response activities.

The more we use information systems, the more important it becomes on how effective we are at incident management. There are multiple factors that compound this need. For example, the overall impact from security incidents is on the rise, as is the failure of existing security controls. Legal and regulatory mandates require increased security vigilance. The sophistication and capabilities of for-profit and nation-state attackers is growing, and they are using more and more zero-day attacks.

Incident Response Concepts

Let's cover some key concepts related to incident management.

Incident handling is a service that covers all processes or tasks associated with handling events and incidents. It involves four functions:

- **Detection and reporting** of incidents and alerts
- **Triage**, which occurs when we categorize, prioritize and assign incidents so that we do not involve unnecessary resources
- **Analysis**, in which we figure out what happened, the size of the threat, the possible damage, and how we are going to recover
- **Incident response**, which are the actions taken to resolve an incident, communicate information, and implement follow-up actions to prevent it from happening again

Effective _incident management_ ensures that incidents are detected, recorded and managed to limit impacts. Recording an incident is important so that we can track what has been done and work to be done can be planned. This enables us to take disciplinary or legal action, because all the forensics information from the incident has been preserved in a format that is acceptable. Additionally, the assigned priority ensures that any resulting work is addressed in an acceptable timeframe. This information can also be checked against known errors to provide possible short-term work-arounds. Incident management may also involve other functions such as vulnerability management and security awareness training.

Incident response is the last step in handling an incident, and carries out mitigation (stop the pain), containment (stop the threat), and recovery (repair the damage) actions.

Incident Response Technology Concepts

There are eight **security principles** the incident response team must understand, which were covered in Section 1, such as CIA, privacy, compliance, etc. Refer back to that section if you need a refresher.

The team must also understand common security vulnerabilities and weaknesses. Software-centric issues include protocol design flaws, such as a man-in-the-middle attack, malicious code, such as trojan horses, implementation flaws such as buffer overflows, and even mis-configuration of systems or applications.

Other weaknesses that the team must understand include physical security issues, phishing attacks resulting from a lack of user awareness, or simple user errors.

The team must be familiar with and understand security issues with the technologies that the Internet itself is built on, including network protocols, such as TCP, IP, UDP, ICMP, and ARP. Network applications and services such as DNS, NFS and SSH need to be well-understood, as are network security issues with firewalls or routers.

The team must be well-versed in operating system (OS) security issues including UNIX, Windows, MAC, Linux, Android, and iOS. General OS issues include hardening systems, reviewing configuration files for weaknesses and effectively managing system privileges. The team must understand common attack methods, how to know if an attack has already occurred, how to determine if that attack was successful, how to analyze the results of an attack, and how to recover from a compromise. Duties outside of the attack life cycle include reviewing log files for anomalies.

Knowledge of how malicious code can propagate is crucial, including the usual methods using CDs, USB drives, email, programs and malicious web sites. Even knowledge of the lesser known propagation methods is important, such as macros, MIME extensions and peer-to-peer file sharing.

And finally, the team must possess some programming skills for two reasons:

1) To be able to detect vulnerabilities
2) To be able to coach developers on secure coding practices

Some poor coding practices the team must understand are lack of input validation, SQL injection, XSS, broken authentication and unvalidated redirects.

This chapter may have included a number of terms that you are unfamiliar with, but an in-depth definition of each is beyond the scope of this book and the exam. But, you need to be very familiar with the details behind each if you are to be a successful CISM candidate.

Chapter 53: Information Security Incident Management – The Goal

The goals of incident management are to:

- Deploy proactive countermeasures to lower the chances of an event from happening
- Handle incidents when they occur so any exposure can be eradicated or contained
- Restore systems to normal operations
- Prevent an incident from recurring by documenting and learning

Strategic Alignment

To ensure that incident management's goals are aligned with the organization, the following components should be examined.

- **Constituency** – who are the stakeholders, and what do they expect?
- **Mission** – if we don't know our mission, how can we hope to identify our goals?
- **Services** – all services provided by the incident management team should be clearly defined for stakeholders
- **Organizational structure** – the incident management team's structure should be the one that best meets the organization's needs
- **Resources** – it is seldom possible to be able to provide all services within one team, and so it more than likely will need to be partially virtual with part-time members
- **Funding** – the right amount of funding will be required to purchase specialized equipment, so the offered services continue to be available
- **Management buy-in** – to be truly effective, the incident management effort must have the full support of senior management

Risk Management

Incident management is the last line of defense for cost-effective risk management. When all prevention efforts fail, incident management steps in to handle the fallout. To deliver value, incident management must seamlessly integrate with business processes and the BCP. It must provide a greater ability to manage risk and provide assurance to stakeholders, and it must become part of an organization's overall strategy to protect critical functions and assets.

Objectives

Some goals of incident management are to detect and diagnose incidents quickly and accurately. This should be followed by activities that contain and minimize damage so that affected services can be restored. Determination of the root cause of an incident is central to this process, and the job is not complete until we have implemented improvements to prevent a recurrence of the incident and documented and reported the entire event properly.

In short, the goal of incident management is to prevent incidents from becoming problems, and problems from becoming disasters. **Figure 42** illustrates the steps to effectively handle incidents.

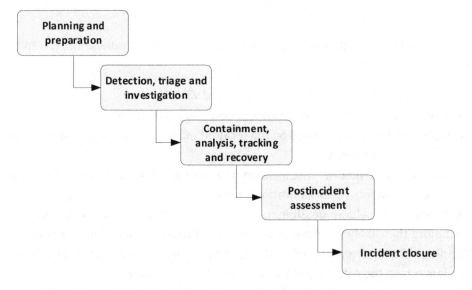

Figure 42: Incident Management Life Cycle Phases

Chapter 54: Information Security Incident Management – The Strategy

Incidents will always be rushed and confusing. To avoid the wrong decisions from being made in the heat of battle, proper planning and well documented procedures should be created well before an incident occurs. This will require significant resources and arriving at a consensus between stakeholders with senior management support will need to reached before those resources are allocated. We can do this in one of two ways:

- **Wait** for the unacceptable consequences of an incident to spur action
- **Create persuasive business cases** detailing how similar incidents in peer organizations resulted in unacceptable consequences

The severity criteria used for incident management should be consistent among incidents. It should be made clear who has the authority to determine the response level, activate the teams, declare a disaster and start the recovery process.

Chapter 55: Information Security Incident Management – Who Does What

The role of an information security manager will vary across organizations, but at a minimum the security manager should be a first responder to any security incident. The manager must also have a good understanding of the BC and DR processes to ensure incident management plans are part of those plans.

Incident Management Organization

Incident management is a subset of risk management and can be viewed as the reactive element. In other words, if our attempts to prevent a threat fail, incident management kicks in to handle the fallout. This means that we will need to create a response and recovery program. This will include meeting with emergency management officials outside of the organization to get a handle on what governmental capabilities exist. From these meetings, we should be able to understand what local emergencies are likely to occur based on history in that geographical region. For example, state authorities will have better insight into how likely our area is to experience earthquakes, recurring floods or tornadoes.

Emergency management activities normally include the following:

- **Recovery** back to an operational status
- **Restoration** of hardware, software and data files
- Ensuring **safety** of personnel
- **Evacuation** of endangered personnel
- Establishment of a **command center**
- Managing **communication** to external parties

Responsibilities

Related to incident management, the responsibilities for the information security manager can be divided into three areas - before an incident happens, while an incident is underway, and after the incident has been handled.

Responsibilities *before* an incident occurs include the development of incident management and response plans and ensuring that both technical and administrative solutions are handled properly – all while taking care of budgeting and development. Maintaining response readiness is crucial, but we need to strike a balanced posture between operational and security processes.

Responsibilities while an incident is *underway* include handling and coordinating incident response activities, making sure the damage and losses do not escalate out of control, and recovering quickly by notifying the correct people to begin the recovery process.

Post-incident responsibilities for the security manager include decreasing the likelihood of recurrence and dealing with legal and law-enforcement issues.

The information security manager will need to define exactly what constitutes a security incident. It is fairly obvious that security incidents should include malicious code attacks, DoS and DDoS attacks, and social engineering attacks. Surveillance and espionage activities, as well as hoaxes, should be added to the list as well. Some less-obvious incidents cover unauthorized access to IT or information resources and unauthorized changes to systems, network devices or information. Many times, a 'malicious' incident actually turns out to be the result of human error. In fact, there are normally twice as many incidents caused by human error as those cause by external breaches.

Senior Management Commitment

To gain senior management support for incident management activities, a business case can be easily created that shows an effective incident management response can be more cost-effective than trying to implement controls for all possible risks. This may allow the business to set a higher level of acceptable risk, thereby lowering mitigation costs.

An incident management team normally is comprised of four roles, which are the information security manager, steering committee, dedicated team members and virtual team members. The information security manager will usually lead the team. The steering committee is usually called the security steering group, or SSG, which serves as an escalation point for the team and approves exceptions to normal activities. Because the breadth of systems the incident management team must cover is wide, it is usually more cost-effective to populate the team with part-time virtual members as opposed to dedicated personnel.

There are four different incident response team models to choose from. We can use the *central IRT model* in which we have only one team. This is best-suited for smaller organizations. For larger organizations, we might choose to use the *distributed IRT model*, which supports multiple teams, each responsible for a different logical or physical segment of the infrastructure. Or, we can choose to employ the *coordinating IRT model*, in which we have multiple distributed teams that manage and implement responses but rely upon a single central team providing all guidance and policy decisions. Finally, we could simply choose to outsource at least a portion of the security team using the _outsourced IRT model_.

If there are virtual team members, these usually will be restricted to business representatives, legal staff, communications staff, or other non-core roles. The permanent members will normally be incident handlers, investigators, forensics experts and IT and physical security.

Roles and Responsibilities

Table 5 lists all roles and responsibilities related to security incident activities.

Position	Roles	Responsibilities
Security steering group	Highest structure of an organization's functions related to information security	1. Takes responsibility for overall incident management and response concept 2. Approves IMT charter 3. Approves exceptions/deviations 4. Makes final decisions
Information security manager	IMT leader and main interface to SSG	1. Develops and maintains incident management and response capability 2. Effectively manages risk and incidents 3. Performs proactive and reactive measures to control information risk level
Incident response manager	IRT leader	1. Supervises incident response tasks 2. Coordinates resources to effectively perform incident response tasks 3. Takes responsibility for successful execution of IRP 4. Presents incident response report and lessons learned to SSG members
Incident handler	IMT/IRT team member	1. Performs incident response tasks to contain exposures from an incident 2. Documents steps taken when executing the IRP 3. Maintains chain of custody and observes incident handling procedures for court purposes 4. Writes incident response report and lessons learned
Investigator	IMT/IRT team member	1. Performs investigative tasks for a specific incident 2. Finds root cause of an incident 3. Writes report of investigative findings
IT security specialist	IMT/IRT team member; subject matter expert in IT security	1. Performs complex and in-depth IT security-related tasks as part of the IRP 2. Performs IT security assessment and audit as a proactive measure and part of vulnerability management
Business managers	Business function owners; information	1. Makes decisions on matter related to information assets and systems when an incident happens, based on IRT/IMT recommendations

	assets and system owners	2. Provides clear understanding of business impact in BIA process or IRP
IT specialists/representatives	Subject matter expert in IT services	1. Provide support to IMT/IRT when resolving an incident 2.Maintain information systems in good condition per company policy and good practices
Legal representative	Subject matter expert in legal	1. Ensures that incident response actions and procedures comply with legal and regulatory requirements 2.Acts as the liaison to law enforcement and outside agencies
HR	Subject matter expert in HR area	1. Provides assistance in incident management or response when there is a need to investigate an employee suspected of causing an incident 2. Integrates HR policy to support incident management or response
PR representative	Subject matter expert in PR area	1. Provides controlled communication to internal and external stakeholders to minimize any adverse impact to ongoing incident response activities and protect the organization's brand and reputation 2. Provides assistance to IMT/IRT in communication issues, thus allowing the team to focus on critical issues
Risk management specialist	Subject matter expert in risk management	1. Works closely with business managers and senior management to determine and manage risk 2. Provides input to incident management
Physical security/facilities manager	Knowledgeable about physical plant and emergency capabilities	1. Responsible for physical plant and facilities 2. Ensures physical security during incidents

Table 5: Security Incident Roles and Responsibilities

Skills

The set of skills that IRT members need to possess can be divided into two groups – personal and technical. Let's cover the personal skills first.

One primary personal skill is **communication**, in both directions – speaking and listening. Communications can take many forms, including email, documentation, notifications and policies and procedures. Members need to be good listeners in order to get all of the necessary details related to an incident. This applies to both in what is being said as well as what is *not* being said, and the targeted audiences include:

- Other team members
- IT staff
- Application owners

- Users of the system
- Technical experts
- Management and other administrative staff
- Human resources
- Law enforcement
- Media and public relations staff
- Vendors

Let's discuss some other important incident response team member skills. **Leadership** skills are essential, as team members must often direct and get support from other members of the organization. The ability to **present** information is crucial, ranging from technical overviews, public conferences and court appearances. Of course, the ability to **follow** policies and procedures is a given, as well as the ability to be a **team** player. An often-overlooked quality is that of possessing **integrity** due to the sensitive nature of the information team members will be expected to handle. Having a healthy level of **self-understanding** in terms of recognizing limitations will go a long way to ensuring success, as will the ability to **cope with stress, solve problems** and **manage time** effectively.

The second group of skills are technical and are comprised of two types. First, **technical foundation skills** refer to the ability of members to understand the basic technologies used in the organization, followed by **incident-handling skills**, which we have already covered in abundance.

Post-Incident Activities and Investigation

The basic, and fairly obvious, principles the security manager should adhere to when approaching post-incident reviews are to identify a problem, create a plan to mitigate the problem and then implement the solution. A less obvious activity in following up on incidents is to calculate the total loss. This provides a very useful metric as it provides a tool to justify the existence of the response team to senior management and will be valuable information if a court case results from an incident.

Identifying Causes and Corrective Actions

For each security event, a review team should examine the evidence and find a root cause for the security failure. This in turn is used to enhance the security program and to prevent a recurrence. This analysis should ask:

- Who was involved?
- What happened?
- Where did the attack originate from?
- When did it happen?
- Why did it happen?
- How was the system vulnerable or how did the attack happen?
- What was the reason for the attack?

In order to ensure a clear record of events is recorded, one or more people should be tasked with incident documentation and preservation of evidence.

Establishing Procedures

It is crucial that the incident handling process adhere to a strict set of rules intended to properly preserve evidence in case legal action is required later. The information security manager should seek out the advice of legal counsel, senior management and law enforcement officials so that processes are in place to preserve evidence and ensure a legal chain of custody while still meeting business goals.

An important concept for incident handlers to internalize is to do nothing that could change, modify or contaminate evidence. Not doing this can easily render valuable evidence inadmissible in a court of law. The initial response by a system administrator should be to retrieve information needed to confirm an incident, followed by the identification of the scope and size of the affected environment. This is followed by determining the degree of loss, modification or damage as well as identifying the possible path or means of attack.

Requirements for Evidence

If care is not taken to keep evidence free of contamination, it may prevent us from carrying out forensics activities required to identify and prosecute the perpetrator. It can also prevent us from understanding how the attack occurred and what changes we should make to stop it next time.

When a computer has been compromised, the usual recommendation is to unplug it to preserve the evidence on the hard drive. This prevents the operating system swap files from overwriting the data as well as stopping the attacker from covering his tracks. However, it is not always the best action to take. By killing power, we risk corruption of data on the disk, and if malware is resident in memory only, that evidence will be lost when power is removed. As both actions are reasonable, the information security manager will need to establish the correct approach and make sure personnel are trained to take that action.

When it comes time for a forensics expert to start analyzing digital media, it is important that the analysis be performed on a copy and never the original data. The original media should be given to an 'evidence custodian' who will store it in a safe and secure location. If the original media is ever changed in any way after the incident, that evidence will no longer be admissible in court.

The copy of a hard drive must be a bit-level image taken by a write-protected cable to prevent even one byte from being written back to the source media. Hash values of both the source and copy are calculated to ensure the copy is exactly the same as the original.

Legal Aspects of Forensic Evidence

The required documentation to establish that evidence is legally admissible in court requires us to follow some very stringent rules. This starts with a chain of custody form tracking the who, what, when, and where of access to the evidence and why the evidence was accessed. All acquiring technicians must sign nondisclosure and confidentiality forms, follow a very specific checklist and maintain a detailed activity log. A case log must be created to outline when requests were received, dates investigations were assigned to investigators, and investigator information. Investigation report templates for investigators to fill out should be used, and a process needs to be established to ensure that all investigations are fair, unbiased and well-documented.

Chapter 56: Information Security Incident Management – Resources That Help

Policies and Standards

The incident response plan, or IRP, must include a documented set of policies, standards and procedures for a variety of reasons. First, we need to ensure that incident management **activities are aligned** with the incident management team (IRT) mission. We need to set correct **expectations**, provide **guidance** for operational needs and maintain a **consistency** of services. Roles and responsibilities must be clearly **understood** and **requirements** for alternate personnel should be set.

Incident Management Systems

Due to the ever-increasing amount of information, automated incident management systems have become more popular. These systems can automate many manual processes by filtering information in real-time and identify pending incidents, resulting in alerts sent to an incident management team, or IRT. These systems can be distributed or centralized. Distributed systems will normally contain multiple detection capabilities such as a network intrusion detection system (NIDS), a host-based intrusion detection system (HIDS) and the ability to sift through appliance logs.

An example of a centralized incident management system is a _security information and event manager_, or _SIEM_. Centralized systems gather logs from across the network and combine the data into a single database that is mined in real-time to detect dangerous patterns.

One key capability that an incident management system provides is to track the status of incidents as they happen, usually by providing a web-based user interface. This means that we will be less likely to overlook an incident, as well as ensuring that it is eventually resolved in some manner.

An effective SIEM will **consolidate input** from multiple systems and **identify** potential and real incidents. This is followed by a **notification** to staff, and incidents will be **prioritized** based on the business impact, which are then **tracked** until closed. Overall, a good SIEM should force us to **implement** effective practice **guidelines**.

Unfortunately, it often takes years to properly configure an incident management system. On the positive side, the following two points highlight the primary benefits of such a system:

- **Operating costs** will go down as we can lower staffing needs and automate many manual processes.
- A properly-configured automated system can drastically decrease the response time to an event, resulting in **lower costs** due to quicker containment and a faster recovery.

Audits

Put simply, audits are performed to make sure an organization is in compliance with policies, standards and procedures. Internal audits are usually carried out by an employed specialist, while external audits are executed by a third party. While most external audits are a result of proving compliance with some type of legal or regulatory rule, they are sometimes required by a business partner.

Related to incident management, an audit can validate that we should not be compromised if an event happens and that we will remain in compliance. It can also show the presence of gaps in response plans.

Outsourced Security Providers

If an organization outsources both IT operations and incident management to the same vendor, there may be some advantages due to tighter integration between the two. The information security manager should consider several things when partially or fully outsourcing security functions. The organization's incident number should be matched to the vendor's incident number, and the organization's change management workflow should be tied with the vendor's. A periodic review of incidents should also be performed with the vendor.

Chapter 57: Information Security Incident Management – Constraints That Hurt

There are no overtly valuable constraints that need to be pointed out for this domain.

Chapter 58: Information Security Incident Management – The Action Plan

The plan for implementation is really handled in the other sections for this domain, so we will skip this chapter.

Chapter 59: Information Security Incident Management – Metrics and Monitoring

Some common KPIs for incident management are the total number of reported incidents, the total number of detected incidents, the number of days without a reported incident, and the average time to resolve. Both KPIs and KGIs must be well-defined and agreed to by relevant stakeholders.

Chapter 60: Information Security Incident Management – What Success Looks Like

How do we know when we have a *good* incident management solution in place? When the following seven statements are true:

- We can deal with **unanticipated events**
- Incidents are **detected quickly**
- Procedures detailing response decisions are **well-documented**
- **Response procedures change** based on the criticality and sensitivity of the asset
- Employees know how to **recognize and report incidents**
- Security is implemented in a **cost-effective manner**
- Response capabilities are **regularly tested and measured**

Now, if the following seven statements are also true then we have a *great* incident management solution:

- Risk level is within **acceptable limits**
- Response teams are **equipped, trained and in-place**
- Incident response procedures, or IRPs, are **in-place and understood by stakeholders**
- **Root causes are fixed** to allow an acceptable interruption window, or AIW
- **Communication flows** to stakeholders as documented in the communication plan
- **Lessons learned are documented** and shared to stakeholders
- Internal and external **stakeholders are confident** the business has control over risks

Acronyms

The following list of acronyms is taken directly from the CISM Review Manual, 15th edition. Not all acronyms are found in this book, but it is recommended that you be familiar with this list in case a term is used on the exam.

AESRM	Alliance for Enterprise Security Risk Management
AIW	Acceptable interruption window
ALE	Annual loss expectancy
API	Application programming interface
AS/NZS	Australian Standard/New Zealand Standard
ASCII	American Standard Code for Information Interchange
ASIC	Application-specific integrated circuit
ASP	Application service provider
ATM	Asynchronous Transfer Mode
AV	Asset value
BCI	Business Continuity Institute
BCM	Business continuity management
BCP	Business continuity planning
BGP	Border Gateway Protocol
BI	Business intelligence
BIA	Business impact analysis
BIMS	Biometric information management and security
BIOS	Basic input/output system
BITS	Banking Information Technology Standards
BLP	Bell-LaPadula
BLP	Bypass label process
BS	British Standard
CA	Certificate authority
CASPR	Commonly accepted security practices and recommendations
CD	Compact disk
CD-ROM	Compact disk-read only memory
CEO	Chief executive officer
CERT	Computer emergency response team
CFO	Chief financial officer
CIM	Computer-integrated manufacturing
CIO	Chief information officer
CIRT	Computer incident response team
CISO	Chief information security officer
CMM	Capability Maturity Model
CMU/SEI	Carnegie Mellon University/Software Engineering Institute
COO	Chief operating officer
COOP	Continuity of operations plan
CORBA	Common Object Request Broker Architecture
COSO	Committee of Sponsoring Organizations of the Treadway Commission

CPO	Chief privacy officer
CPU	Central processing unit
CRM	Customer relationship management
CSA	Control self-assessment
CSF	Critical success factor
CSIRT	Computer security incident response team
CSO	Chief security officer
CSRC	Computer Security Resources Center (USA)
CRO	Chief risk officer
CTO	Chief Technology officer
CVE	Common vulnerabilities and exposures
DAC	Discretionary access controls
DBMS	Database management system
DCE	Distributed control environment
DCE	Data communications equipment
DCE	Distributed computing environment
DCL	Digital command language
DDoS	Distributed denial of service
DES	Data Encryption Standard
DHCP	Dynamic Host Configuration Protocol
DMZ	Demilitarized zone
DNS	Domain name system
DNSSEC	Domain Name Service Secure
DoS	Denial of service
DOSD	Data-oriented system development
DR	Disaster recovery
DRII	Disaster Recovery Institute International
DRP	Disaster recovery planning
EDI	Electronic data interchange
EER	Equal error rate
EFT	Electronic funds transfer
EF	Exposure factor
EGRP	External Gateway Routing Protocol
EIGRP	Enhanced Interior Gateway Routing Protocol
EU	European Union
FAIR	Factor analysis of information risk
FAR	False-acceptance rate
FCPA	Foreign Corrupt Practices Act
FIPS	Federal Information Processing Standards (USA)
FISMA	Federal Information Security Modernization Act
FSA	Financial Security Authority (USA)
GLBA	Gramm-Leach-Bliley Act (USA)
GMI	Governance Metrics International
HD-DVD	High definition/high-density-digital video disc
HIDS	Host-based intrusion detection system

HIPAA	Health Insurance Portability and Accountability
HIPO	Hierarchy Input-Process-Output
HR	Human resources
HTML	Hypertext Markup Language
HTTP	Hypertext Transfer Protocol
I/O	Input/output
ICMP	Internet Control Message Protocol
ICT	Information and communication technologies
ID	Identification
IDEFIX	Integration Definition for Information Modeling
IDS	Intrusion detection system
IEC	International Electrotechnical Commission
IETF	Internet engineering task force
IFAC	International Federation of Accountants
IIA	Institute of Internal Auditors
IMT	Incident management team
IP	Internet Protocol
IPF	Information processing facility
IPL	Initial program load
IPMA	International Project Management Association
IPRs	Intellectual property rights
IPS	Intrusion prevention system
IPSec	Internet Protocol Security
IRP	Incident response plan
IRT	Incident response team
IS	Information systems
ISF	Information Security Forum
ISO	International Organization for Standardization
ISP	Internet service provider
ISSA	Information Systems Security Association
ISSEA	International Systems Security Engineering Association
IT	Information technology
ITGI	IT Governance Institute
ITIL	Information Technology Infrastructure Library
JCL	Job control language
KGI	Key goal indicator
KLOC	Kilo lines of code
KPI	Key performance indicator
KRI	Key risk indicator
L2TP	Layer 2 Tunneling Protocol
LAN	Local area network
LCP	Link Control Protocol
M&A	Mergers and acquisitions
MAC	Mandatory access control
MAO	Maximum allowable outage

MIME	Multipurpose Internet mail extension
MIS	Management information system
MitM	Man-in-the-middle
MTD	Maximum tolerable downtime
MTO	Maximum tolerable outage
NAT	Network address translation
NCP	Network Control Protocol
NDA	Nondisclosure agreement
NIC	Network interface card
NIDS	Network intrusion detection system
NIST	National Institute of Standards and Technology (USA)
NPV	Net present value
OCSP	Online Certificate Status Protocol
OCTAVE	Operationally Critical Threat, Asset and Vulnerability Evaluation
OECD	Organization for Economic Co-Operation and Development
OEP	Occupant emergency plan
OSPF	Open Shortest Path First
PaaS	Platform as a Service
PAN	Personal area network
PCI	Payment Card Industry
PDCA	Plan-Do-Check-Act
PKI	Public key infrastructure
PMBOK	Project Management Body of Knowledge
PoS	Point-of-sale
PPPoE	Point-to-point Protocol over Ethernet
PRA	Probabilistic risk assessment
PSTN	Public switched telephone network
PVC	Permanent virtual circuit
QA	Quality assurance
RACI	Responsible, accountable, consulted, informed
RAID	Redundant array of inexpensive disks
ROI	Return on investment
ROSI	Return on security investment
RPO	Recovery point objective
RRT	Risk Reward Theorem/Tradeoff
RSA	Rivest, Shamir and Adleman (RSA stands for the initials of the developers last names)
RTO	Recovery time objective
S/HTTP	Secure Hypertext Transfer Protocol
SaaS	Software as a Service
SABSA	Sherwood Applied Business Security Architecture
SCADA	Supervisory Control and Data Acquisition
SDLC	System development life cycle
SDO	Service delivery objective
SEC	Securities and Exchange Commission (USA)
SIEM	Security information and event management

SIM	Security information management
SLA	Service level agreement
SMART	Specific, measurable, achievable, relevant, time-bound
SMF	System management facility
SOP	Standard operating procedure
SPI	Security Parameter Index
SPICE	Software process improvement and capability determination
SPOC	Single point of contact
SPOOL	Simultaneous peripheral operations online
SQL	Structured Query Language
SSH	Secure Shell
SSL	Secure sockets layer
SSO	Single sign-on
TCO	Total cost of ownership
TCP	Transmission Control Protocol
TLS	Transport layer security
UDP	User Datagram Protocol
URL	Uniform resource locator
USB	Universal Serial Bus
VAR	Value at risk
VoIP	Voice-over IP
VPN	Virtual private network
XBRL	Extensible Business Reporting Language
XML	Extensible Markup Language
XSS	Cross-site scripting

Definitions

The following list of terms and definitions is taken directly from the CISM Review Manual, 15th edition. Not all terms are found in this book, but it is recommended that you be familiar with this list in case a term is used on the exam.

Acceptable interruption window
The maximum period of time that a system can be unavailable before compromising the achievement of the organization's business objectives

Acceptable use policy
A policy that establishes an agreement between users and the organization and defines for all parties the ranges of use that are approved before gaining access to a network or the internet

Access controls
The processes, rules and deployment mechanisms that control access to information systems, resources and physical access to premises

Access path
The logical route that an end user takes to access computerized information. Typically, it includes a route through the operating system, telecommunications software, selected application software and the access control system.

Access rights
The permission or privileges granted to users, programs or workstations to create, change, delete or view data and files within a system, as defined by rules established by data owners and the information security policy

Accountability
The ability to map a given activity or event back to the responsible party

Address Resolution Protocol (ARP)
Defines the exchanges between network interfaces connected to an Ethernet media segment in order to map an IP address to a link layer address on demand

Administrative control
The rules, procedures and practices dealing with operational effectiveness, efficiency and adherence to regulations and management policies

Advanced Encryption Standard (AES)
The international encryption standard that replaced 3DES

Alert situation
The point in an emergency procedure when the elapsed time and the interruption is not resolved. The organization entering into an alert situation initiates a series of escalation steps.

Algorithm
A finite set of step-by-step instructions for a problem-solving or computational procedure, especially one that can be implemented by a computer.

Alternate facilities
Locations and infrastructures from which emergency or backup processes are executed, when the main premises are unavailable or destroyed. This includes other buildings, offices or data processing centers.

Alternate process
Automatic or manual process designed and established to continue critical business processes from point-of-failure to return-to-normal

Annual loss expectancy (ALE)
The total expected loss divided by the number of years in the forecast period yielding the average annual loss

Anomaly detection
Detection on the basis of whether the system activity matches that defined as abnormal

Anonymous File Transfer Protocol (AFTP)
A method of downloading public files using the File Transfer Protocol (FTP). AFTP does not require users to identify themselves before accessing files from a particular server. In general, users enter the word "anonymous" when the host prompts for a username. Anything can be entered for the password such as the user's email address or simply the word "guest." In many cases, an AFFP site will not prompt a user for a name and password.

Antivirus software
An application software deployed at multiple points in an IT architecture. it is designed to detect and potentially eliminate virus code before damage is done, and repair or quarantine files that have already been infected.

Application controls
The policies, procedures and activities designed to provide reasonable assurance that objectives relevant to a given automated solution (application) are achieved

Application layer
in the Open Systems interconnection (OSI) communications model, the application layer provides services for an application program to ensure that effective communication with another application program in a network is possible. The application layer is not the application that is doing the communication; it is a service layer that provides these services.

Application programming interface (API)
A set of routines, protocols and tools referred to as "building blocks" used in business application software development. A good ADI makes it easier to develop a program by providing all the building blocks related to functional characteristics of an operating system that applications need to specify, for example, when interfacing with the operating system (cg. provided by Microsoft Windows, different versions of UNIX). A programmer utilizes these APIs in developing applications that can operate effectively and efficiently on the platform chosen.

Application service provider (ASP)
Also known as managed service provider (MSP), it deploys, hosts and manages access to a packaged application to multiple parties from a centrally managed facility. The applications are delivered over networks on a subscription basis.

Architecture
Description of the fundamental underlying design of the components of the business system, or of one element of the business system (e.g., technology), the relationships among them, and the manner in which they support the organization's objectives

Asymmetric key
A cipher technique in which different cryptographic keys are used to encrypt and decrypt a message

Attack signature
A specific sequence of events indicative of an unauthorized access attempt. Typically, a characteristic byte pattern used in malicious code or an indicator, or set of indicators, that allows the identification of malicious network activities.

Audit trail
A visible trail of evidence enabling one to trace information contained in statements or reports back to the original input source

Authentication
The act of verifying the identity (i.e., user, system)

Authorization
Access privileges granted to a user, program or process, or the act of granting those privileges

Availability
Information that is accessible when required by the business process now and in the future

Backup center
An alternate facility to continue IT/IS operations when the primary data processing (DP) center is unavailable

Baseline security
The minimum security controls required for safeguarding an IT system based on its identified needs for confidentiality, integrity and/or availability protection

Benchmarking
A systematic approach to comparing an organization's performance against peers and competitors in an effort to learn the best ways of conducting business. Examples include benchmarking of quality, logistic efficiency and various other metrics.

Bit
The smallest unit of information storage; a contraction of the term "binary digit"; one of two symbols "0" (zero) and "I" (one) that are used to represent binary numbers

Bit copy
Provides an exact image of the original and is a requirement for legally justifiable forensics

Bit-stream image
Bit-stream backups, also referred to as mirror image backups, involve the backup of all areas of a computer hard disk drive or other type of storage media. Such backups exactly replicate all sectors on a given storage device including all files and ambient data storage areas.

Botnet
A large number of compromised computers that are used to create and send spam or viruses or flood a network with messages such as a denial-of-service attack

Brute force attack
Repeatedly trying all possible combinations of passwords or encryption keys until the correct one is found

Business case
Documentation of the rationale for making a business investment, used both to support a business decision on whether to proceed with the investment and as an operational tool to support management of the investment through its full economic life cycle

Business continuity plan (BCP)
A plan used by an organization to respond to disruption of critical business processes. Depends on the contingency plan for restoration of critical systems.

Business dependency assessment
A process of identifying resources critical to the operation of a business process

Business impact
The net effect, positive or negative, on the achievement of business objectives

Business impact analysis (BIA)
Evaluating the criticality and sensitivity of information assets. An exercise that determines the impact of losing the support of any resource to an organization, establishes the escalation of that loss over time, identifies the minimum resources needed to recover and prioritizes the recovery of processes and supporting system Tins process also includes addressing: income loss

unexpected expense, legal issues (regulatory compliance or contractual), interdependent processes and loss of public reputation or confidence

Business Model for Information Security (BMIS)
A holistic and business-oriented model supports enterprise governance and management information security, and provides a common language for information security professionals and business management

Capability Maturity Model Integration (CMMI)
Contains the essential elements of effective processes for one or more disciplines. It also describes path an evolutionary improvement path from ad hoc, immature processes, to disciplined, mature processes with improved quality and effectiveness

Certificate (certification) authority (CA)
A trusted third party that serves authentication infrastructures or enterprises and registers entities and issues them certificates

Certificate revocation list (CRL)
An instrument for checking the continued validity of the certificates for which the certification authority (CA) has responsibility. The CRL details digital certificates that are no longer valid. The time gap between two updates is very critical and is also a risk in digital certificates verification.

Certification practice statement
A detailed set of rules governing the certificate authority's operations. It provides an understanding of the value and trustworthiness of certificates issued by a given certificate authority (CA). Stated in terms of the controls that an organization observes, the method it uses to validate the authenticity of certificate applicants and the GAS expectations of how its certificates may be used.

Chain of custody
A legal principle regarding the validity and integrity of evidence. It requires accountability for anything that will be used as evidence in a legal proceeding to ensure that it can be accounted for from the time it was collected until the time it is presented in a court of law. This includes documentation as to who had access to the evidence and when, as well as the ability to identify evidence as being the exact item that was recovered or tested. Lack of control over evidence can lead to it being discredited. Chain of custody depends on the ability to verify that evidence could not have been tampered with. This is accomplished by sealing off the evidence, so it

cannot be changed, and providing a documentary record of custody to prove that the evidence was, at all times, under strict control and not subject to tampering.

Chain of evidence
A process and record that shows who obtained the evidence, where and when the evidence was obtained, who secured the evidence, and who had control or possession of the evidence. The "sequencing" of the chain of evidence follows this order: collection and identification, analysis, storage, preservation, presentation in court, return to owner.

Challenge/response token
A method of user authentication that IS carried out through use of the Challenge Handshake Authentication Protocol (CHAP). When a user tries to log onto the server using CHAR the server sends the user a "challenge," which is a random value. The user enters a password, which is used as an encryption key to encrypt the "challenge" and return it to the server. The server is aware of the password. It, therefore, encrypts the "challenge value and compares it with the value received from the user. If the values match, the user is authenticated. The challenge/response activity continues throughout the session and this protects the session from password sniffing attacks. In addition, CHAP IS not vulnerable to "man-in-the-middle" attacks because the challenge value is a random value that changes on each access attempt,

Change management
A holistic and proactive approach to managing the transition from a current to a desired organizational state.

Checksum
A mathematical value that is assigned to a file and used to "test" the file at a later date to verify that the data contained in the file have not been maliciously changed.
A cryptographic checksum is created by performing a complicated series of mathematical operations (known as a cryptographic algorithm) that translates the data in the file into a fixed string of digits called a hash value, which is then used as the checksum. Without knowing which cryptographic algorithm was used to create the hash value, it is highly unlikely that an unauthorized person would be able to change data without inadvertently changing the corresponding checksum. Cryptographic checksums are used in data transmission and data storage. Cryptographic checksums are also known as message authentication codes, integrity check values, modification detection codes or message integrity codes.

Chief information officer (CIO)
The most senior official of the enterprise who is accountable for IT advocacy, aligning IT and business strategies, and planning, resourcing and managing the delivery of IT services, information and the deployment of associated human resources. In some cases, the CIO role has been expanded to become the chief knowledge officer (CKO) who deals in knowledge, not just information. Also see chief technology officer.

Chief information security officer (CISO)
Responsible for managing information risk, the information security program, and ensuring appropriate confidentiality, integrity and availability of information assets

Chief security officer (CSO)
Typically, responsible for physical security in the organization although increasingly the CISO and CSO roles are merged.

Chief technology officer (CTO)
The individual who focuses on technical issues in an organization

Cloud computing
An approach using external services for convenient on-demand [T operations using a shared pool of configurable computing capability. Typical capabilities include infrastructure as a service (IaaS), platform as a service (PaaS) and software as a service (SaaS) (cg, networks, servers, storage, applications and services) that can be rapidly provisioned and released with minimal management effort or service provider interaction. This cloud model is composed of five essential characteristics (on-demand self-service, ubiquitous network access, location independent resource pooling, rapid elasticity, and measured service). It allows users to access technology-based services from the network cloud without knowledge of, expertise with, or control over, the technology infrastructure that supports them and provides four models for enterprise access (private cloud, community cloud, public cloud and hybrid cloud).

COBIT 5
Formerly known as Control Objectives for Information and related Technology (COBIT); now used only as the acronym in its fifth iteration. A complete, internationally accepted framework for governing and managing enterprise information and technology (IT) that supports enterprise executives and management in their definition and achievement of business goals and related IT goals. COBIT describes five principles and seven enablers that support enterprises in the

development, implementation, and continuous improvement and monitoring of good IT-related governance and management practices.

Earlier versions of COBIT focused on control objectives related to IT processes, management and control of IT processes and IT governance aspects. Adoption and use of the COBIT framework are supported by guidance from a growing family of supporting products.

COBIT 4.1 and earlier

Formerly known as Control Objectives for Information and related Technology (COBIT). A complete, internationally accepted process framework for IT that supports business and IT executives and management in their definition and achievement of business goals and related IT goals by providing a comprehensive IT governance, management, control and assurance model. COBIT describes IT processes and associated control objectives, management guidelines (activities, accountabilities, responsibilities and performance metrics) and maturity models. COBIT supports enterprise management in the development, implementation, continuous improvement and monitoring of good IT-related practices.

Common vulnerabilities and exposures (CVE)

A system that provides a reference method for publicly known information-security vulnerabilities and exposures. MITRE Corporation maintains the system, with funding from the National Cyber Security Division of the United States Department of Homeland Security.

Compensating control

An internal control that reduces the risk of an existing or potential control weakness resulting in errors and omissions

Computer forensics

The application of the scientific method to digital media to establish factual information for judicial review. This process often involves investigating computer systems to determine whether they are or have been used for illegal or unauthorized activities. As a discipline, it combines elements of law and computer science to collect and analyze data from information systems (cg, personal computers, networks, wireless communication and digital storage devices) in a way that is admissible as evidence in a court of law.

Confidentiality

The protection of sensitive or private information from unauthorized disclosure

Configuration management
The control of changes to a set of configuration items over a system life cycle

Content filtering
Controlling access to a network by analyzing the contents of the incoming and outgoing packets and either letting them pass or denying them based on a list of rules. Differs from packet filtering in that it is the data in the packet that are analyzed instead of the attributes of the packet itself (e. g, source/target IP address, transmission control protocol [TCP] flags).

Contingency plan
A plan used by an organization or business unit to respond to a specific systems failure or disruption

Continuous monitoring
The process implemented to maintain a current security status for one or more information systems or for the entire suite of information systems on which the operational mission of the enterprise depends.
The process includes: 1) the development of a strategy to regularly evaluate selected IS controls/metrics, .2) recording and evaluating IS-relevant events and the effectiveness of the enterprise in dealing with those events, 3) recording changes to IS controls, or changes that affect IS risks, and 4) publishing the current security status to enable information-sharing decisions involving the enterprise.

Control
The means of managing risk, including policies, procedures, guidelines, practices or organizational structures which can be of an administrative, technical, management or legal nature

Control center
Hosts the recovery meetings where disaster recovery operations are managed

Controls policy
A policy defining control operational and failure modes (e.g., fail secure, fail open, allowed unless specifically denied, denied unless specifically permitted)

Corporate governance
The system by which enterprises are directed and controlled. The board of directors is responsible for the governance of their enterprise. It consists of the leadership and organizational structures and processes that ensure the enterprise sustains and extends strategies and objectives.

COSO
Committee of Sponsoring Organizations of the Treadway Commission. Its report "Internal Control-Integrated Framework" is an internationally accepted standard for corporate governance. See WWW. coso.org.

Cost-benefit analysis
A systematic process for calculating and comparing benefits and costs of a project, control or decision

Countermeasures
Any process that directly reduces a threat or vulnerability

Criticality
A measure-of the impact that the failure of a system to function as required will have on the organization

Criticality analysis
An analysis to evaluate resources or business functions to identify their importance to the organization, and the impact if a function cannot be completed or a resource is not available

Cryptographic algorithm
A well-defined computational procedure that takes variable inputs, including a cryptographic key, and produces an output

Cryptographic strength
A measure of the expected number of operations required to defeat a cryptographic mechanism

Cryptography
The art of designing, analyzing and attacking cryptographic schemes

Cyclical redundancy check (CRC)
A method to ensure that data have not been altered after being sent through a communication channel

Damage evaluation
The determination of the extent of damage that is necessary to provide for an estimation of the recovery time frame and the potential loss to the organization

Data classification
The assignment of a level of sensitivity to data (or information) that results in the specification of controls for each level of classification. Levels of sensitivity of data are assigned according to predefined categories as data are created, amended, enhanced, stored or transmitted. The classification level is an indication of the value or importance of the data to the organization.

Data custodian
The individual(s) and/or department(s) responsible for the storage and safeguarding of computerized data

Data Encryption Standard (DES)
An algorithm for encoding binary data. it is a secret key cryptosystem published by the National Bureau of Standards (NBS), the predecessor of the US National Institute of Standards and Technology (NIST). DES and its variants have been replaced by the Advanced Encryption Standard (AES).

Data integrity
The property that data meet with a priority expectation of quality and that the data can be relied on

Data leakage
Siphoning out or leaking information by dumping computer files or stealing computer reports and tapes

Data leak protection (DLP)
A suite of technologies and associated processes that locate, monitor and protect sensitive information from unauthorized disclosure

Data mining
A technique used to analyze ex1stmg information, usually with the intention of pursuing new avenues to pursue business

Data normalization
A structured process for organizing data rate tables in such a way that it preserves the relationships among the data

Data owner
The individual(s), normally a manager or director, who has responsibility for the integrity, accurate reporting and use of computerized data

Data warehouse
A generic term for a system that stores, retrieves and manages large volumes of data. Data warehouse software often includes sophisticated comparison and hashing techniques for fast searches, as well as advanced filtering.

Decentralization
The process of distributing computer processing to different locations within an organization

Decryption key
A digital piece of information used to recover plain text from the corresponding cipher text by decryption

Defense in depth
The practice of layering defenses to provide added protection. Defense in depth increases security by raising the effort needed in an attack. This strategy places multiple barriers between an attacker and an organization's computing and information resources.

Degauss
The application of variable levels of alternating current for the purpose of demagnetizing magnetic recording media. The process involves increasing the alternating current field gradually from zero to some maximum value and back to zero, leaving a very low residue of magnetic induction on the media. Degauss loosely means: to erase.

Demilitarized zone (DMZ)
A screened (firewalled) network segment that acts as a buffer zone between a trusted and untrusted network. A DMZ is typically used to house systems such as web servers that must be accessible from both internal networks and the Internet.

Denial-of-service (DOS) attack
An assault on a service from a single source that floods it with so many requests that it becomes overwhelmed and is either stopped completely or operates at a significantly reduced rate

Digital certificate
A process to authenticate (or certify) a party's digital signature; carried out by trusted third parties

Digital code signing
The process of digitally signing computer code to ensure its integrity

Disaster declaration
The communication to appropriate internal and external parties that the disaster recovery plan is being put into operation

Disaster notification fee
The fee the recovery site vendor charges when the customer notifies them that a disaster has occurred, and the recovery site is required. The fee is implemented to discourage false disaster notifications.

Disaster recovery plan (DRP)
A set of human, physical, technical and procedural resources to recover, within a defined time and cost, an activity interrupted by an emergency or disaster

Disaster recovery plan desk checking
Typically, a read-through of a disaster recovery plan without any real actions taking place. Generally involves a reading of the plan, discussion of the action items and definition of any gaps that might be identified.

Disaster recovery plan walk-through
Generally a robust test of the recovery plan requiring that some recovery activities take place and are tested. A disaster scenario is often given and the recovery teams talk through the steps they would need to take to recover. As many aspects of the plan should be tested as possible.

Discretionary access control (DAC)
A means of restricting access to objects based on the identity of subjects and/or groups to which they belong. The controls are discretionary in the sense that a subject with a certain access permission is capable of passing that permission (perhaps indirectly) on to any other subject.

Disk mirroring
The practice of duplicating data in separate volumes on two hard disks to make storage more fault tolerant. Mirroring provides data protection in the case of disk failure because data are constantly updated to both disks.

Distributed denial-of-service (DDoS) attack
A denial-of-service (DOS) assault from multiple sources

Domain name system (DNS)
A hierarchical database that is distributed across the Internet that allows names to be resolved into IP addresses (and vice versa) to locate services such as web and email servers

Dual control
A procedure that uses two or more entities (usually persons) operating in concert to protect a system resource so that no single entity acting alone can access that resource

Due care
The level of care expected from a reasonable person of similar competency under similar conditions

Due diligence
The performance of those actions that are generally regarded as prudent, responsible and necessary to conduct a thorough and objective investigation, review and/or analysis

Dynamic Host Configuration Protocol (DHCP)
A protocol used by networked computers (clients) to obtain IP addresses and other parameters such as the default gateway, subnet mask and IP addresses of domain name system (DNS) servers from a DHCP server. The DHCP server ensures that all IP addresses are unique (e.g., no IP address is assigned to a second client while the first client's assignment is valid [its lease has not expired]). Thus, IP address pool management is done by the server and not by a human network administrator.

Electronic data interchange (EDI)
The electronic transmission of transactions (information) between two enterprises. EDI promotes a more efficient paperless environment. EDI transmissions can replace the use of standard documents, including invoices or purchase orders.

Electronic funds transfer (EFT)
The exchange of money via telecommunications. EFT refers to any financial transaction that originates at a terminal and transfers a sum of money from one account to another.

Encryption
The process of taking an unencrypted message (plain text), applying a mathematical function to it (encryption algorithm with a key) and producing an encrypted message (cypher text)

Enterprise governance
A set of responsibilities and practices exercised by the board and executive management with the goal of providing strategic direction, ensuring that objectives are achieved, ascertaining that risks are managed appropriately and verifying that the enterprise's resources are used responsibly

Exposure
The potential loss to an area due to the occurrence of an adverse event

External storage
The location that contains the backup copies to be used in case recovery or restoration is required in the event of a disaster

Fail-over
The transfer of service from an incapacitated primary component to its backup component

Fail safe
Describes the design properties of a computer system that allow it to resist active attempts to attack or bypass it

Fall-through logic
An optimized code based on a branch prediction that predicts which way a program will branch when an application is presented

Firewall
A system or combination of systems that enforces a boundary between two or more networks typically forming a barrier between a secure and an open environment such as the Internet

Flooding
An attack that attempts to cause a failure in a system by providing more input than the system can process properly

Forensic Copy
An accurate bit-for-bit reproduction of the information contained on an electronic device or associated media, whose validity and integrity has been verified using an acceptable algorithm

Forensic examination
The process of collecting, assessing, digital evidence to assist in the identification of an offender and the method of compromise

Guideline
A description of a particular way of accomplishing something that is less prescriptive than a procedure

Harden
To configure a computer or other network device to resist attacks

Hash function
An algorithm that maps or translates one set of bits into another (generally smaller) so that a message yields the same result every time the algorithm is executed using the same message as input. It is computationally infeasible for a message to be derived or reconstituted from the result produced by the algorithm or to find two different messages that produce the same hash result using the same algorithm.

Help desk
A service offered via telephone/Internet by an organization to its clients or employees that provides information, assistance and troubleshooting advice regarding software, hardware or networks. A help desk is staffed by people who can either resolve the problem on their own or escalate the problem to specialized personnel. A help desk is often equipped with dedicated customer relationship management (CRM) software that logs the problems and tracks them until they are solved.

Honeypot
A specially configured server, also known as a decoy server, designed to attract and monitor intruders in a manner such that their actions do not affect production systems

Hot site
A fully operational offsite data processing facility equipped with hardware and system software to be used in the event of a disaster

Hypertext Transfer Protocol (HTTP)
A communication protocol used to connect to servers on the World Wide Web. Its primary function is to establish a connection with a web server and transmit hypertext markup language (HTML), extensible markup language (XML) or other pages to the client browsers.

Identification
The process of verifying the identity of a user, process or device, usually as a prerequisite for granting access to resources in an information system

Impact analysis
A study to prioritize the criticality of information resources for the organization based on costs (or consequences) of adverse events. In an impact analysis, threats to assets are identified and potential business losses determined for different time periods. This assessment is used to justify the extent of safeguards that are required and recovery time frames. This analysis is the basis for establishing the recovery strategy.

Incident
Any event that is not part of the standard operation of a service and that causes, or may cause, an interruption to, or a reduction in, the quality of that service

Incident handling
An action plan for dealing with intrusions, cybertheft, denial-of-service attack, fire, floods, and other security-related events. It is comprised of a six-step process: Preparation, Identification, Containment, Eradication, Recovery, and Lessons Learned.

Incident response
The response of an enterprise to a disaster or other significant event that may significantly affect the enterprise, its people or its ability to function productively. An incident response may include evacuation of a facility, initiating a disaster recovery plan (DRP), performing damage assessment and any other measures necessary to bring an enterprise to a more stable status.

Information security
Ensures that only authorized users (confidentiality) have access to accurate and complete information (integrity) when required (availability)

Information security governance
The set of responsibilities and practices exercised by the board and executive management with the goal of providing strategic direction, ensuring that objectives are achieved, ascertaining that risks are managed appropriately and verifying that the enterprise's resources are used responsibly

Information security program
The overall combination of technical, operational and procedural measures, and management structures implemented to provide for the confidentiality, integrity and availability of information based on business requirements and risk analysis

Integrity
The accuracy, completeness and validity of information

Internal controls
The policies, procedures, practices and organizational structures designed to provide reasonable assurance that business objectives will be achieved, and undesired events will be prevented or detected and corrected

Internet protocol
Specifies the format of packets and the addressing scheme

Internet service provider (ISP)
A third party that provides individuals and organizations access to the Internet and a variety of other Internet-related services

Interruption window
The time the company can wait from the point of failure to the restoration of the minimum and critical services or applications. After this time, the progressive losses caused by the interruption are excessive for the organization.

Intrusion detection
The process of monitoring the events occurring in a computer system or network to detect signs of unauthorized access or attack

Intrusion detection system (IDS)
Inspects network and host security activity to identify suspicious patterns that may indicate a network or system attack

Intrusion prevention system (IPS)
Inspects network and host security activity to identify suspicious patterns that may indicate a network or system attack and then blocks it at the firewall to prevent damage to information resources

IP Security (IPSec)
A set of protocols developed by the Internet Engineering Task Force (IETF) to support the secure exchange of packets

ISO/IEC 15504
ISO/IEC 15504 *Information Technology-Process assessment.*
ISO/IEC 15504 provides a framework for the assessment of processes. The framework can be used by organizations involved in planning, managing, monitoring, controlling and improving the acquisition, supply, development, operation, evolution and support of products and services.

ISO/IEC 17799
Originally released as part of the British Standard for Information Security in 1999 and then as the Code of Practice for Information Security Management in October 2000, it was elevated by the International Organization for Standardization (ISO) to an international code of practice for information security management. This standard defines information's confidentiality, integrity

and availability controls in a comprehensive information security management system. The latest version is ISO/IEC 17799:2005.

ISO/IEC 27001
An international standard, released in 2005 and revised in 2013, that defines a set of requirements for an information security management system. Prior its adoption by the ISO, this standard was known as BS 17799 Part 2, which was originally published in 1999

ISO/IEC 27002
A code of practice that contains a structured list of suggested information security controls for organizations implementing an information security management system. Prior to its adoption by ISO/IEC, this standard existed as BS 77799.

ISO/I EC 31000
ISO 31000:22009 *Risk Management-Principles and guidelines.*
Provides principles and generic guidelines on risk management. It is industry- and sector-agnostic and can be used by any public, private or community enterprise, association, group or individual.

IT governance
The responsibility of executives and the board of directors; consists of the leadership, organizational structures and processes that ensure that the enterprise's IT sustains and extends the organization's strategies and objectives

IT steering committee
An executive management-level committee that assists the executive in the delivery of the IT strategy, oversees day-to-day management of IT service delivery and IT projects and focuses on implementation aspects

IT strategic plan
A long-term plan (i.e., three- to five-year horizon) in which business and IT management cooperatively describe how IT resources contribute to the enterprise's strategic objectives (goals)

IT strategy committee
A committee at the level of the board of directors to ensure that the board is involved in major IT matters and decisions. The committee is primarily accountable for managing the portfolios of

IT-enabled investments, IT services and other IT resources. The committee is the owner of the portfolio.

Key goal indicator (KGI)
A measure that tells management, alter the fact, whether an IT process has achieved its business requirements; usually expressed in terms of information criteria

Key performance indicator (KPI)
A measure that determines how well the process is performing in enabling the goal to be reached. A KPI is a lead indicator of whether a goal will likely be reached, and a good indicator of capability, practices and skills. It measures an activity goal, which is an action that the process owner must take to achieve effective process performance.

Key risk indicator (KRI)
A subset of risk indicators that are highly relevant and possess a high probability of predicting or indicating important risk

Least privilege
The principle of allowing users or applications the least amount of permissions necessary to perform their intended function

Mail relay server
An electronic mail (email) server that relays messages so that neither the sender nor the recipient is a local user

Malicious code
Software (e.g., Trojan horse) that appears to perform a useful or desirable function, but actually gains unauthorized access to system resources or tricks a user into executing other malicious logic

Malware
Software designed to infiltrate, damage or obtain information from a computer system without the owner's Consent. Malware is commonly taken to include computer viruses worms Trojan horses, spyware and adware. Spyware is generally, used for marketing purposes and, as such, is not malicious although it is generally unwanted. Spyware can, however, be used to gather information for identity theft or other clearly illicit purposes.

Mandatory access control (MAC)
A means of restricting access to data based on varying degrees of security requirements for information contained in the objects and the corresponding security clearance users or Programs acting on their behalf

Man-in-the-middle attack (MITM)
An attack strategy in which the attacker intercepts the communication stream between two parts of the victim system and then replaces the traffic between the two components with the intruder's own system, eventually assuming control of the communication

Masqueraders
Attackers that penetrate systems by using the identity of legitimate users and their login credentials

Maximum tolerable outage (MTG)
Maximum time the organization can support processing in alternate mode

Media access control (MAC)
Applied to the hardware at the factory and cannot be modified, MAC is a unique, 48-bit, hard-coded address of a physical layer device, such as an Ethernet local area network (LAN) or a wireless network card.

Message authentication code
An American National Standards Institute (ANSI) standard checksum that is computed using the Data Encryption Standard (DES)

Message digest
A cryptographic checksum, typically generated for a file that can be used to detect changes to the file; Secure Hash Algorithm-1 (SHA-I) is an example of a message digest algorithm.

Mirrored site
An alternate site that contains the same information as the original. Mirror sites are set up for backup and disaster recovery as well as to balance the traffic load for numerous download requests. Such download mirrors are often placed in different locations throughout the Internet.

Mobile site
The use of a mobile/temporary facility to serve as a business resumption location. They can usually be delivered to any Site and can house information technology and staff.

Monitoring policy
Rules outlining or delineating the way in which Information about the use of computers, networks, applications and information is captured and interpreted.

Multipurpose Internet mail extension (MIME)
A specification for formatting non-ASCII messages so that they can be sent over the Internet. Many email clients now support. MIME, which enables them to send and receive graphics, audio and video files via the Internet mail system. In addition, MIME supports messages in character sets other than ASCII.

Net present value (NPV)
Calculated by using an after-tax discount rate of an Investment and a series of expected incremental cash outflows (the initial investment and operational costs) and cash inflows (cost savings or revenues) that occur at regular periods during the life cycle of the investment. To arrive at a fair NPV calculation, cash inflows accrued by the business up to about five years after project deployment also should be considered.

Network address translation (NAT)
Basic NATs are used when there is a requirement to interconnect two IP networks with incompatible addressing. However, it is common to hide an entire IP address space, usually consisting of private IP addresses, behind a single IP address (or in some cases a small group of IP addresses) in another (usually public) address space. To avoid ambiguity in the handling of returned packets. A one-to-many NAT must alter higher level information such as Transmission Control Protocol (TCP)/User Datagram Protocol (UDP) ports in outgoing communications and must maintain a translation table so that return packets can be correctly translated back.

Network-based intrusion detection (NID)
Provides broader coverage than host-based approaches but functions in the same manner detecting attacks using either an anomaly-based or signature-based approach or both

Nonintrusive monitoring
The use of transported probes or traces to assemble information, track traffic and identify vulnerabilities

Nonrepudiation
The assurance that a party cannot later deny originating data; that is, it is the provision of proof of the integrity and origin of the data and can be verified by a third party. A digital signature can provide nonrepudiation.

Offline files
Computer file storage media not physically connected to the computer; typically tapes or tape cartridges used for backup purposes

Open Shortest Path First (OSPF)
A routing protocol developed for IP networks. It is based on the shortest path first or link state algorithm.

Open Source Security Testing Methodology
An open and freely available methodology and manual for security testing

Outcome measure
Represents the consequences of actions previously taken; alien referred to as a lag indicator. An outcome measure frequently focuses on results at the end of a time period and characterizes historical performance. It is also referred to as a key goal indicator (K01) and is used to indicate whether goals have been met. Can be measured only after the fact and, therefore, is called a lag indicator.

Packet
Data unit that is routed from source to destination in a packet- switched network. A packet contains both routing information and Port data. Transmission Control Protocol/Internet Protocol (TCP/IP) is such a packet-switched network.

Packet filtering
Controlling access to a network by analyzing the attributes of the incoming and outgoing packets, and either letting them pass or denying them based on a list of rules

Packet sniffer
Software that observes and records network traffic

Packet switched network
Individual packets follow their own paths through the network from one endpoint to another and reassemble at the destination.

Partitions
Major divisions of the total physical hard disk space

Passive response
A response option in intrusion detection in which the system simply reports and records the problem detected, relying on the user to take subsequent action

Password cracker
A tool that tests the strength of user passwords searching for passwords that are easy to guess. It repeatedly tries words from specially crafted dictionaries and often also generates thousands (and in some cases, even millions) of permutations of characters, numbers and symbols.

Penetration testing
A live test of the effectiveness of security defenses through mimicking the actions of real-life attackers

Personally Identifiable Information (PII)
Information that can be used alone or with other sources to uniquely identify, contact or locate a single individual

Pharming
This is a more sophisticated form of a man-in-the-middle (MITM) attack. A user's session is redirected to a masquerading web site. This can be achieved by corrupting a domain name system (DNS) server on the Internet and pointing a URL to the masquerading web site's IP address.

Phishing
This is a type of electronic mail (email) attack that attempts to convince a user that the originator is genuine, but with the intention of obtaining information for use in social engineering. Phishing attacks may take the form of masquerading as a lottery organization advising the recipient or the user's bank of a large win; in either case, the intent is to obtain account and personal identification number (PIN) details. Alternative attacks may seek to obtain apparently innocuous business information, which may be used in another form of active attack.

Platform as a Service (PaaS)
Offers the capability to deploy onto the cloud infrastructure customer-created or acquired applications that are created using programming languages or tools supported by the provider

Policy
Overall intention and direction as formally expressed by management

Port
A hardware interface between a CPU and a peripheral device. Can also refer to a software (virtual) convention that allows remote services to connect to a host operating system in a structured manner.

Privacy
Freedom from unauthorized intrusion or disclosure of information of an individual

Private key
A mathematical key (kept secret by the holder) used to create digital signatures and, depending on the algorithm, to decrypt messages or files encrypted (for confidentiality) with the corresponding public key

Procedure
A document containing a detailed description of the steps necessary to perform specific operations in conformance with applicable standards. Procedures are defined as part of processes.

Proxy server
A server that acts on behalf of a user. Typically, proxies accept a connection from a user, decide as to whether or not the user or client IP address is permitted to use the proxy, perhaps perform additional authentication, and then complete a connection to a remote destination on behalf of the user.

Public key
In an asymmetric cryptographic scheme, the key that may be widely published to enable the operation of the scheme

Reciprocal agreement
Emergency processing agreements among two or more organizations with similar equipment or applications. Typically, participants promise to provide processing time to each other when an emergency arises.

Recovery action
Execution of a response or task according to a written procedure

Recovery point objective (RPO)
Determined based on the acceptable data loss in case of a disruption of operations. It indicates the earliest point in time to which it is acceptable to recover data. It effectively quantifies the permissible amount of data loss in case of interruption.

Recovery time objective (RIO)
The amount of time allowed for the recovery of a business function or resource after a disaster occurs

Redundant Array of Inexpensive Disks (RAID)
Provides performance improvements and fault-tolerant capabilities, via hardware or software solutions, by writing to a series of multiple disks to improve performance and/or save large files simultaneously

Redundant site
A recovery strategy involving the duplication of key information technology components, including data or other key business processes, whereby fast recovery can take place

Request for proposal (RFP)
A document distributed to software vendors requesting them to submit a proposal to develop or provide a software product

Residual risk
The remaining risk after management has implemented risk response

Resilience
The ability of a system or network to resist failure or to recover quickly from any disruption, usually with minimal recognizable effect

Return on investment (ROI)
A measure of operating performance and efficiency, computed in its simplest form by dividing net income by the total investment over the period being considered

Return on security investment (ROSI)
An estimate of return on security investment based on how much will be saved by reduced losses divided by the investment

Risk
The combination of the probability of an event and its consequence. (ISO/IEC 73). Risk has traditionally been expressed as Threats x Vulnerabilities = Risk.

Risk analysis
The initial steps of risk management: analyzing the value of assets to the business, identifying threats to those assets and evaluating how vulnerable each asset is to those threats. It often involves an evaluation of the probable frequency of a particular event, as well as the probable impact of that event.

Risk appetite
The amount of risk, on a broad level, that an entity is willing to accept in pursuit of its mission

Risk assessment
A process used to identify and evaluate risk and potential effects. Risk assessment includes assessing the critical functions necessary for an organization to continue business operations, defining the controls in place to reduce. organization exposure and evaluating the cost for such controls. Risk analysis often involves an evaluation of the probabilities of a particular event.

Risk avoidance
The process for systematically avoiding risk, constituting one approach to managing risk

Risk mitigation
The management and reduction of risk through the use of countermeasures and controls

Risk tolerance
The acceptable level of variation that management is willing to allow for any particular risk while pursuing its objective

Risk transfer
The process of assigning risk to another organization, usually through the purchase of an insurance policy or outsourcing the service

Robustness
The ability of systems to withstand attack, operate reliably across a wide range of operational conditions and to fail gracefully outside of the operational range

Role-based access control
Assigns users to job functions or titles. Each Job function or title defines a specific authorization level

Root cause analysis
A process of diagnosis to establish origins of events, which can be used for learning from consequences, typically of errors and problems

Rootkit
A software suite designed to aid an intruder in gaining unauthorized administrative access to a computer system

Secret key
A cryptographic key that is used with a secret key (symmetric) cryptographic algorithm, that is uniquely associated with one or more entities and is not made public. The same key is used to both encrypt and decrypt data. The use of the term "secret" in this context does not imply a classification level, but rather implies the need to protect the key from disclosure.

Secure hash algorithm (SHA)
A hash algorithm with the property that is computationally infeasible I) to find a message that corresponds to a given message digest, or Z) to find two different messages that produce the same message digest

Secure shell (SSH)
Network protocol that uses cryptography to secure communication, remote command line login and remote command execution between two networked computers

Security information and event management (SIEM)

SIEM solutions are a combination of the formerly disparate product categories of SIM (security information management) and SEM (security event management). STEM technology provides real-time analysis of security alerts generated by network hardware and applications. SIEM solutions come as software, appliances or managed services, and are also used to log security data and generate reports for compliance purposes. Capabilities include:

- **Data aggregation:** SIEM/LM (log management) solutions aggregate data from many sources, including network, security. servers, databases and applications, providing the ability to consolidate monitored data to help avoid missing crucial events.
- **Correlation:** Looks for common attributes, and links events together into meaningful bundles. This technology provides the ability to perform a variety of correlation techniques to integrate different sources, in order to turn data into useful information.
- **Alerting:** The automated analysis of correlated events and production of alerts, to notify recipients of immediate issues.
- **Dashboards:** SIEM/LM tools take event data and turn them into informational charts to assist in seeing patterns or identifying activity that is not forming to a standard pattern.
- **Compliance:** SIEM applications can be employed to automate, the gathering of compliance data, producing reports that adapt to existing security, governance and auditing processes.
- **Retention:** SIEM/SIM solutions employ long-term storage of historical data to facilitate correlation of data over time, and to provide the retention necessary for compliance requirements.

Security metrics

A standard of measurement used in management of security-related activities

Segregation/separation of duties (SOD)

A basic internal control that prevents or detects errors and irregularities by assigning to separate individuals the responsibility for initiating and recording transactions and for the custody of assets. Segregation/separation of duties is commonly used in large IT organizations so that no single person is in a position to introduce fraudulent or malicious code without detection.

Sensitivity

A measure of the impact that improper disclosure of information may have on an organization

Service delivery objective (SDO)
Directly related to business needs, SDO is the level of services to be reached during the alternate process mode until the normal situation is restored.

Service level agreement (SLA)
An agreement, preferably documented, between a service provider and the customer(s)/user(s) that defines minimum performance targets for a service and how they will be measured

Session key
A single-use symmetric key used for a defined period of communication between two computers, such as for the duration of a single communication session or transaction set

Shell programming
A script written for the shell, or command line interpreter, of an operating system; it is often considered a simple domain-specific programming language. Typical operations performed by shell scripts include file manipulation, program execution and printing text. Usually, shell script refers to scripts written for a UNIX shell, while COMMANDCOM (DOS) and cmd.exe (Windows) command line scripts are usually called batch files. Others, such as AppleScript, add scripting capability to computing environments lacking a command line interface. Other examples of programming languages primarily intended for shell scripting include digital command language (DCL) and job control language (JCL).

Sniffing
The process by which data traversing a network are captured or monitored

Social engineering
An attack based on deceiving users or administrators at the target site into revealing confidential or sensitive information

Split knowledge/split key
A security technique in which two or more entities separately hold data items that individually convey no knowledge of the information that results from combining the items; a condition under which two or more entities separately have key components that individually convey no knowledge of the plain text key that will be produced when the key components are combined m the cryptographic module

Spoofing
Faking the sending address of a transmission in order to gain illegal entry into a secure system

Software as a service (SaaS)
Offers the capability to use the provider's applications running on cloud infrastructure. The applications are accessible from various client devices through a thin client interface such as a web browser (e.g., web-based email).

Standard
A mandatory requirement, code of practice or specification approved by a recognized external standards organization, such as International Organization for Standardization (ISO)

Symmetric key encryption
System in which a different key (or set of keys) is used by each pair of trading partners to ensure that no one else can read their messages. The same key is used for encryption and decryption.

System owner
Person or organization having responsibility for the development, procurement, integration, modification, operation and maintenance, and/or final disposition of an information system

Threat
Anything (e.g., object, substance, human) that is capable of acting against an asset in a manner that can result in harm. A potential cause of an unwanted incident. (ISO/IEC 13335)

Threat agent
Methods and things used to exploit a vulnerability. Examples include determination, capability, motive and resources.

Threat analysis
An evaluation of the type, scope and nature of events or actions that can result in adverse consequences; identification of the threats that exist against information assets. The threat analysis usually also defines the level of threat and the likelihood of it materializing.

Threat assessment
The identification of types of threats to which an organization might be exposed

Threat event
Any event where a threat element/actor acts against an asset in a manner that has the potential to directly result in harm

Threat model
Used to describe a given threat and the harm it could to do a system if it has a vulnerability

Threat vector
The method a threat uses to exploit the target

Token
A device that is used to authenticate a user, typically in addition to a user name and password. A token is usually a device that displays a pseudo random number that changes every few minutes.

Total cost of ownership (TOC)
Includes the original cost of the computer plus the cost of: software, hardware and software upgrades, maintenance, technical support, training, and certain activities performed by users

Transmission Control Protocol (TCP)
A connection-based Internet protocol that supports reliable data transfer connections

> **Scope Notes:** Packet data are verified using checksums and retransmitted if they are missing or corrupted. The application plays no part in validating the transfer.

Trusted system
A system that employs sufficient hardware and software assurance measures to allow its use for processing simultaneously a range of sensitive or classified information

Tunneling
Commonly used to bridge between incompatible hosts/routers or to provide encryption; a method by which one network protocol encapsulates another protocol within itself

Two-factor authentication
The use of two independent mechanisms for authentication, (e.g., requiring a smart card and a password); typically, the combination of something you know, are or have

Uniform resource locator (URL)
The global address of documents and other resources on the World Wide Web. The first part of the address indicates what protocol to use; the second part specifies the IP address or the domain name where the resource is located (e.g., http://www.isaca.org).

Virtual private network (V PN)
A secure private network that uses the public telecommunications infrastructure to transmit data. In contrast to a much more expensive system of owned or leased lines that can only be used by one company, VPNs are used by enterprises for both contracts and wide areas of intranets. Using encryption and authentication, a VPN encrypts all data that pass between two Internet points maintaining privacy and security.

Virus signature files
The file of virus patterns that is compared with existing files to determine if they are infected with a virus or worm

Voice-over IP (VoIP)
Also called IP Telephony, Internet Telephony and Broadband Phone, a technology that makes it possible to have a voice conversation over the Internet or over any dedicated Internet Protocol UP) network instead of over dedicated voice transmission lines

Vulnerability
A weakness in the design, implementation, operation or internal controls in a process that could be exploited to violate system security

Vulnerability analysis
A process of identifying and classifying vulnerabilities

Warm site
Similar to a hot site, but not fully equipped with all of the necessary hardware needed for recovery

Web hosting
The business of providing the equipment and services required to host and maintain files for one or more web sites and provide fast Internet connections to those sites. Most hosting is "shared," which means that web sites of multiple companies are on the same server to share/reduce costs.

Web server
Using the client-server model and the World Wide Web's Hypertext Transfer Protocol (HTTP), Web server is a software program that serves web pages to users.

Wide area network (WAN)
A computer network connecting different remote locations that may range from short distances, such as a floor or building, to long transmissions that encompass a large region or several countries

Worm
A programmed network attack in which a self-replicating program does not attach itself to programs, but rather spreads independently of users' action

Wi-Fi protected access 2 (WPA2)
The replacement security method for WPA for wireless networks that provides stronger data protection and network access control. It provides enterprise and consumer Wi-Fi users with a high level of assurance that only authorized users can access their wireless networks. Based on the ratified IEEE 802.1 Ii standard, WPA2 provides government-grade security by implementing the National Institute of Standards and Technology (NIST) FIPS 140-2 compliant advanced encryption standard (AES) encryption algorithm and 802.1X-based authentication.

Index

Made in the USA
Middletown, DE
12 March 2019